CW00322271

HC

Part of the Pattern

Part of the Pattern

Memoirs of a Wife at Westminster

EDNA HEALEY

ISIS
LARGE PRINT
Oxford

First published in Great Britain 2006
by
Headline Review, an imprint of
Headline Book Publishing

Published in Large Print 2007 by ISIS Publishing Ltd.,
7 Centremead, Osney Mead, Oxford OX2 0ES
by arrangement with
Headline Book Publishing,
a division of Hodder Headline

British Library Cataloguing in Publication Data
Healey, Edna
    Part of the pattern: memoirs of a wife at Westminster.
    – Large print ed.
    1. Healey, Edna
    2. Politicians' spouses – Great Britain – Biography
    3. Large type books
    4. Great Britain – Politics and government – 20th
    century
    I. Title
    941'.082'092

ISBN 978–0–7531–9414–0 (hb)
ISBN 978–0–7531–9415–7 (pb)

Printed and bound in Great Britain by
T. J. International Ltd., Padstow, Cornwall

Extracts from *The Time of My Life* are reprinted by permission of Peters Fraser & Dunlop on behalf of Denis Healey. The publishers are grateful to Hutchinson for permission to quote Mary Wilson's poem "The Lunarnaut" and to Weidenfeld and Nicolson for permission to quote from *The Damburst of Dreams* by Christy Nolan.

Dedication

Once again to Denis with grateful thanks for sixty years of married happiness and to all my family. They have always given me loving support.

Contents

INTRODUCTION AND ACKNOWLEDGEMENTS

I initially declined invitations to write my autobiography: having lived since my marriage for six decades in the shadow of great and interesting people, I know I do not rate an autobiography. However, when I reflected that I have been lucky to watch, from a privileged position, many of the men, women and events which have so profoundly changed our world, I thought some of the memories of a varied life might be worth recording.

So this is a memoir written in the evening of a long life by one who remembers much — and forgets more. It is not a political history, although there are some chapters which record political events and personalities. It is partly a social history, for my childhood is a world away; it is partly a travel book with glimpses of China, Borneo and Russia thirty years ago; but mostly it is about people I cannot forget and do not want forgotten.

As I walk in memory through the gallery of the past, I pause longer before some of the portraits — my beloved but tragic sister, Ivy, the amazing crippled writer, Christy Nolan, Audrey and Jim Callaghan, Lord and Lady Longford and others whose lives I do not want to be "writ in water".

My chief source has been Denis's own autobiography, *The Time of My Life*, often and rightly described as the best political autobiography of the period, and his unpublished diary, kept daily though briefly (and often illegibly). These remind me of the progress and pattern of our lives through six decades of happy marriage. It is supplemented by our daughter Jenny's more lively diaries, also written daily over many years. My own diaries tend to go blank after 7 January but I have found my notes from lectures and my own books and documentaries useful reminders.

It would be impossible to mention all those who, in conversation or in their own biographies or autobiographies, have helped me. I owe the greatest debt to Ed Pearce, whose biography of Denis brilliantly describes the political background of the period and is a discerning and generous portrait of the man.

I have also been most grateful to other biographers of Denis, particularly Giles Radice for his skilful presentation of the three "crown princes", Denis, Roy Jenkins and Tony Crosland, in his *Friends and Rivals*, for his published diaries and for sparing time to read my political chapters, as did Roy Hattersley whose writings have been of constant interest and inspiration. The works of my good friend, the late Roy Jenkins, light the long years we have spent in politics with a matchless brilliance. I mourn his loss; I valued his friendship and that of his wise wife, Jennifer. The thought-provoking works of the late Tony Crosland have been inspiration to me, as to many others, and his wife Susan's biography of him has been a deeply moving portrait of a remarkable pair.

I was most delighted that the wives of three prime ministers, Mary Wilson, Cherie Blair and Norma Major, spared time to talk to me and that I was privileged to count a fourth, Audrey Callaghan, as my friend. Cherie's own study of Prime Ministers' wives, *The Goldfish Bowl*, has been most useful. They have given me some understanding of the problems of life at the top and of the importance of holding on to their own work. I am grateful to Mary Wilson's publishers for permission to publish extracts from her books of poetry.

I wish it were possible to mention all those who have talked to me about the past, especially my friends in the Forest of Dean who remember our childhoods in the Baptist chapel in Coleford, but I have the deepest debt to my old friend Dr Cyril Hart, OBE, the great authority on the history of the Forest of Dean. His detailed *Coleford: The History of a West Gloucester-shire Forest Town*, is a mine of information.

My Oxford days have been well documented by contemporaries, some of whom have remained our friends all our lives. In particular the biographies and autobiographies of Roy Jenkins, Tony Crosland, Ted Heath, Chris Mayhew and Nicholas Henderson have revived memories of our shared political student life. I have relied on my own vivid memories for the meeting at Oxford with Denis Healey, my teaching years in his home town of Keighley, our courtship and separation during the war. I eternally regret that I never kept his wartime letters from Italy though, like his diaries, they were so brief that, as I always said, I could have pinned them without embarrassment on the school notice board.

I have read with great interest the autobiographies of other politicians — particularly of Jack Ashley and Roy Mason — whose lives so well illustrate the diversity of the Labour Party in my time.

I would like to remember with particular gratitude my friends from the world beyond Westminster, lifelong friends from the Forest of Dean who have always loyally supported and encouraged me. In particular I am grateful to my academic friends, Professor Michael Slater whose encyclopaedic knowledge of Dickens and his world has inspired me; my good friend Desmond King-Hele, the great authority on Erasmus Darwin who opened a new chapter of history to me. Above all, Randal Keynes, great-great-grandson of Emma and Charles Darwin, who for many years has given me the greatest assistance, access to his family papers and to his profound knowledge and understanding of the Darwin family. I have greatly valued my long friendship with the great Lord Asa Briggs, who has kindly read most of my published work and offered valuable advice. Friends like these have given me inspiration and a welcome release from the wearisome world of politics.

I owe my deepest thanks of all to my editor, Celia Kent: her patience and constant encouragement have been beyond the call of duty. Gillian Somerscales, my copy editor, has dealt sensitively with a wordy author.

Without my secretary, Cheryl Lutring, this book would never have been finished. Her competence and kindly support have been beyond praise. My housekeeper Carroll has stayed us with coffee and kindness throughout our long sessions.

Finally, I owe the deepest debt to Denis. His enduring love and encouragement have been my greatest support and he has suffered with exemplary patience my absences. I have been fortunate in having access to his extensive library and even more to his exceptional mind.

CHAPTER
ONE

THE FOREST OF DEAN,
1918–1936

I was born in Coleford, a small market town on the edge of the ancient and magical Forest of Dean. Once the Forest covered 100,000 acres in a triangle of land between the Severn and the Wye and, though now it has shrunk to about 24,000 acres, there are still extensive woodlands of oak and beech where the bracken grows tall and seas of bluebells dazzle the eye as they did when I was young. The boundaries have changed and Coleford, once in the heart of the Forest, is now at its edge; but Colefordians still fiercely claim their right to be called Foresters.

Until I was eighteen the rivers Severn and Wye were the boundaries of my world, outside which I rarely ventured. Occasionally there would be a visit to Bristol across the Severn, or to south Wales across the Wye. There were rare holidays with an old deaf aunt in Cheltenham, thirty miles distant. My mother's cousin Aunt Lil was a dressmaker and took me once to visit her client, a lady in a grand house. I have never forgotten my childhood impressions of Cheltenham — the wide promenade, the space and the light and the flowers, and the satinwood furniture of that elegant room. Gloucester, twenty miles away, was our metropolis, with a Woolworths and a Bon Marché which provided a delectable meal for ninepence. To those distant delights we went either by red-and-white bus or, occasionally, by railway. Coleford then had two railway stations, one for goods and one for passengers.

Though my geographical boundaries were limited, the Forest's temporal horizon stretched back to what the old records call "tyme out of mynde", and from earliest childhood I absorbed its ancient history almost without knowing. My earliest memories are of idyllic family picnics at Symonds Yat. Sometimes we took the bus to the famous great rock around which the Wye meanders through green meadows and from which you can see seven counties. Here, to my mind, you could still catch the scent of the fashionable ladies of the eighteenth century who rowed downriver to Chepstow in the days when the French troubles made the Grand Tour dangerous and the beauty of the Wye was discovered. More often we walked up the Staunton Road to where an overgrown woodland path led to the meadows downstream on the banks of the Wye. Now a chain bridge spans the river, but then my mother would call, "Mr Brown! Mr Brown!" and the farmer poled his boat across from his house. I still hear that clear, strong voice echoing from the rocky heights of the Forest to the grassy banks on the other side.

We did not realize when we took our candles to the caves above the Wye at Symonds Yat that in paleolithic times early man had lived there with mammoths. Nor did I know that on the calm river bank there had been a fierce battle between Celts and Saxons. We still call that meadow "the Slaughter". On the road between Coleford and Staunton a strange six-foot stone stood beside the road. We called it the Blood Stone and believed that if we stuck a pin in it at midnight it would bleed. Alas, we were never there at midnight! I believed, and still do, that it was a marker signing our secret way through the thick Forest to the Wye below Symonds Yat. Further along the road to Monmouth there were more strange stones at the side of the road: in Staunton a weird rock we called The Frog's Mouth was the keeper of the way up the hill to the Buckstone at the highest point in the Forest. It was a huge slab of rock on a narrow pivot. Once it had bucked or rocked until rough lads had pushed it down the hill, and in my time it was cemented in place.

Our playgrounds were reminders of past ages: Bronze, Iron, pre-Roman. We played Druids and Romans among the ancient stones. One had a convenient hollow for the head in our games of sacrificial rites; a gully carved in the top was for the blood to run down. Way down below us, glinting in the sunlight, the Romans marched their way up the River Wye from Chepstow to Monmouth, sending us running into the woods in panic. In our games we followed the invaders, Roman, Saxon, Viking and Norman, through a network of hollow-ways and old tracks among the woods. Everywhere there were reminders of the past; everywhere we were reminded of our deep roots in history.

★ ★ ★

Over the years I have kept in close contact with my family in Coleford: my sister Doreen lives there still, and I go back to my old home whenever I can. When I drive down the road from Gloucester along the Severn Valley, my heart leaps at the sign to "The Forest of Dean". That is the quicker way I take when I am alone, but when Denis is with me we follow the river to Newnham where he and his brother, Terry, spent many idyllic holidays in his boyhood. Here his mother and her sister, Dolly, were born; and here his grandfather was the stationmaster, signalman and ticket collector at the tiny village halt. I might have seen the two wild Yorkshire boys as the train chugged along the now defunct railway from Coleford to Gloucester, but train rides were rare and expensive. More often we took the red-and-white bus along the road where the Blaisdon plums dangled from the trees over the road, and did not go through Newnham. This small town has a particular resonance for Denis that it does not have for me: he remembers the daffodils at the roadside, and on each visit he goes to photograph the grave where his grandparents lie in a quiet churchyard overlooking the river.

Then we take the narrow road from Newnham up into the Forest, never failing to stop at the gap in the hedge at Pleasant Stile, with its breathtaking distant view of the Severn winding through meadow-land. Denis's long-suffering, devoted Aunty Dolly had often climbed there with her two young nephews. Small, with a crooked spine, the archetypal faithful spinster aunt, she remained an important part of our lives right up to her death. Possessed of a warm heart as well as a tongue that could be crisp when necessary, she had looked after her parents until they died, and then generously devoted herself to her sister, her sister's children and their children in turn. It was not easy: there was one shaming moment when the two boys were discovered competing in a pee-shooting contest out of the bedroom window. When we pass through Newnham, Denis never fails to point out the window to me.

Denis claims in his autobiography that he loves the Forest as much as I do. This is not strictly true. Newnham was holiday for him; his formative years were spent among the moors and stone walls of Yorkshire, and it was that environment that shaped his character as the Forest did mine. Indeed, I never felt the Severn-side boundary of my world was truly part of the Forest of Dean: it was too pastoral, though it had its dramatic moments. Twice a year, at the vernal and autumnal equinoxes, a six-foot wall of water called the Severn Bore reached its maximum height as it swept up the river, and once a year elvers swarmed their way on their mysterious route up from the sea. My brothers would bring home pails of them — a grey, wriggling mass which my mother would fry to a delicious crisp.

My road home lies through Cinderford, Coleford's competitor for the title of Capital of the Forest. It cannot claim any of the beauty of the honey-and-gold Cotswold villages: like many of the Forest towns, Cinderford is a long, straggling street with no centre, and the grey houses and grey slate roofs can seem

5

dismal, especially on a rainy day. The guidebook calls it "almost totally haphazardly built as a settlement for quarry and iron foundry workers". But it must be remembered that Dean Forest is not merely a romantic idyll: it was a workplace where iron, coal and stone were hewn out of the ground. Part of the attraction of the Forest for me is that behind its beauty there is rough reality.

From now on the road to Coleford is layered deep in memories. Turn the soil and fragments appear, memories and old records joining to make a pattern outside time.

The road passes Dilke Hospital, named after the Forest's late-Victorian Member of Parliament, Sir Charles Dilke. Sir Charles's career in public life suffered badly from scandal in his private affairs; but Foresters, ever realists, forgave him his trespasses and many remembered him kindly. My aunt recalls how he sat in their kitchen at Parkend. Alas, all she can recall is that he wore a handsome black coat with a huge astrakhan collar. But for me "Dilke" is not a Member of Parliament; it is the hospital in which my mother died. I will never forget the day of her funeral when the beech trees, afire in the autumn sun, lit her way through the woods.

After the hospital the road passes the eighteenth-century Speech House, now a hotel but once the building where the Forest of Dean free miners held their court. Here they closely defended their ancient rights, conferred on them, as Margaret Mushet recorded, "by King Edward I for the assistance they gave as engineers in his wars with the Scots at Berwick-upon-Tweed". Foresters had been famous as skilled miners since pre-Roman times. A record of 1610 sets out the miners' rights, but it is a transcript of an earlier document. Certainly by 1244 Dean miners were allowed to dig for iron and coal and had other rights. In 1673 a document entitled "the miners lawes and privileges" proclaimed: "bee itt in minde and remembrance what the customes and ffranchises have beene that were granted tyme out of Minde and after in tyme of the excellent and Redoubted Prince King Edward unto ye miners of the Fforest of Deane and the Castle of St Briavell and the bounds of the said Fforest". It affirmed the miners' rights to take iron ore and coal in the Forest "without withsaying of any man", along with other rights: to build roads to carry coal to the nearest King's highway, and to take timber for their use without payment. A Forester had the right to call himself a free miner if he had worked in a quarry or mine for a year and a day. This could have been a stone quarry or an iron or coal mine. He then could apply for a "gale" — a strip of land on which to dig a mine. There are still small mines owned by free miners. Perhaps my father could have become a free miner. He was born within the Hundred of St Briavels and had worked in a stone quarry for more than a year and a day. Now the road runs into my father's home territory. I remember him carrying me on his shoulders through the Speech House woods to his old home in Parkend two miles away. My brother remembers, though I do not, how our grandmother, wearing her best black dress

7

and a lace cap, greeted us with wide open arms. In the faded sepia photograph my grandparents look a fine pair. I wish I had known them: he upright and handsome, sporting a flower in his buttonhole as my father often did; she sitting comfortably, radiating warmth and affection.

My grandmother, Mary Ann Trafford, came from a family whose roots were deep in the Forest. My father's sisters liked to think they were descended from the Norman French de Traffords, and it is not impossible. Certainly, during the sixteenth and seventeenth centuries the Lydney Traffords were closely involved as managers with the dominant Lydney family descended from Admiral Sir John Wintour, the godson of Queen Elizabeth. His grandson, the famous — or, to the Foresters, infamous — Sir John Wintour, had friends at court and served as secretary to Queen Henrietta Maria from 1638; but he had as many enemies in the Forest, where his financial dealings were regarded with suspicion, his Catholicism was viewed askance by the Nonconformists, and his fervent support for King Charles I was unwelcome at the outbreak of the Civil War, when the Foresters were inclined to hold themselves aloof from the fighting. An enterprising character with a striking personality that later impressed Samuel Pepys and John Evelyn, he showed Charles I what a fortune could be made from the iron in the Forest of Dean. Elizabeth had valued the Forest for its oaks, a priceless source of timber for her ships. John Evelyn wrote that the Spanish commanders of the Armada, in the Great Expedition of 1588, were ordered "not to leave a tree standing in the Forest of Dean". In the seventeenth century Sir John showed the Stuarts that the Forest also had plentiful wood for charcoal burning, abundant water, and excellent iron to be mined at nearby Cinderford. Charles I leased to him all "The King's Ironworks" in the Dean and made his fortune. In these works the Trafford family was involved, it is said, "in a managerial capacity".

Like the Wintours, some of the Traffords were Catholic and were doubtless involved when, in the Civil War, Wintour stoutly defended his house against the Parliamentarians and, when defeated, burned it down rather than allow the King's enemies to take it. He fled to France; but at the Restoration his loyalty was rewarded, and once again he was received at court. The Trafford family, too, were still involved in the iron industry. One branch remained Catholic and apparently took part in the doomed Jacobite Rebellion of 1715, after which they fled to America.

In 1858 iron mining in the Forest came to an end, and the iron miners turned increasingly to coal mining and stone quarrying. My father worked as a crane driver in the stone quarry near the little village of Parkend, where he belonged to the band and learned to play many instruments. In my childhood he superintended my piano lessons and taught me to play the clarinet. He often walked up the woodland road to Coleford to court the lively little Rose Crook. A keen musician himself, he was certainly charmed by the lovely voice that won my mother the title of "Nightingale of the Forest". Was he perhaps in the audience when, in the character of Maid Marion, she brought the house down at a Coleford concert? "Carriages at Ten" the programme said, she recalled, and how "the gentry from Newland clapped and shouted 'Hear, hear!' ". He took her to Coleford dances where, as she remembered, he always wore white gloves. Lively even in her nineties, she could demonstrate how they danced the cakewalk, to the amazement of her grandchildren.

Returning to the road home from Gloucester, we drive now through the hamlet of Broadwell, where, as a girl, I walked to my first dances in the Memorial Hall. There my brothers taught me to waltz. If they saw me a wallflower, they would cross the floor and, with exaggerated courtesy, ask: "May I have the pleasure?" And pleasure it was — like my father and mother, they were both fine dancers. In my flame-coloured taffeta, I was a queen. But the long windy walk home at midnight was hard on the feet.

And so to Coleford down the Gloucester Road which, in the Middle Ages, had followed the Poolway Brook from the King's Fishpool. We pass the eighteenth-century Poolway Villa where my friend Jocelyn lived; in the coach house and stables of the oldest house in Coleford, the neighbouring Poolway House, our gang had its den. There we acted out the film *Disraeli*, which we had seen at Coleford cinema, with Dennis Horwood taking George Arliss's part. Is there still, I wonder, a hole in the ceiling where once my sister's foot appeared alarmingly from the attic?

From the corner of Gloucester Road the last stretch leads home along what we used to call Back Lane, now

Bank Street. During the Civil War the Royalist troops from Monmouth passed this way on their way to Gloucester and were met by Cromwell's men stationed at Coleford. Apparently Back Lane ran with blood and, from a window in the inn on the site of the King's Head, a silver bullet was fired which killed the King's colonel (I cannot believe a Forester would have wasted good silver like this).

In my childhood, walking up Back Lane we passed the Spout, our original source of water, to which we used to see the great farm horses lumbering down for their evening drink. We passed the meeting house of the Plymouth Brethren, some cottages and a sweet shop. There were few cars then, and those would be laid up on bricks in the winter. So in the right season we could play marbles on the dusty road or bowl our great iron hoops or spin tops. Once mine flew up to break a cottage window. As a new Girl Guide I knew I must not run away, so I counted to ten — and then fled. At the top of the lane was our house, part of a somewhat gaunt yellow-washed terrace of three-storeyed houses — converted, as I later learned, from the old workhouse. It spanned the apex of a triangle where Back Lane met the main street, St John's Street.

Now I pause with a sigh: our house and its neighbours are gone, demolished to make a wider road. Did this small space hold all my childhood and youth? Where is the low stone wall surrounding the apex of that triangle, where on summer nights my friends and I sat and chatted for long goodnights? Where are my father's row of kidney beans and soldierly ranks of

11

onions? Where is the stony garden path down to the shed, the coal house and the lavatory? I remember the night walks down the path, slapped by the frozen sheets on the line, a candle in a jamjar with a string handle. Where is the jackdaw, who knew me a coward, with its wicked eyes glinting, that would chase me down the garden path and besiege me in the garden shed?

A group of neat little houses has replaced the terrace I knew, and there are shops and a Chinese takeaway! As I stand on the dead grey roadway I hear my mother singing the Indian Love Lyrics and her clear, true voice rising above my thumping accompaniment: "Pale hands I loved, beside the Shalimar . . . where are you now, where are you now?"

I was born in a cottage in Newland Street, near the little pottery where my maternal grandfather had worked: I was the fourth child, after an elder sister and two brothers. When I was two, we moved to the house in Back Lane, and it was here that my younger sister, Doreen, arrived. Though the addition to the family was most unwelcome at the time, she proved to be my mother's greatest and lifelong support, and has always been my most loyal and most loved companion. Here I lived happily for the first eighteen years of my life.

In those days between the wars we lived in another world, spoke a different language, accepted different customs. But I, and many of my generation, were forever moulded by the values of those times. It is because they should not be forgotten that I try to recapture the people and places and life of years now long past.

12

★   ★   ★

Coleford lies in a shallow dip in the hills and, unlike other Forest towns, has a centre, with a clock tower (all that remains of the octagonal Victorian chapel) on The Tump. In my day it stood beside the Town Hall, where concerts and dances were held, and a market hall, where a penny would buy liquorice or a slab of nutty chocolate or coconut ice or gobstoppers that rainbowed to an aniseed pip in the centre. Now market and hall are demolished and the clock tower stands alone.

In early times three brooks were forded here, and the main roads to Coleford from Monmouth, Gloucester and Chepstow still follow the line of the brooks as they cross the Forest from the Severn to the Wye. One of the old brooks was, in my childhood, an open sewer, past which we walked holding our noses, and the others caused many a serious flood in Coleford, and in our house. One night we came home from chapel to find the ground floor under water. I still remember the smell of dank linoleum as we mopped up in the kitchen.

Because there was a steep slope from Back Lane to St John's Street, the ground floor of our house was a semi-basement. Steep steps descended to our front door. Inside a small hall held a larder and coal cellar under the stairs. At the back was the kitchen, the heart of the house. Here we cooked, ate, had our Saturday baths and sat in the evenings. The only heat in the house came from the kitchen coal fire in its black grate, burnished bright every day by my mother. The small front room was always called "the other room".

13

There were two bedrooms at the top of the house, one for the girls and one for the boys. My parents' bedroom was on the first floor, next to it was the small sitting room with a piano, a horsehair settee and velvet-covered armchairs. On Sundays and at Christmas we lit a fire in the little grate with a green velvet fringe over the mantelpiece, and watched all the comings and goings in the street outside.

We had none of the amusements or conveniences of the modern world. We had no radio until I was sixteen, no television, no refrigerator or vacuum cleaner. The house was cold; in winter the water in our bedroom jugs froze. Instead of hot-water bottles we had bricks, heated in the kitchen oven. We knelt on the cold lino to say our prayer, "Gentle Jesus, meek and mild . . .", and jumped into the icy bed to the grateful warmth of the brick in its singed brown paper wrapping. The kitchen and sitting room were gas-lit, otherwise we carried candles. I did my homework by the light of an oil lamp in the front room, wearing my coat.

Adjoining the back of the house was the back kitchen with a bread oven, which was never used, and a large copper set in stone, which on Mondays boiled water for washing and on Saturday nights for baths, and at every Christmas time for eight Christmas puddings. In my childhood there was no drinking water laid on; it had to be brought in pails from a standpipe in St John's Street. This was a job for my brothers, who carried the pails home and impressed us by swinging the full buckets over their heads to demonstrate centrifugal force. Secretly we hoped that one day the force would fail!

Water for washing came from the iron pump over the stone sink in the back kitchen. To make it work you poured water into the top, then a quick push on the handle would prime the pump and bring up the water. But for me it rarely did. I was always ham-fisted.

Outside the back door was a small knot of flowers, which my mother tended with love, and my father's vegetable garden. At the bottom of the garden stood the shed where he mended our shoes and made wine, the coal house, and the lavatory with its shiny seat and neat squares of newspaper on a string. Once a week the night-soil man came: the windows were shut while he carried our bucket up to his cart and tipped the contents into the bigger, rusty bucket at the back of his horse-drawn wagon. His wife kept a shop where she sold faggots and green peas. These we never fancied.

In the house next door Coleford's first telephone exchange was established in our neighbour's sitting room, as was sometimes done in the country at this time. At the age of fifteen my sister started her long and successful career as a telephonist here, and since our back doors adjoined, the telephone exchange was an extension of our world. Mrs Hooper, the caretaker telephonist, shared her room with a huge board and a tangle of cords and plugs. Her kitchen was in the next room. Once an engineer tried to go in to man a line. "You can't!" shouted my sister. "Granny's having her bath!" Pink-cheeked, white-haired, this comfortable old lady became a surrogate "granny".

There was no wall between our garden and that of the telephone exchange, but there was a wall dividing us from the third house which opened on to St John's Street. This was the coffee tavern — so called because the temperance campaigners wanted to offer a convivial alternative to pubs for those who had signed the pledge. In my day it was a rather dingy café where we bought our ice-creams; the coffee was made from Camp extract. We often heard Mr Gardner, the owner, singing as he turned the handle of his ice-cream maker in the shed adjoining our gardens. I used to peer through a hole in his wall and wonder at the huge pile of woollen waste heaped there.

I wish I had known more about the past of this building but Dr Cyril Hart, in his superb book *Coleford*, has carefully unravelled the history of the workhouse from which the three houses were created.

The first workhouse in Coleford was established in June 1774 by the parish council at Newland, in order to give work to the poor of the parish of Newland. A certain Mr Timothy Mitchell, "serge clothier in the county of Wiltshire", apparently proposed that he should "employ the poor of the parish of Newland at constant work at spinning and otherwise relating to the trade of serge clothing . . . until the said number of sixty be completed . . . And after the first year to employ a hundred or more . . . and of these to teach some of them the art or mystery of weaving, allowing them for their work in spinning according to the market rate at Tetbury."

Dr Hart says that it is not known where in Coleford this first workhouse was set up, or for how long it continued. But I believe it was in an outhouse behind the coffee tavern; perhaps that would explain the immense pile of wool shoddy.

That original ambitious workhouse has disappeared from the records, but on 18 August 1785, the Newland parish vestry decided to establish a large workhouse, which was completed in November 1786. Again it was planned to train weavers there. The subscription list was headed by the lord of High Meadow manor — Lord Gage — with a donation of fifty pounds. An ancestor of his, Thomas, Viscount Gage, had in 1713 married Maria Theresa Hall, granddaughter and heiress of the wealthy Catholic ironmaster Benedict Hall, and so acquired the vast High Meadow estate, which included the house, half of Coleford and the site of our old home. The Gage family will reappear in my later life.

I do not remember being bored. There was always the "Rec" — the recreation ground created in memory of a remarkable Colefordian, Captain Angus Buchanan VC, who, though blind, crowned his many battle honours with a new career as a solicitor. I remember him being led around Coleford. The Rec was a lively place: my brothers played golf and my sisters and I belonged to a tennis club. There were swings, roundabouts, a slide and "giant strides". We helped to plant lines of trees which now have grown to a magnificent avenue.

Sometimes in the evening I would go next door and sit with Granny Hooper while she minded the telephone switchboard and had her supper with "just a tot" of Guinness. She knew the private life of every subscriber.

"There he goes," she would say, "ringing from a call box so his wife can't hear."

"Who?" I would ask.

"I darsen't tell you, my dear — it would be as much as my job would be worth."

Imagining was better than watching a soap opera.

Then there was the annual fair, held in the centre of Coleford on 21 and 22 June. It was the high spot of the year, for which we saved for months. For twopence, you could ride up and down your kingdom on a huge white horse, or queen it around, splendid in a red velvet dragon.

Dad always took us. My mother would never come to the fair. Unaccountably, she said: "I can't bear it. It makes me feel so sad."

There was plenty to watch from the window of our little first-floor sitting room. "Here she comes," my critical mother would say: "hold my head for my behind is coming." Just opposite, at the top of Back Lane, was the Independent Chapel — a handsome building dated 1842, built by the successors of Cromwell's "preaching captains". In our day we called it the Congregational Chapel or "the Congs". Outside it stood the Wayfarer's Pulpit and board bearing a text. My favourite was "foot-steps in the sands of time are not made by sitting down". On Sundays a large congregation streamed out to the sound of the organ. Immediately opposite, the Masons' Arms held its vociferous gatherings on Saturday nights. I remember the particularly raucous laughter after the refrain, "with his cock-a-doodle-doo". I never understood why my mother disliked this jolly song!

The juxtaposition of pub and chapel was typical of Coleford. In the centre alone there were nine pubs, with many more in the outlying districts. There were almost as many chapels, including the Baptist, Independent, Wesleyan and Methodist, and the Plymouth Brethren Meeting House. There had even been a Chapel of the Countess of Huntingdon's Connexion. One small Catholic church and one Victorian Anglican church were swamped by the Nonconformists.

In our house at 9 Bank Street we seven lived most happily — if most simply. My elder sister, Ivy, helped take care of us younger ones. As in so many large families, the eldest daughter was the "little mother". Ivy was intelligent and hard-working and a competent pianist, but over-sensitive — an early sign of the instability that would ruin her later life and sometimes caused friction with my mother, although they loved and admired each other.

My brothers, Bert and Victor, also helped, grumbling and singing "Jerusalem" as they rocked "this blessed baby" in her pram. They had their own jobs: chopping sticks, carrying in the coal and fetching water. The two boys were very different. The eldest, Bert, was sensitive, quiet, withdrawn. After my father's death he stayed at home to take care of my mother, working as a dental mechanic in Monmouth. Victor started as a driver of a petrol lorry and finished his career with Esso. He loved the Forest and until his eighties went back in the autumn to pick hazelnuts and chestnuts. A generous and affectionate brother, he would always have some treat for me in his greatcoat pockets. During the war, he found his tour in India the most exciting time of his life, explored the jungle, went snake-hunting with an Indian guide and sent his wife a snakeskin which she had made into shoes.

Whenever bands came marching through Coleford my father would carry me on his shoulders to see them pass. It's a pity he never developed his musical skills. He could conduct as well as play many instruments — clarinet, trumpet, double bass — and, for a while, continued playing some music with friends in the little sitting room. My brother Victor remembers lugging the double bass up the narrow stairs. But as he grew older and his health weaker, he must have found his work in the stone quarry extremely exhausting. Early every morning he went off with his can of cold tea and sandwiches — and sometimes a raw egg which, to my horror, he would suck. Daily he walked the two miles to work. When the family grew he supplemented the kitchen garden at Bank Street with the produce of an allotment nearby; so on summer evenings he would work here too, digging potatoes, planting onions, picking the plums that hung in swags from the Victoria plum tree.

Blue-eyed, fair-haired, he was a good-looking man, with an upright, soldierly carriage, and a moustache he sometimes waxed. I see him now shaving by the stone sink in the old back kitchen, sharpening his razor on the leather strop — sometimes he threatened us with it, but we never believed him. His was the gentlest of natures.

My father loved flowers: he always wore one in the buttonhole of his Sunday suit, and knew where to find the rarest orchids. Once he took my brother Vic and me to see a clump of bee orchids on the old golf course and made us promise not to tell anyone where they were. He swore by his herbal remedies — tea made from agrimony or elderflowers, the flowers laid out to dry on yellowing newspaper. The elderflower tea was a foul concoction, the thought of which cured a cold immediately. Much better was the cider, heated by a red-hot poker, and better still the parsnip or elderberry wine he made. In the album of the memory I see him holding up the bottle to the light: "How's that for clarity?" he would say.

Was it my mother's beautiful singing voice that first attracted him? Or her shapely small hands and feet of which she was always most proud, and a complexion that only Icilma face cream was allowed to touch? Or her lively charm and infectious laugh? When, as frequently happened, one of us fell down the narrow stairs, we would find her helpless with laughter at the bottom. At one school concert when I with three companions and the music master were proudly playing madrigals on our recorders, my mother, finding the sight and the tootling irresistibly funny, started laughing and infected her whole row. Finally the whole

21

audience collapsed. We gave up. She apologized for what she called "seeing the funny side".

All her life music was her greatest joy. She and her friend Nora Morris sang duets, and my mother sang most of the solos from the oratorios that the Baptist choir performed so well. However busy her day had been, at the end of it she would always revive herself in song — with the help of a spoonful of honey. She and Nora grew old in music together. When Nora was dying, she sent for mother to sing to her; and when she herself was in her last days we found her lying in bed, her lips silently moving. "Go away," she said, "I'm singing my way through the *Messiah*."

She mellowed in old age, but she could be a fierce little bantam. I think my father was a little afraid of her — and we often were. She was a perfectionist, and the house was immaculate. The kitchen stove had to be black-leaded every afternoon before she would take her rest. The beds had to be perfectly made (not an easy task). Our mattresses were heavy flock and had to be turned every day. When she had nothing better to do, we claimed, she would whitewash the back kitchen. She made the curtains and steadfastly refused to put the pattern on the inside. She would say, "No, always put the best side towards London." The pattern had to be outside, so that the neighbours could see it. She was very angry with a relative who was seen out shopping in the morning. "How can she go out in the morning?" she would say. "When does she do her work?" Her week had its own rhythm. Monday was washday; Tuesday, ironing; Wednesday, bedrooms; Thursday, sitting room and kitchen; Friday, baking. If she allowed herself to go shopping, it was on Saturday.

Sunday was special. Dressed in our best clothes with hats and gloves, we walked through the town to chapel, admiring our reflections in the drawn blinds of the shop windows — we had no long mirror at home. Shops were closed on Sundays; even the swings and roundabouts in the recreation ground were chained up. I never forgot my mother's horrified voice as she saw the jeans and duffel coats of our children: "But it's Sunday!" We did not mind our more restricted lives; in any case, it was a busy day, with Sunday School and chapel in the morning, chapel again in the evening. In the winter we all went round to the Gwilliams' house to sing around the piano. Mr and Mrs Gwilliam were our surrogate Uncle Hubert and Aunty Jin. They lived over their tobacconist's shop in the Market Square and were our kindest friends in good times and bad. She was a Londoner, always trim and neat, but his roots were deep in the Forest. He told us of the little green men that he swore had been seen in the mines, and how, walking to his work as a carpenter in the early morning, he was once accompanied by a Roman soldier who was walking on an invisible path at a higher level.

After chapel on summer evenings Dad joined us for walks in the Staunton woods, showed us the flowers, found butterfly orchids by their scent, taught us to ease horsefly bites with crushed plantain leaves. As we grew up, the walks after chapel would be taken with boyfriends — in winter through the frosty fields; in spring through bluebell woods. The modern generation would not understand the innocence of those walks. I was not even kissed until I was sixteen, and I heard of adventures in the tall bracken with incomprehension.

The year had its pattern too. There were primroses and daffodils to be picked in the spring, wild strawberries in summer, and in the autumn apples and plums in the allotment, blackberries in the hedgerows, and hazelnuts to be pulled down with our sticks from pliant branches. There were shiny chestnuts in their prickly green husks to be picked up from the rich, deep earth and little blue bilberries hiding under the rocks. Those were the gathering years.

Beyond the supporting frame of my family were a host of aunts and honorary relatives.

The three youngest of my father's sisters were always an important part of our lives. There was little work for girls in Parkend at this time and, like many others, the Edmunds girls went into service in London and acquired the style, accent and manners of their grand ladies. Aunt Lil went to London as a maid in the household of a Lady Spires. Intelligent and charming, in time she became the valued secretary and companion of her employer and travelled with her. She bought us our piano, on which a photograph always stood showing her draped in a Spanish shawl, leaning on a verandah and holding a guitar. She was generous to her younger brother and his children, sending exotic little presents and offering to pay for my elder brother's education at grammar school — an offer he obstinately refused. She finally came back to marry a carpenter, her childhood sweetheart, and lived in a little house in Bristol. When we visited her we felt she had found a happy end to her exotic life.

Aunt Polly Perks, we never knew her proper name, followed Lil to London and married a captain in the Guards. They came back to live in a pleasant house with an orchard in Chepstow, where we often visited. She brought back with her the accent of the period — "blooses" for blouses and "gals" for girls — and the lavender scent of a now-vanished world that clung to the tiny slippers she showed us, and the faded satins and silks that hung in her wardrobe. She adopted the lifestyle of her former employers and served tea from a silver teapot with elegant china, sitting in basket chairs on the lawn. My mother thought this "swank". In our childhood, gardens were for growing vegetables, not to be wasted on grass. Handsome Uncle Jack was something of a ladies' man and was always embarrassingly affectionate to his young nieces. You avoided climbing the apple trees when he was around. Their son, Patrick, never married and died intestate, leaving his tiny fortune to be divided among his relatives. Our minuscule legacy, long awaited, became the family joke.

Of the three, however, it was Aunt Min who, with her husband and children, remained closest to us throughout her life. The youngest Edmunds daughter, Min had stayed at home to look after her mother and cycled round the Forest roads selling insurance. She caught the eye of a young Scottish officer, Hugh Robertson, a captain in the Seaforth Highlanders, who after the First World War came to study at the Parkend Forestry School. They married and she followed him to Oxford, where he took his degree. Fair-haired, blue-eyed and stylish, she leans on her parasol in the family photograph, the very epitome of the elegant Edwardian. To her dying day her hats were memorable creations. She was generous and warm-hearted; we loved her and forgave her incurable snobbery. Uncle Hugh, handsome, courteous and kind, was to my mother always the beau ideal of a Scottish gentleman. In later life she would reprimand my brothers: "Uncle Hugh would never come to the table in his shirtsleeves." She would never allow us to laugh at Aunty Min's grand ways: "Remember, she is your father's sister." However, she often took offence at trifles herself, as when Min called her carpets "rugs".

I remember little of moment from my early schooldays. I recall the smell of the lavatories across the playground at the Church of England Infants' School, which I attended between the ages of four and seven, but I also remember the heavenly scent of a white rose just beyond the playground as I sat on the cold iron fence, listening to the chant "The farmer has a wife" . . . All my life I have searched for that rose.

I do, however, remember distinctly one incident, because it became part of family legend, recounted by Miss Gwilliam, the headmistress. I was five. We were knitting in the big room of the Victorian school. Miss Gwilliam inspected and held up my long strip of knitting, which was full of holes. "And what do you think this is?" she asked. "That's all right," I replied brightly, "it's all part of the pattern." Somehow it is a typical remark — and so I have chosen it as the title of this book.

Similarly, little remains of my time from seven to eleven at the Church of England Girls' Junior School on Lord's Hill, though I do remember the three big rooms and an icy cold cloakroom where at playtime we huddled under a pile of coats. Outside was the "glory hole" where a little green man had once been seen among the rubbish. I also remember fascinating lessons on "Latin roots" and learning that the word for our "Tump" was derived from *tumulus*. We had no library, but book boxes came from Gloucester, with limp-backed copies of Dickens's novels smelling of must. I remember the shame of being taken to the big room, as a seven-year-old, to show off to a big hapless girl, because I knew, and she did not, that "Japan is a chain of islands in the Far East" — "She is only seven and you are eleven!" Later I was mocked in my turn in the big room: "Edna Edmunds holds her needle like a shovel." No one ever succeeded in teaching me to sew, though I did learn one hemming stitch which has served me well enough.

At the age of eleven, I won a scholarship to Bell's Grammar School and wore with pride my green gymslip and blazer, and the panama hat held on with cutting elastic. Bell's was one of the oldest grammar schools in the country, and was originally housed beside the lovely thirteenth-century Church of All Saints at Newland, set among green hills and meadows and rightly known as the "Cathedral of the Forest". The school badge — three palmers' shells and motto "*per ardua ad astra*" — suggests that there had been a pilgrim among its founders. Edward Bell gave the school its name in 1630, but he re-endowed an earlier school, founded in 1445 by a wealthy landowner, Robert Greyndour, and his wife Jane. In fact, it is Jane who deserves the credit since Robert, who must have planned the charitable foundation, died in 1443. Obviously a devout and competent lady, two years after his death she obtained the royal licence from Henry VI for the foundation "of a perpetual chantry at the altar of St John and St Nicholas" in Newland Church. Unusually, the foundation provided for the education of the poorer children of Newland's parish, which at that time included Coleford. An "honeste and discrete prieste sufficientlie learned in the art of grammar" should "kepe and teche a gramer scoole ther, half free forever, that is to saie, to take of scolers lernynge gramer 8d the quarter, and other(s) lernynge letters and to rede 4d the quarter, within a house there called the chauntrie house or scool house". The "discrete" priest should have a salary of £10 4s 2d per annum. This was roughly equivalent to that of the headmaster of Eton (founded around the same time). The chantry was endowed with lands to the value of £12 a year. The reward for the Greyndours was that the priest should daily pray for their souls and "all other Christian soules".

We often walked to Newland along the old Burial Path, now almost completely overgrown. In the days before Coleford cemetery was built, coffins were carried from Coleford to Newland Church graveyard. For me, the slippery moss-grown path to the ancient church always held a rare magic. The ghost of a grey lady haunted our path and in the church, we claimed, we could still smell the incense from pre-Reformation days drifting across the wide aisles.

In the south chapel, Robert and Jane Greyndour lie in the dappled shadows. Above them, engraved brasses show him in full armour and his lady wearing the horned head-dress of the fifteenth century. Higher up a brass engraving of an iron miner in working dress, holding a candlestick in his mouth: by chance or design, a reminder that their school was intended to serve the poor as well as the rich.

For more than a century the Greyndour School flourished, providing a classical education as well as instruction in reading and writing, surviving Henry VIII's assault on the monasteries. Even when the chantries were abolished under Edward VI the school was allowed to continue; for otherwise, it was said, "it would be a great loss, for there is not any other Gramer scole free, nor otherwise, not by a grete distance to have their children brought upp virtuously in lerninge". Robert and Jane Greyndour deserve to be remembered.

By the middle of the sixteenth century, though, the old grammar school was struggling — until the old chantry properties, including the school, were bought by Edward Bell, who re-endowed the old school, stipulating that it should be a free grammar school for the children of Newland parish and establishing trustees to build and endow a house for the school and master. The school survived the Civil War, when the sole trustee was the Catholic Benedict Hall of High Meadow House — grandfather of the Maria Theresa Hall who inherited the house and married an ancestor of the present Lord Gage, who will reappear later in the pattern of my life. By the nineteenth century it was in the doldrums again, though the trust remained in existence. The old school building needed expensive repairs and there was no playground — except the graveyard. At that time, the trustees made some shrewd deals, and in the summer of 1876 a new school was built on Lords Hill at a cost of £1,884; it was in this large, red-brick Victorian house, planned to accommodate the headmaster and thirty boys, that I attended grammar school from 1929 to 1936. By my time the headmaster, then John Hough, had moved across the road (it was under his predecessor, Mr Hodder, that the school had begun to admit girls), but the main school still had the comfortable feel of a home, especially in the summer when the windows were thrown wide open and the sixth-form room was filled with the scent of the borders of white pinks — and, when the mind wandered, we could admire the distant Welsh hills.

With the energy and determination for which he was famous, John Hough built an assembly hall, prefabricated buildings for the first classes and a tin hut for a chemistry laboratory. This blew up with a spectacular explosion in my time. Much of the work he did himself with the help of the boys: an indefatigable bodger, his pockets were always full of string and nails. As a headmaster he was not perfect (we had no library), but if he wielded the cane with enthusiasm, it was never with brutality. He would take on any challenge and, above all, had the good sense and judgement to appoint the stimulating young teachers to whom I owe my subsequent career.

There was no theatre in Coleford, though travelling players sometimes came. But John Hough's wife was a professional actress, so the annual Shakespeare production was well performed in the Assembly Hall. I longed to be Lady Macbeth, but because I was small and skinny had to settle for Macduff's son, with the single line: "He has kill'd me, mother: run away, I pray you!"

The first three years at Bell's left little of permanent interest, and my memories grow clearer only from the age of fourteen, when I moved up to the "big school". But one master, who taught me geography, deserves to be remembered. S. D. Morgan (Sammy) was a Quaker, and had been a conscientious objector during the First World War. Usually mild and benevolent, his handsome face could sometimes contort with sudden rages and he would send books and pencils flying through the air. Waste of time or talent roused him to a black fury: "You are going down the drain!" he would shout. He could not bear to see the young men standing for hours on a corner of the Market Square "watching all the girls go by". So, with immense dedication, he campaigned and worked to create the Coleford Community Centre — and his portrait still hangs there. Whenever, on holiday in the mountains, I see a glacial U-shaped valley, I hear again the squeak of his chalk on the blackboard as he copied out his interminable notes, and smile with affection.

The Forest of Dean, as a Royal Forest, was extra-parochial and therefore fell outside the domain of the pre-Reformation churches, like those of Newland and Staunton, both dating from the thirteenth century. Though some well-intentioned priests made missionary journeys into the depths of the Forest, the miners and colliers were too work-begrimed to be welcomed among the Sunday-suited congregations, and if they did come to church were expected to stand in the aisles. It is not surprising that there were few weddings in the Forest: it was a long way to the unwelcoming churches. So, though the free miners had their own ceremonies, there were many natural children and Foresters gained a reputation — sometimes deserved — for immorality. The old workhouse took care of many scores of illegitimate children.

Coleford had a chapel on the Tump, but it was only a chapel-of-ease under the great church at Newland. It was damaged in the Civil War, enlarged in 1743, and replaced in 1821 by an octagonal chapel — remaining Coleford's only Anglican place of worship until the large Victorian redstone church was built in 1878–80. Thereafter, in 1882, it was demolished, leaving the clock tower isolated on the Tump, where it still stands.

Meanwhile, the field was open for an army of Nonconformist chapels of differing persuasions. There were Baptist communities from as early as 1653, probably influenced by Cromwell's "preaching captains" in the Civil War. It may be that since Coleford shopkeepers provisioned Cromwell's army, they took in his religion as they gave out their supplies. Certainly when, during the Protectorate, Coleford asked to be licensed as a market town, the application was granted, in spite of the opposition of Royalist Monmouth, which was afraid of losing custom. So the shopkeepers of Coleford flourished, and in time were able to give financial support to the new Baptist chapel.

Throughout the eighteenth century the Baptists remained, but only as little groups meeting in an old barn or private houses and carrying out their baptisms in Cannock Brook. Then in 1799 the remarkable William Bradley founded the first Baptist chapel. A middle-class, highly intelligent man who had a scheme for a Severn tunnel, he braved the colliers and miners in the depths of the Forest, where he was pelted with filth, rotten eggs and dead cats. Nonconformity was linked with revolution at this time, and distrust was increased by the traditional attitude of Foresters to the outsiders they called foreigners. Nevertheless, by 1804 Mr Bradley's initial thirteen members, ancestors of some of my friends, had grown to seventy-eight, and the first chapel premises were built on the site of an old silk factory with which Bradley was connected and which he had probably helped to finance. Known in 1837 as the Baptist Meeting House, it was a small building, incorporating the minister's house, with a baptistery and a cemetery behind it. During the

33

nineteenth century the Baptists flourished in Coleford and in 1842, inspired by the example of the handsome chapel the Independents had built, the elders applied for a licence to build a Baptist chapel. By 1857 they had raised £3,000, and in 1858 the present Baptist chapel was opened with a membership of 240, along with 500 in the Sunday School. Its opening on 5 October was celebrated by a dinner at the Angel Hotel at 2s 6d a head. The old Meeting House became the Sunday School and the chapel flourished.

After my family and friends, the most important influence in my early life was this Baptist chapel and Sunday School. I learned more there than I did in my early years at school. It was more than a church, more than a school: it was a community centre that filled our week, and our year was brightened by its outings, anniversaries, "treats" and concerts. On the anniversary of the foundation of the Sunday School movement we paraded behind a brass band through the streets of Coleford, under a banner bearing the portrait of its founder, the Gloucester printer Robert Raikes. Thanks to him, the Nonconformist Sunday School became a powerful influence throughout the country, affecting thousands of children at home and abroad. In later life I discovered how powerful this Nonconformist tradition has been in the lives of many distinguished men and women of my generation. Sometimes, as in the case of Tony Crosland, who was brought up as a strict Plymouth Brother, it produced a contrary reaction. But James and Audrey Callaghan were both Sunday School teachers, and Margaret Thatcher, Geoffrey Howe, Roy

Jenkins and many others were influenced by the Nonconformist ethos.

In my time the Baptist chapel and Sunday School dominated Newland Street almost as far as the hamlet of Whitecliff. The chapel itself was a surprisingly impressive building, with twin turrets modelled, it was said, on the cathedral at Amiens. Next to the chapel itself was the caretaker's cottage and then came the Sunday School, the old Meeting House. As a child I was always puzzled by the gravestones at the rear, marking the old Nonconformist burial ground.

In 1887 the Sunday School had been enlarged to include the primary school which I attended from the age of four. Since the chapel itself is now altered beyond recognition, it is worth recalling what it once was. In recent years it has been divided horizontally: now the chapel is upstairs and the Sunday School below. In my day the spacious interior, which was planned to seat 800, had upstairs two galleries, for girls on one side and boys on the other facing each other, with the choir and organ in the middle. Downstairs the pulpit rose above a platform that concealed the baptistery, where two or three times a year baptisms were performed. Above the pulpit in letters of gold, the inscription read: "O worship the Lord in the beauty of holiness". The word "beauty" was significant. Some Nonconformist sects rejected music as part of the Devil's seductive evil, but in our chapel hymns and anthems were sung with enthusiasm. When, one holiday, I took my children to chapel they were

35

astonished to hear the congregation singing in perfect harmony.

Beside the organ, in a dark corner, was the organ blower's cubby-hole. My brothers had the concession, and for twopence a week would pump the lever which provided the power for the organ. If they became immersed in their comics and forgot to blow, the organ would wail into silence until the organist rapped and called "Wind!" Many years later, when writing the life of Mary Livingstone, I understood exactly the meaning of her sister's complaint, "Missionary wives are the organ blowers" — for without them the music stopped.

The choir was at the heart of the chapel. My mother had sung in it since she was a little girl, reading the music from "tonic sol fa". She and her friend Nora sang duets like little angels, but often plagued the excellent choirmaster of the day until he called "Rose Crook and Nora Morris — OUT!" In my day the choirmistress, Miss Emily Taylor, was a remarkable lady. Henry James might have written her life. The daughter of a successful Coleford businessman, Mr Terrett-Taylor, she had been sent to school at Bristol, where she had a good education with special training in music. She was engaged to be married, but on the eve of her wedding she decided she was not in love and cancelled the ceremony. She remained single, devoting the rest of her life to the service of the chapel and the community. Had there been a lord of the manor in Coleford, she would have made an excellent lady. She was not only the choirmistress but the superintendent of the Sunday School, a Justice of the Peace, a much admired member of the community and a secretary of the Bell's Grammar School Trust. Her home, Forest House, had once belonged to the famous metallurgist David Mushet, whose son Robert in 1856 perfected the Bessemer process of self-hardening steel. The house has since become a hotel and guests now dine where once we stood at her piano and rehearsed our pieces for the chapel concerts.

On Friday nights Miss Taylor conducted choir practice with some crispness. The chapel had a long history of musical excellence, and she kept up the tradition. She sometimes sang duets with my mother in her pleasant contralto voice. In my memory she stands immortal, white hair escaping round her still handsome face, tapping with her baton in the choir gallery above the clock. I never hear the *Messiah* without seeing her again and hearing the familiar voices around me: the clear true tenor of John Horwood behind me; in front, my mother and Aunty Nora singing the duets as they have done all their lives in the sweetest harmony; the full bass of Ted Mansfield still breaking in out of time in the pause in the Hallelujah Chorus.

The minister, the Reverend Frank Hearn, came to us from Melksham with his wife and two daughters, Joan and Gladys; all of them played an important part in my formative years. Mr Hearn was an intelligent man who preached tidy and interesting Sunday sermons. Unable to afford a university education, he had gained his diploma in religious studies from an Oxford University correspondence course. Like many Nonconformists he had a passionate interest in science, and was an astronomer *manqué*. I often found him in his book-lined study in the manse working on his telescope, or grinding the glass lens with infinite care, following the instructions from an American manual. Finally the great day came when his telescope was ready. He told Joan to call her friends to come and see the great miracle — the mountains of the Moon. When, in later years, I talked in 10 Downing Street with the first astronauts to walk on the Moon, I thought of the Baptist minister in his back garden and wished he could have been with us.

His wife, a warm, practical lady, still carried a touch of the accent of her east London childhood. The girls were seldom allowed to visit the Coleford cinema, not just because it was a bad influence but because she saved every penny so that they could have an annual family holiday. Highly intelligent, Mrs Hearn sometimes took her husband's place in the pulpit, where the congregation considered her a better preacher than him. "She speaks to the heart," they said. She was frequently invited to preach at the little chapels in the surrounding villages — where she never allowed the congregations to forget to pay her expenses. "A labourer is worthy of his hire," she would say, as her daughter remembers. Joan, attractive, blonde, blue-eyed, lively and intelligent, was and remains one of my best friends, as was her self-effacing sister, Gladys.

The late John Horwood was one of the most memorable chapel characters. Descended from one of the early founders of the chapel, he carried on the family tradition with distinction. For many years he was the chapel chancellor and keeper of accounts. His mother, gentle Mrs Horwood, ran the primary class in the Sunday School; his sister, Joyce, dedicated all her spare time to the chapel, teaching in the Sunday School, running the Girls' Life Brigade, decorating the chapel, even varnishing the pews. Her brother and my particular friend, Dennis, married Joan Hearn; together, they were the leaders of the little gang of my childhood. Dennis himself became a Baptist minister.

Other families reached back far into the past. Their names — Trotter, Provis, Locke, Cullis — recur again and again in the records of Coleford. Surrounded by such continuity, I grew up with a sense of stability, security and deep roots.

I remember so many other remarkable characters. There was Mr Kilby, the village blacksmith: "a mighty man was he", in his leather apron among the sparks and hissing hooves — and on Sundays in his best suit he was mightier still. He led prayers in the vestry in a tremendous voice, challenging the Almighty. "O Lord our heavenly Father, thou knowest . . ." and the Lord had better watch out if he did not. There were no intermediaries in the Baptist chapel, no priests to pardon confessions. Prayers were direct, and Mr Kilby spoke to God as man to man.

One of the gentlest of saints was Mrs Lydia Salter, who took us on Saturday expeditions. She knew magical places deep in the woods where the best blackberries grew; she knew the secret way to the "Hearkening Rock" in the woods near Staunton. Miles below, the Wye was just visible, winding its way towards

39

Monmouth. "Put your ear to the great stone slab," she said, "and you can hear people talking at The Haze," a big house on the other side of the river. They never spoke to us.

She climbed with us over her garden wall to picnic under the big oak in the rushy field beyond it. On winter afternoons she made us splendid teas with tinned peaches, and we played snakes and ladders, and obscure literary games that involved shouting, "I have Percy Bysshe Shelley!" "Who has got Sir Walter Scott?" We were the children she never had, and in turn we loved her dearly. When I went up to Oxford she gave me a silver serviette ring engraved with my initials, which she could ill afford. I prize it still.

The years of my childhood were not all sunshine and roses. Though we were shielded from most of the troubles around us, I was aware of the hard lives that others had. On the dark winter mornings we watched the colliers (as we called those who mined coal; "miners" dug for iron) sitting on their heels outside our house waiting for the bus to take them to the mines. The accounts of pit accidents gave me many nightmares. Then there was a dark, dirty house from which sometimes we heard screams and wailings, where a bruised wife died and an illegitimate child was born. Gossip was silenced when we came into the room. Outside the school gates was a cottage where a poor mad girl was chained in the yard. I shut my ears to her sobs and whimpers. I hated passing another house where a shambling mad girl would come out to hug us. "She loves children," her mother would say, but I would ask to get in the pram with my younger sister. I never knew of a divorce in my youth, but sometimes a woman would unaccountably kill herself. A girl had thrown herself into the well in the garden of the White House, at the top of the recreation ground; and a friend's mother hanged herself. No one told us why.

In 1930 tragedy struck home. During the slump my father lost his job as a crane driver in the stone quarry. I read his testimonial — "a sober and industrious workman" — and never forgot my fury at the patronizing tone of the letter, nor the hurt at seeing him standing in the queue at the Labour Exchange. I hated being called out in front of the class to receive my free milk because my father was unemployed. When a dear old lady from the chapel gave me sixpence at Coleford Fair Day "because your Dad's out", I felt shame and anger, not gratitude.

For a time after that my father worked at home, mending our shoes with old car tyres, peeling potatoes, and digging in our allotment in Boxbush Road. I never heard him grumble. Then came the wonderful day when I came home to a shout from my mother: "Dad's got a job!"

He had been put in charge of the new waterworks. Coleford was growing and the water supply was inadequate, so a station was installed at Redbrook to pump water up to a reservoir at the Buckstone — the highest point in the area. It was opened with great ceremony in October 1932 and described with enthusiasm. But when I went to visit my father there I always found it depressing, dark and dank. He walked to work and in the summer evenings I would go to meet him, often reading my homework as I walked down the green valley. *Villette* is indissolubly linked in my memory with dark Redbrook.

On 14 June 1932 it was my fourteenth birthday, and I felt I wanted to make it somehow special. I told my father I would walk to work with him in the early morning. "I'll bet you don't," he said. But I got up with him, watched him light the fire in the cold kitchen and take my mother her tea. She thought I was mad.

We walked in silence up over the recreation ground and down to Cherry Orchard, where the road drops steeply to Redbrook. I waited there to watch him down the hill. He had once found a rare orchid in a quarry at the bottom of the hill, and now said he would look for it and signal to me if it was still there. But when he looked back it was thumbs down; his orchid had gone. We waved goodbye and I walked home.

The next winter he fell ill with pneumonia — the Redbrook damp and the daily climb home had finished him. In a snowy January the fire was lit for the first time in the little grate in my parents' bedroom. His friends laid straw in the road outside, as they did in those days, to muffle the sound of the carts. I plumped up his pillows and he thanked me, saying, "Ah — a bed of roses!" I gave him his birthday present — a tin of brilliantine — so that he would not go bald, and some hard pears. This month he would be fifty-two. I could not stand listening to his painful gasping for breath, so I walked down to the bus stop to wait for the bus to bring breathing apparatus from Gloucester. Early the next morning he died.

They laid him in the little sitting room and shut the door. "Would you like to see him?" my mother asked. My elder sister shook her head. But I wish I had said "yes".

On the day of the funeral my younger sister and I were sent out to friends. I sat in their cold sitting room and tried to drink a mug of cocoa with skin on top. My brothers told me of their walk to the cemetery, and how all the men in the street had taken off their hats. That week the headline in the local paper read: "Quite a shadow was cast over Coleford with the death of Ted Edmunds."

Throughout the day my mother held firm, but when it was all over she broke down. "He'll be so cold up in that cemetery," she said. In the years to come she rarely spoke of him; it was too painful. Though she was still young, she never remarried. It was unthinkable: "I'll never find another mate like him." When, at the Gwilliamses' house on Sunday nights, we gathered around the piano and they called for a song — "Rose, sing 'Smiling Through' " — she shook her head and said, "Not that, not that." The last words were too poignant: "If ever I'm left in this world all alone . . . those two eyes of blue, come smiling through for me." Sentimental the old ballads may be, but they can tear at the heart.

The death of my father was more of a watershed in my life than I realized at the time. I had taken so much of the chapel teaching without thought; had cheerfully sung, "There's a home for little children above the bright blue sky," and, kneeling on the cold bedroom floor, repeated after my mother, "Gentle Jesus, meek and mild / Look upon a little child / Pity my simplicity / Suffer me to come to thee." It was comforting, though I did not understand. In the Sunday School primary room, a picture of Jesus showed him enfolding children of all colours in his arms. Kindness, gentleness, tolerance and an all-embracing love were the ideals of good Christians. These were the excellent values that I willingly but unthinkingly absorbed.

In due course the Reverend Hearn encouraged our group to be baptized. I completely accepted the Baptist belief that no godparents should make promises on behalf of a baby, that each has to commit himself when old enough to understand.

Later, when, researching the life of Emma Darwin, I read of the puzzling refusal of Emma and Charles to stand as godparents to a cousin's baby, I understood. But I used my father's death as an excuse to put off the moment. I had not come to terms with pain and death. Eventually, however, persuaded by the minister and my friends, I agreed to be baptized with Gladys Hearn and others of our group.

I dreaded the ceremony. It always seemed disturbingly apocalyptic: the dim, gas-lit chapel, the familiar platform removed to reveal the steps down into the baptistery; then the splash, the peal of the organ and the burst of "Hallelujah!" from the choir. I suspect my mother felt the same. I do not think she had ever been baptized: she would have found the ceremony immodest and slightly indecent. Characteristically, she warned me, "Mind you don't catch your death." However, as I stepped down into the water and the minister expertly rocked me backwards under the surface, she sang her "Hallelujah!" with the rest. Our dear Mrs Salter waited at the other side with a black shawl and took me to the vestry to be dried (behind a screen) before the fire. I wish I could say I felt transformed. I did not; but it had been a rite of passage and an important one.

At fourteen I was small and skinny and late in developing. My mother told me nothing about sex, and when at last I had my first period she merely said, "I expect the girls at school have told you all about it," and handed me a square of terry towelling with loops and an elastic girdle.

My ignorance was profound and, surprisingly, I had no curiosity. I had never seen a naked body: we always dressed and undressed modestly under our nightgowns. The school having no library, let alone any art books, I saw no pictures of nudes, and Christ was always decently covered on the cross. The headmaster did not believe in teaching biology, so botany took its place; and the birds and bees were not helpful.

I was sixteen before I received the most tentative of kisses on a cold cheek as I walked with a young man through the starlit frosty fields on a Sunday night after chapel — traditionally the courting time — and it was not until my last year at school that I had a real, but totally innocent, romance. My friend Joyce and I, walking round the town on a Saturday night, were pursued and caught by two likely lads from Monmouth. Mine was an airman, stationed at Basra and home on leave. For me it was exciting and exotic: it gave me a partner at the local dances, and to be picked up from school in his secondhand car gave me a new and elevated status.

My mother tried without success to stop the attachment, but we kept it going, mostly by correspondence when he returned to Basra. She need not have worried; in those days innocence was a stout protector. When I left for Oxford, my young airman warned me that if, as he feared, war broke out, as a navigator he would be killed in the first few weeks. He was right. I never saw him again.

In the years between fourteen and eighteen I began to wake up in many ways. I took the School Certificate early and then had three stimulating years in the sixth form, taught by three dedicated teachers who literally changed my life.

Miss Lamin, young and pretty with a plait of golden hair, taught me French, sang charming French songs, and read the poems of Victor Hugo and Lamartine. I can still hear her quiet precise voice reading "*Quand je serai bien vieille, le soir à la chandelle*". Now that I am *bien vieille*, it is still one my favourite poems and I remember every word.

Robert (Bobby) Noble had come to Bell's straight from Oxford and taught us history. Not only was there no school library, there was at that time no public library in Coleford — but he brought us books from

Gloucester and lent us his own copy of *Mother India*, with the warning that perhaps we should not take it home, lest our parents be shocked. He opened our eyes to art and taught us how to frame postcards of great paintings. Until he came our art mistress had set us to draw, week after week, a jug, a bowl of fruit and a huge peacock feather. Most of all he shared his love of music, revived the school orchestra in which I had once played the clarinet, and taught us to sing madrigals and play recorders. After he left the school, as County Musical Director he began the tradition of carol singing around the Christmas tree in Trafalgar Square. Serious and good-looking, with big blue eyes and fair hair, he had a sexless kind of innocence that aroused a maternal desire to protect him from the rougher Forest lads.

I owe most, however, to the English mistress, Miss Joan Davis. It was she who decided that I must try for a scholarship to Oxford University. She persuaded my mother that, should I gain a place, the school would find enough scholarships and grants and the Education Department would provide a loan. My elder sister and some of her friends had been similarly aided to take a teacher's diploma at Cheltenham Training College, and Ivy was by now teaching at an elementary school in Birmingham. My mother saw the Oxford proposal as a step in the same direction, only along a higher road. It would take three years to get a degree and a further year at the Oxford Education Department to get a diploma. I should then be qualified to teach in a secondary school. It would not be easy, but my mother was prepared to manage. Ivy and my brothers were working and my younger sister Doreen had started her career in the telephone exchange next door.

More worldly-wise friends saw problems of which we were quite unaware. Mr Hearn came in a for a quiet talk. "Oxford University", he gently explained, was "for aristocrats and public-school boys, and the girls would be from schools like Cheltenham Ladies College. Edna would be out of place." He meant well, but my mother was adamant. "If they say at school she should go to Oxford, then she must try for Oxford." Not long down from Oxford himself, Bobby Noble came, blushing with embarrassment, to tell us what kind of clothes I should need — but he was encouraging. And so the application forms were duly filled in.

Ted Heath noted in his memoirs that there were similar concerns when he had gone up to Oxford. "I was the first member of my family ever to go to a university and my parents were, naturally, delighted. But I already suspected that they were also apprehensive about the financial difficulties that they were facing. They had also wondered, they told me some time later, whether our humble background would put me at a permanent disadvantage compared with many of my contemporaries . . . In those days, overcoming class differences was not easy." At that time accents marked class differences more than they do today. Ted Heath, Margaret Thatcher and Roy Jenkins all took pains to acquire new tones. Recently, listening to a recording of Philip Toynbee addressing the Oxford Union, I was reminded of the cut-glass public-school accents of this time.

Some years later the playwright Dennis Potter made a similar progress from miner's son in the Forest of Dean to Oxford student, but found the transition difficult. Unlike him, but like Heath, I soon adjusted. After my first term my Coleford friends told me I had lost my Forest accent. In fact, it is still there.

Until this time I believe my friend Joan, the minister's daughter, was the first girl to go from Bell's to any university. She went up to Bristol to read history the year ahead of me. But no one had raised their sights to Oxford. At this time — 1936 — there were only four women's colleges, and the competition was intense. It was a more ambitious project than I realized. I was profoundly ignorant about the higher reaches of academic life, and when asked to choose between St Hugh's and St Hilda's on the application form I thought of my uncle Hugh and followed his name. I would need Latin for the entrance exam, and Latin had disappeared from the school centuries ago with Mr Edward Bell. But, thanks to the headmaster, Mr Hough, who brushed up his Latin and coached me, I learned enough for scholarship purposes in a year — and forgot it as fast afterwards!

Miss Davis brought mountains of books from Gloucester Library in her battered old car. We read *Antony and Cleopatra* in her sitting room in the evenings. I begged to read Cleopatra aloud, and was the queen in her burnished barge on the waters of the Nile. She took us to Stratford to see the play (the set Shakespeare text that year) but I was disappointed. No one ever rivalled the queen of my mind, nor mourned

49

her Antony as Joan Davis did. "The soldier's pole is fallen and there is nothing left remarkable beneath the visiting moon."

One weekend she took a group of us to the Friends' Holiday Guest House to freshen our minds before the Higher School examination. It was in Llandogo on the Wye, upriver from the spot where Wordsworth had composed his unforgettable "Lines Written above Tintern Abbey". Here we saw again for ourselves the "steep and lofty cliffs", the "hedgerows, hardly hedgerows, little lines of sportive wood run wild", the "sounding cataract", the "tall rock, The mountain, and the deep and gloomy wood . . .".

Joan Davis never married — she lost the love of her life — but those of us who were taught by her owe her a priceless inheritance. Many years later one of her old scholars heard me lecture, and came up to tell me that she heard throughout the voice of Joan Davis. Now, whenever I ask successful men or women of distinction, "Who taught you at school?", I recognize the sudden glow as they remember their Miss Davis, without whom their lives would have been so different.

In 1936, thanks to Miss Davis and those other gifted teachers appointed by John Hough, I won a place at St Hugh's College, Oxford. I still remember rushing out, waving the telegram, to my mother who was hanging the washing on the line.

So that September my brothers carried my trunk up to Coleford's goods railway station. I followed later on the red-and-white bus to Gloucester, where I changed to the coach for Oxford. I was eighteen and a new world awaited.

Looking back, I think what a privileged childhood I had. I was fortunate in my family and friends, in my chapel background, in my teachers and, above all, in spending those seminal early years in the incomparable beauty of the Forest of Dean.

After I had written my first book, I went with Denis to see Joan Davis. She had not long to live and was in bed in a nursing home near Tintern Abbey in the Wye Valley. With the old enthusiasm undiminished, she discussed my book and Denis's autobiography, and gave us both brisk advice. Then I suddenly realized that the home had once been the Friends' Holiday Guest House to which she had brought us long ago. Sitting by her bed, I heard again her lovely voice reading in the old sixth-form classroom and smelt the pinks under the open windows.

> Once again
> Do I behold these steep and lofty cliffs,
> That on a wild secluded scene impress
> Thoughts of more deep seclusion . . .
> These beauteous forms,
> Through a long absence, have not been to me
> As is a landscape to a blind man's eye:
> But oft . . . I have owed to them . . . feelings too
> Of unremembered pleasure . . .

Her voice is fading now, but the words come back with a new meaning.

>   For I have learned
> To look on nature, not as in the hour
> Of thoughtless youth; but hearing oftentimes
> The still, sad music of humanity . . .
>   . . . And I have felt
> A presence that disturbs me with the joy
> Of elevated thoughts; a sense sublime
> Of something far more deeply interfused
> . . .
> A motion and a spirit, that impels
> All thinking things, all objects of all thought,
> And rolls through all things.

CHAPTER
TWO

OXFORD, 1936–1940

[T]he majority of women students are embryo school-mistresses who take everything literally, make copious notes at lectures, talk to one another about the lecturer afterwards, do not bother about their personal appearances, carry hundreds of books in the little wicker baskets in front of the handlebars of their bicycles. They think about the examinations, and any who think about other things are unlikely to earn the approval of dons.

John Betjeman, *An Oxford University Chest*

I suppose there was some truth in Betjeman's rather sour sketch of "undergraduettes". In our serviceable tweed suits, flat shoes and lisle stockings, few of us aspired to sartorial elegance, though I remember one who regularly received packages from Italy, each containing twelve pairs of silk stockings — this before nylons were introduced. Many of us were at Oxford on grants and loans, so our clothes came from Marks & Spencer, not Knightsbridge. My friend Daphne included me in a witty verse on our contemporaries: "in Marks [Marx] and Spencer [Edmund Spenser] was her joy".

53

Another jaundiced observer of the female student, Christopher Hobhouse, noted that we were "perpetually awheel". Well, of course we were. Bikes were very necessary. St Hugh's was a mile up the Banbury Road; how else should we get to lectures? And while it is true that most of our dons there were spinsters — for they were the generation who lost their sweethearts in the trenches of the First World War — in my experience they bore no resemblance to their caricature.

What these cavilling men did not realize was that we were not grimly "cabined, cribbed, confined". I was free, for the first time in my life, in the most beautiful city I had ever seen. Yes, we worked — who would not, surrounded by the unimagined riches of the Bodleian Library? But we also walked on Cumnor Hill and punted on the river, even though I could not swim. I remember even now the delight of the throw and thrust of the long pole and the pull of the boat through the green meadows.

Then there were all those young men who sent notes by college messengers with invitations to "tea and cinnamon toast" in their rooms. Hobhouse sniffed loftily that "little danger lurks in the path of the 'undergraduette' ": in his view, "about half the men in Oxford are no more adventurous than new-born lambs; the rest, if they adventure at all, look in other directions than St Hilda's or St Hugh's". In fact, they were happy to be good friends. Accustomed to the company of boys at home and at school, I enjoyed their undemanding companionship. My public-school friends found it interesting that my school had been co-educational —

thinking it, I suppose, an experimental school like Bedales — but the schools in the Forest of Dean had taken both boys and girls.

As for our supposedly dismal little rooms — pictured by Hobhouse as "minute green-and-yellow bed-sitter[s] opening off an echoing shiny corridor", where he imagined us drinking "cocoa and Kia-Ora" instead of "claret and port" — neither he nor Betjeman could know the sheer joy of my first room, in a house along St Margaret's Road. It was indeed a bed-sitting room — but it was a large, comfortable, ground-floor room with huge windows opening on to the street. "Easy to climb out and in," said my worldly-wise friends. But who would want to? This was the first room that I'd had all to myself. The bathroom was on the first floor, the bath itself huge, almost frighteningly deep. I left the door unlocked when I took my first real bath in case I should be unable to get out and have to call for help! In my second year I moved into college: my small modern berth there was bright enough, but could not compare with the exhilaration of that first "room of my own".

The other delight was the college garden, lovingly created and tended by Miss Rogers. Here in the spring and summer I could find a seat enclosed by scented bushes or a green lawn where I could lie and read or write in peace. It may seem strange that, coming from the country, I should find this a new experience, but at home gardens were for growing vegetables, not for sitting in. On my first spring holiday at home I took a chair outside and sat beside the rhubarb to write. My mother thought me mad — and even madder when I took with me a cup of black coffee. We rarely opened our bottle of Camp essence of coffee. "Without milk!" she said in horror. "It'll turn your inside black."

On the whole, however, my first year at Oxford was an extension of my Coleford life. I played hockey for St Hugh's, as I had done for Bell's, and joined the Bach Choir — where Ted Heath was already established among the basses — and the Baptist John Bunyan Society. This was mainly a social group, meeting on Sundays for tea at the home of Dr Wheeler Robinson in the Cornmarket, where his wife presided over a teatable with a silver urn, and students, mostly from Keble, handed round tea and sandwiches. If we held theological discussions, I regret to say I do not remember. But we also met occasionally to sing Gilbert and Sullivan operas, and went to tea on summer afternoons at the house of a Baptist lady at Littlemore, just east of Oxford. The friendship of fellow Baptists in that first year was comforting.

I went often to college chapel on Sundays, but the service was Anglican and, repeating the Creed, I realized how little I had thought about the beliefs on which my religion had been based. In the first vacation I took my doubts to Mr Hearn, the Baptist minister. Did he really believe in the Virgin Birth? Or the Resurrection of the Body? And what was the Holy Ghost? I wish I could remember the advice he gave, but he was a rational man and I felt he sympathized. Gradually I lost touch with the John Bunyan Society. When we all parted at the end of my third year, some wit passed round a little note: "Sic transit gloria Edmundi."

Betjeman mocked our earnest attendance at lectures, but he failed to understand that for country bumpkins like me they were important. I cycled in cap and flapping gown through the gates of the Groves of Academe to another world where the people (students and dons) and the places (ancient colleges and halls, and above all the Bodleian Library) alike were all part of the magical Oxford experience. No printed article could compare with the dramatic lecture given by C. S. Lewis on "The Prolegomenon to the Middle Ages" — even the title intoxicated. He always ended with a flourishing phrase and a swirl of gown as he left the platform. I have never forgotten Nevill Coghill's lectures on Chaucer and his lucid exposition of *Troilus and Criseyde*.

In our first year we had to take a preliminary examination hurdle, Pass Moderations, entailing lectures by Marcus Todd with a Latin paper to be written on Pliny. Professor Todd, a gentle, precise man whose courtesy was legendary, would greet late students with an apology for having his lectures in such a difficult place — Oriel College. He gave me a lifelong love of classical history. I would meet Pliny again many years later at the site of his garden on Lake Como. Helen Darbishire's lectures on Wordsworth were equally memorable, reawakening my memories of "Lines Written above Tintern Abbey" on the Wye. Now, listening to her reading *The Prelude* in her northern accent, I was transported to the Lake District.

57

The Oxford system of tutorials, however, was even more important than the lectures. On arrival we were allotted a tutor who guided us in pairs through the three-year course, setting our programme of work, later on sending us to other colleges for tutorials. Daphne Thomas — my tutorial partner — and I read our weekly essays to Miss Ethel Seaton. Seated with her cat by the cosy coal fire in her sitting room on the Parks Road, Miss Seaton was one of the spinsters so unfairly caricatured by Betjeman. Patiently she understood my ignorance and led me out of it. Daphne and I were primly shocked by Chaucer's cheerful vulgarity; Miss Seaton, "old spinster" as she may have been, taught us to accept his realism.

Our syllabus was limited: English Literature began with Anglo-Saxon but ended with the Romantics. The novel was excluded, along with modern poetry. However, I was drawn to the direct vigour of the Anglo-Saxon poets and was honoured by our tutor, Mrs Martin Clark, who invited me to special after-dinner tutorials on Old Norse. The knowledge I gained here was unexpectedly useful in later years when I was teaching in Yorkshire, helping me to understand their dialect in which "laking" meant playing and "spice" meant sweets.

For other tutorials we were sent to men's colleges — to Balliol for sessions on Keats and Shelley. Best of all were the illuminating hours with Edmund Blunden, the poet, author and critic who was at this time a Fellow of Merton College. I had read his *Undertones of War*, reminiscences of his experiences in the First World War.

58

It seemed difficult to believe that this sensitive and easy-going man had suffered the trauma of trench warfare in the Battle of the Somme, fighting with a courage that had won him the Military Cross. I know of no one, except my own husband, who could so communicate his love of literature after the bruising of war. He held his tutorials among his books in his own sitting room in north Oxford, where we sat with glasses of sherry — an unaccustomed sophistication — while he roamed around the shelves, taking down volumes and reading at random. It was here that I first heard the voice of Dr Johnson booming across the centuries. Blunden was an example of the true educator, drawing out and leading on young minds. Alas, I have lost the book of his own poems he gave me.

I had gone up to Oxford from a school with no library, in a town which had no public library nearer than Gloucester, so the libraries, bookshops and museums of Oxford opened doors to an undiscovered country. I spent the happiest hours in the Bodleian Library at desks rubbed smooth by generations of students, intoxicated by the smell of ancient leather, and realizing again and again the profound depth of my ignorance.

From my new friends I was also to realize, in my innocence, how unaware I was of real life and of the world. In my second year, I went for a week's holiday to Paris with my boyfriend at that time. Handsome, very clever and kind, he was older than me. One of my worldly-wise girlfriends shocked me profoundly when she took it for granted that we would be sleeping

59

together. In fact we had a happy and perfectly platonic week, visiting the opera, hearing Wanda Landowska playing her harpsichord at the Conservatoire, eating unfamiliar dishes outside cafés on the Champs Elysées. If it was a disappointing week for him, he kindly never showed it. However, soon after our return the attachment ended.

It was the influence of friends rather than dons or tutors that did most to shape my life in these years. It was an exceptional time, and it brought forth men and women of exceptional quality. I was fortunate that I could count among those I came to know many whose rising careers I would watch with interest over the years to come. I wish I had had the prescience to have marked their characters more carefully — so often I catch only a snapshot in the memory, though sometimes even the body language captured in that is revealing. I have a particularly vivid memory of walking along the High with Tony Crosland and Roy Jenkins. Tony wears his famous long camel overcoat, upright, handsome head thrown back. Roy, head bent, turns deferentially to him. I wish I could recall some profound remarks made by these two — the future Chancellor of the Exchequer and Foreign Secretary — but all I recall is my puritanical shock when Tony said briskly, "I must go and have a pee." As his friends later told me, he would have said it deliberately to shock; I expect it was the quickest way to get rid of me.

Then in another snapshot I see the young Nico Henderson standing at the corner of the Broad, absent-mindedly pondering, his hair ruffled, his bow tie at an angle: not long ago I listened with admiration and affection to Sir Nicholas Henderson, Her Majesty's erstwhile ambassador in Paris, as he stood in Westminster Abbey to give the funeral oration in memory of Lord Jenkins of Hillhead — our old friend Roy of Oxford days. So he had stood a few months earlier in Westminster Cathedral, speaking in memory of my dear friend Elizabeth, Lady Longford. I had not known her at Oxford, but my memory holds an unforgettable image of the young don Frank Pakenham, in Home Guard uniform, speaking in a demonstration against conscription. In memory, Frank stands before some forgotten stage, helping somewhat ineffectually to produce a performance of *Winterset* and consoling me after the director, Leo Pliatzky, had mocked my awkward acting. Leo, a friend of Iris Murdoch, became my closest friend for some years until I deserted him for Denis Healey. He had a brilliant mind, and was sensitive, funny and brave. Proud of his Jewish name, he steadfastly refused to change it to Green as his family had done. As a poor boy he had been forced to leave school to work in a warehouse in Manchester, until Harold Laski heard of him and sponsored him through his years at Oxford. When, during the Labour government of 1974–9, Denis became Chancellor of the Exchequer, Leo — then Sir Leo Pliatzky, a Treasury knight — was one of his team. But I never saw him again after we parted. He married happily, but in his last years became almost blind and died of cancer, mourned by many of his old, now distinguished, Oxford friends. I did not hear of his death until Roy

Jenkins told me. It was typical of Roy that he took the trouble to visit Leo in hospital in his last days. I shall always regret that I did not know of his illness. I should have liked to have wished him goodbye.

I am sorry that I lost touch over the years with my St Hugh's friends. Though they came from backgrounds so different from mine — educated at Bedales, Cheltenham, Roedean — I was always at ease with them and was grateful, especially at the beginning, for their warm friendship. I owe a particularly deep debt of gratitude to my two friends Dorothy Townend and Jack Dawes, whose Yorkshire practical sense and generosity helped me through a difficult patch during the war years.

In my second year I became increasingly involved in the world of Oxford politics.

Politics had played little part in my Coleford days. Parliament was infinitely removed and rarely mentioned, though I do remember chanting, "Vote, vote, vote for good old Wignall!" without the slightest idea who he was. My father had been in a reserved occupation during the Great War so there were no family memories of the agony of trench warfare, though war poetry and my Quaker friends made me a pacifist. My father's unemployment during the slump left me angry, but the levers of power were held far away — as uncontrollable as thunder.

However, in my Oxford years — 1936 to 1940 — students were more politically active than at almost any time. These were the years of the "gathering storm": the rise of fascism in Germany and Italy, the support of

Hitler and Mussolini for General Franco in the Spanish Civil War, and the German invasion of Austria. After Chamberlain's pathetic attempt to hold back Hitler's marching army with the Munich Agreement in September 1938, the invasion of Czechoslovakia in March 1939 and the attack on Poland, the storm would break, and the Second World War would be upon us all.

For us students it was a period of constant excitement, fervent marches and demonstrations, and a passionate desire to save a whole world that stretched from China in the Far East to Europe on our doorstep. My first political meeting, in 1936, was a Labour Club gathering held to declare opposition to Japan's aggression in China, which it had invaded in 1934. It was a Sunday night, so I wore my Sunday coat and a hat which was quickly removed by my mocking new friends. We were to burn our silk stockings in protest. Since I had never possessed a pair, I could happily agree.

Never again would good and evil, right and wrong be so clearly differentiated. Nor were domestic affairs ignored. In 1936 the unemployed of Jarrow made their long walk to Downing Street. I watched with amusement some of my wealthy student friends marching in the rain through Oxford, collars turned up, caps pulled well down, waving banners declaiming "We Want Work", and remembered my distress at the sight of my father in the queue outside the Labour Exchange during the slump.

In October 1938 Oxford had its chance to protest against Chamberlain's Munich Agreement. Following the death of the sitting MP a by-election was called.

Quintin Hogg (later Lord Hailsham), the official Conservative candidate, stood in support of Chamberlain, but the Conservative Party was deeply divided. Many members of the Oxford University Conservative Association, led by Ted Heath, were passionately opposed to the Munich Agreement and the government's official policy, and supported Dr Lindsay, Master of Balliol, who stood as an Independent Progressive. Ted Heath's banner read: "A Vote for Hogg is a Vote for Hitler". Years later, at Denis's eightieth birthday party in the House of Lords, he would recall with amusement the days when they had electioneered shoulder to shoulder against Quintin Hogg.

This was the first time I had taken part in a political campaign, and I did so because the Spanish Civil War had been for me, as for so many of our generation, a political birth. Ted Heath felt equally deeply, as he recalled in his autobiography, *The Course of My Life*: "We were to witness a conflict which aroused, in our generation, passions every bit as fierce as those stirred up by the war in Vietnam thirty years later." He was at this time a leading figure among Conservative students and chairman of the Federation of University Associations. In that capacity he had been invited to Spain with three other Oxford undergraduates by the Republican government, which had been fighting for two years against General Franco's fascists. He returned from Barcelona — where he had met Jack Jones, later leader of the Transport and General Workers' Union, then in the British contingent of the International Brigade at the front — convinced of the justice of the Republican cause: "we saw for ourselves that the Republican government was introducing progressive social reforms and encouraging a bracing, democratic atmosphere among its people. Most of the men we met were not extremists, by any token, rather they were practical, hard-nosed individuals. All of us were hardened in our resolve to put their case as forcefully as we could back in the United Kingdom."

Though I was at this time profoundly ignorant about world politics in general, I too felt deeply about Spain, seeing the Republican government as the first defence against a tide of fascism sweeping from Germany and Italy. I saw the conflict quite simply as a battle against evil — accounts of the persecution of the Jews filled me with horror. I was moved to write a poor poem beginning, "We have lived too long in the sun", describing devils creeping out of the dark and hiding the sun, and finishing: "And we cannot see, we cannot see in the dark." I had even given a lecture one vacation at the Friends' Meeting House in Coleford, with all the sublime confidence of an eighteen-year-old, called "Which Way to Peace?", the theme of which was the importance of British support for the Spanish Republican government. I was therefore delighted when Dr Lindsay, for whom I had the deepest admiration, agreed to stand in the Oxford by-election.

If, in later years, Balliol students taught by Dr Lindsay reached the heights in their professions, it was, as they all recognized, mainly due to his influence. Denis Healey and Ted Heath write of him in the same way. An idealist, a Christian Socialist, he had the supreme gift of drawing out the best in his students, not stamping them in his own mould but helping them to find themselves. As a parliamentary candidate, he inspired students of all shades of political opinion, and his campaign was widely and enthusiastically supported. The official Labour candidate, Patrick Gordon-Walker, reluctantly stood down in his favour.

Throughout the campaign there were enthusiastic meetings, at many of which I heard Ted Heath — now a supremely confident and persuasive speaker. I should like to record that, canvassing as I did in north Oxford, I met him on the doorsteps; but if I did, neither of us remembered.

The result was to be declared late at night, and we had to be in college by twelve. So we arranged that our friends should cycle past our windows and shout up the result. The philosophy don asked us to come and tell her the news. Accordingly, after the depressing shouts of "The Hog's won!", I knocked on her door. Standing in her woolly dressing gown, she responded: "Oh, I'm so sorry, I did want Dr Lindsay to win — though I voted for Mr Hogg." The philosophy of the ivory tower indeed.

Always more swayed by values than party dogma, I was happy with Dr Lindsay's supporters in the Popular Front Movement, but I was typical of those of us in the Labour Party who became Communists for a short time. It seemed that only the Communists saw the importance of Spain and took seriously the growing menace of fascism. We were "bed and breakfast Communists", joining on Spain and leaving when Russia invaded Finland. In between we enjoyed the camaraderie of the Party, sang political songs with enthusiasm, and blindly admired the great "Russian experiment" to bring equality to the "masses". I am afraid that it was not until many years later, when I wrote the life of Jenny, Karl Marx's wife, that I actually read *Das Kapital*; but I doubt whether many others among my Communist friends had either. There were summer schools for Party members but I remember nothing of our studies, though I was impressed at the time by one fellow student, later to become the great Marxist historian Eric Hobsbawm.

Moments of disillusion were quick in coming. I had marched through the streets of Oxford behind a banner bearing the portrait of a handsome youth we believed had been killed in Spain. He had not, and was nothing like his Byronic portrait. But when a comrade tried to persuade me that "whether or not mines had been laid in the Hormuz channel depended on whether or not it was in the interests of the Soviet Union that they should have been so laid", I gave up. However, many good friends shared the Communist experience with me and we all learned something from it, particularly the methods of Communist infiltration, since we were instructed to join all societies and work hard in them to reach the top. Some were "moles" — secret Communists. Sometimes it seemed an amusing game; but for some, like our Czech friends, it was deadly serious, with later harrowing consequences.

One of my friends, then a "mole", was what they called a "culture boss". I chaired a college Labour Club meeting when he came to talk about art. Denis Healey

— black-haired, red-cheeked and already sporting the eyebrows that were to become famous — impressed me deeply with a lecture on Picasso and modern art. I knew little about painting, but in my enthusiasm for Spain I had been moved by Picasso's *Guernica*. I found Denis impressive but alarmingly omniscient. At that time we both had other partners. I watched him punting on the river with his girlfriend and, in my tweeds and lisle stockings, envied her shorts and sandals. Once, when we travelled up to London in the same railway carriage to a demonstration, he told me that he spent some holidays in the Forest of Dean. But until after Oxford, when I went to teach in his home town of Keighley, we were merely casual friends, and though we occasionally met at Ruskin dances, dancing was not one of his many skills and I am afraid I did not seek him out as a partner. I did, though, exchange admiring glances with the leader of the jazz band "The Bandits", Denis Rattle. Many years later, I would meet him after a concert conducted by his son, the world-famous Simon Rattle, and remember with amusement the old days.

During my last year at St Hugh's, Britain was slowly moving towards war. In January 1939 Franco entered Barcelona: the Republican President resigned and the Spanish Civil War was over. For many years some of us felt unable to take holidays in Spain while Franco was there. The relentless march of events swept on. On 15 March 1939 Hitler marched into Prague, and on 31 March Chamberlain pledged support for Poland. In April Mussolini occupied Albania; in May Mussolini

68

and Hitler signed their pact, and Britain sought to make a similar pact with Russia. In June, King George VI and Queen Elizabeth visited America in a bid to win the support of Roosevelt. On 1 September Germany invaded Poland, and at 11 a.m. on 3 September Chamberlain declared war. I vividly remember hearing his voice on the radio as I sat by the kitchen fire, and can still feel the cane under my hands as I gripped the arms of the basket chair.

Then, for months, nothing seemed to happen. In June 1939 I had taken my degree — a worthy second — and was preparing to move on to the Oxford Department of Education for a year, to get my teaching diploma. Denis volunteered for the army immediately war broke out, but was sent back to Oxford to finish his degree. (He achieved a double first in Greats. Measured against his extraordinary mind, my second took its rightful place.) This was the pattern for many of our friends who had been pacifists in their youth, had argued against conscription, but now saw this as a conflict between good and evil. Perhaps nothing would ever seem so clear-cut again.

For me, the most useful part of my diploma year was the term I spent in teaching practice at Monmouth Girls' High School, during a flu epidemic when one by one the teachers fell ill and I gamely stood in for them. I realized then that the only way to learn to teach is to do it. While I was taking my final examinations, France fell: the history and theory of education seemed increasingly irrelevant.

CHAPTER
THREE

WARTIME, 1940–1945

They have a quick perception of character, and a keen sense of humour; the dwellers among them must be prepared for certain uncomplimentary, though most likely true, observations, pithily expressed. Their feelings are not easily roused, but their duration is lasting . . . Sometimes the sour rudeness amounts to positive insult. Yet, if the "foreigner" takes all this churlishness good-humouredly or as a matter of course, and makes good any claim upon their latent kindliness and hospitality, they are faithful and generous, and thoroughly to be relied upon.

Mrs Gaskell on the Yorkshire character, in
The Life of Charlotte Brontë (1857)

The next three years were to be my introduction to the distinctive Yorkshire character. In September 1940 I went up to Denis's home town, Keighley in Yorkshire, for an interview at the Girls' Grammar School. The headmistress, Mrs Kirk, was the mother of Ken, one of our mutual Oxford friends. And so a new chapter in my life began at their home in Riddlesden, a small village two miles outside Keighley, on the Bradford road, and on the edge of Ilkley Moor. It was a comfortable, solid, stone semi-detached house. The big windows looked down to the Aire Valley and across to the Brontë parsonage in Haworth. Riddlesden itself had a church and a manorial hall with gardens and a small lake. When in 1992 Denis became Lord Healey, he took his title from this village, where he spent a happy childhood with doting parents and an admiring younger brother, Terry.

Denis's father, William, was the principal of Keighley Technical College. He came from Todmorden on the Lancashire border, where he had been one of a large, poor family, his parents having arrived from Ireland in the early part of the century. Will made his way to Leeds University by his own efforts and chose to study technical education because it would more easily earn him a living; however, though he became a good teacher and was admired and remembered with affection by his students, I suspect that his real love was the arts. He had kept a commonplace book in which he wrote poetry and theatre reviews that were published in local newspapers. Like Patrick Brontë, Charlotte's father, he combined Irish sentiment with Yorkshire realism, a mixture of qualities that Denis inherited. Though Will was a generous host — on my first visit he immediately offered me his best Drambuie — his humour could be disconcerting, and his mood often difficult to judge: late arrivals would be greeted with "Punctuality is the courtesy of kings". Mrs Healey's patience with him was monumental. She laughed loyally at his oft-repeated jokes — indeed, more often

71

than not, she would incur his wrath by absent-mindedly laughing before the punchline!

I was immediately attracted to Win Healey on that very first visit: a remarkable woman, handsome and stylish with glossy black hair braided round her ears. She had been born and brought up in Newnham in Gloucestershire. Perhaps it was our common Gloucestershire background that created this rapport. Highly intelligent with a hunger for learning, in a later age she would have gone to university; as it was, she had trained as an elementary-school teacher and had taught in Gloucester. At the time I met her, she was an enthusiastic member of the local WEA class on literature and, though not particularly musical, was struggling to understand modern music. Ambitious for both boys, she understood that Terry, lively and outgoing but not in the least bookish, was overshadowed by the brilliant Denis, and sent him from Bradford Grammar School to Pangbourne to be trained for the navy. When I first met him he was a good-looking naval officer, who, unlike Denis, loved a party — which Mrs Healey, the soul of hospitality, loved to provide. He could not match Denis's proficiency as a pianist, but he was encouraged to perform on and to compose for the clarinet.

Denis, however, was guided by his mother with all the power of her strong personality. He went to the best concerts and plays that Leeds and Bradford could provide, and on their rare visits to London, when they accompanied Will to educational conferences, she booked visits to theatres and museums every afternoon

72

and evening. In later years, Lord Longford would repeatedly say to me, "Denis is the greatest polymath I have ever known." For the impetus and the encouragement behind this extraordinary breadth of knowledge and interest, it is Win Healey we have to thank.

She did not, however, allow him to become a frowsty bookworm. When the wind swept the rain across the moors, she would wake him up with a "Come along, Denis, it's a lovely day for a walk". Nor was she uncritical. In later years, when interviewers would question her, she would say: "Oh, he always thought he was right, always thought he knew it all." But she did like to imagine that he could read fluently when he was two.

My first impressions of Keighley were somewhat daunting, and I was to discover that the Yorkshire character had not much changed since Mrs Gaskell had so shrewdly described it in 1857. Indeed, I was to recognize this portrait again and again in my Yorkshire friends — and in none more than Denis himself.

I had not, however, come to Keighley in search of him. Ken Kirk had told me of the vacant post and encouraged me to apply. Hearing that one of Denis's Oxford friends was coming up for an interview, Mrs Healey invited me to stay overnight. Attracted by her warm welcome, the comfort of their home with its books, pictures and music, the wild beauty of Ilkley Moor rising up behind the house, and the valley views across to Haworth and Brontëland, I hoped to get the job.

But next morning, as the bus rattled down the hill and along the Aire Valley to the school two miles away, I realized I was in a foreign land. The voices in the bus were harsh and unintelligible; the town itself smoky, industrial; the grey stone houses along the road solid and uncompromising. The wind blew harshly down from the high moors, and there were no hedges, only grey stone walls where blackened sheep huddled out of the wind.

The school secretary who welcomed me looked blue with cold as she led me along the chilly corridor. By now my enthusiasm had evaporated and I decided that, should the managers offer me the job, I would refuse it. This was not my country. However, with true Yorkshire bluntness the chairman told me that the committee was not sure that I was ready for the position, but thought that I might in time become worthy of them. Humbled, I agreed to start the same month.

I shared digs in a comfortable, solid house on the Skipton Road with Miss Bruce, who taught French — a lovely gentle girl with flowing blonde hair. The house, bright and shining, was run by plump and comely Miss Mattock, who cooked wholesome Yorkshire meals and cared for us like a mother.

I stayed at the school for two years, gradually learning to understand and love the girls and to accept their directness. "Eeh, Miss Edmunds, you look right dozy this morning, go and put some lipstick on" — so one brought me to earth one morning as I soared in the

74

poetry of Keats. Some of the girls came from Haworth and, on summer evenings, did their homework on the tombstones in the churchyard, where the grey headstones were laid flat like tables. Half a century later, I made a broadcast for the BBC programme *Down Your Way* in that rook-haunted churchyard. The curator of the Brontë Museum spoke movingly about infant mortality in Haworth and, to my delight, I recognized her. She was one of my old girls.

I learned more than I taught in Keighley. The headmistress, Mrs Kirk, was exceptional. Unconventional, she allowed me to let "Birnam wood come to Dunsinane" over the desks, teach civics, take classes into the fields to plan new towns. Outside toilets, the girls told me, are essential if you get home while your mother is at work. I learned too from the outstanding teachers. Sensitive Peggy Jones introduced me to Dylan Thomas; I was so glad that in her old age she was able to join us at Riddlesden Hall to welcome "Lord Riddlesden". Her unmarried sister Beryl, a progressive intellectual, later bravely went to London to give evidence for the defence in the obscenity trial which followed the publication by Penguin of the unexpurgated text of *Lady Chatterley's Lover*. Seonaid Robertson was an inspired art mistress to whom adventures happened. Determined to catch a "heavy breather" who plagued the staff with indecent telephone calls, she made up her homely face and, with a bow of ribbon in her hair and an improbably short skirt, kept an assignation with him — and handed him over to the police. Elsie Farrar, the wise head of the history department, persuaded me to teach history, unqualified as I was, and gave me a lasting love of the subject. With these valued colleagues I spent many a weekend walking in the Dales, to Bolton Abbey and, in the spring, to the Grass Woods at Appletreewick, where the bluebells reminded me of the Forest of Dean.

In my first year at Keighley it was often hard to remember that there was a war on, but we were reminded by our fire-watching duties. The staff and senior girls took turns to sleep in the school and we were all given fire drill. Bombs were dropped on Bradford, but our nights, though uncomfortable, were quiet.

During my early months in Yorkshire I saw Ken Kirk, the headmistress's son, from time to time on school occasions, and once or twice I was surprised to see, at the back of the school hall, Denis Healey with him. Still awaiting call-up after completing his degree, Denis joined the Home Guard before eventually entering the army at Uniacke Barracks outside Harrogate. He was actually enjoying the physical exercise when he ruptured himself and was hospitalized. Hence his unexpected presence in Yorkshire. There followed at the end of 1940 a period of training at the Artillery Depot in Woolwich, and in 1941 Gunner Healey became a railway checker on Swindon Station, counting soldiers getting on trains and getting off. Finally he found it easier to make up the figures and use those of the ticket collectors — until he found that they were inventing them too. He has always said it was good experience for a future Chancellor of the Exchequer.

By this time our friendship had grown into a closer attachment. Denis had broken with his girlfriend and I with my Oxford friend, Leo Pliatzky. I deeply regret now the insensitivity of the "Dear John" letter I wrote to Leo. I did not know that he would receive it when he was fighting abroad; only many years later did I hear how deeply he had been hurt. Once in those later years my son saw him on television and asked me the unanswerable question: "If you had married him, who should I have been?"

By now Denis and I were often seeing each other when he was at home. Sometimes on summer evenings we would cycle up into the Dales after school — always getting me back to Miss Mattock and my digs by midnight. Sometimes he would meet me from Swindon for a lyrical weekend in the Cotswolds. When he was posted to Sheffield we would walk on the Derbyshire Peaks, or I would watch with amusement his excursions to a secondhand bookshop that was closing down, where the widow was selling off a treasure trove of books and pamphlets. Denis, a favoured visitor, would be allowed to sit and sort through the dusty piles and afterwards be given a basin of water and towel. As far as he is concerned, heaven is made of hours like these. I marvel now at my patience.

In 1942 Denis moved, at his own request, to Scotland to train as a military landing officer or beachmaster, and was sent to join the Americans for a landing in Algeria. On the way back he caught severe bronchitis and was sent to hospital and then home. I remember walking up a snowy hill behind his house on Ilkley Moor with him when he could scarcely breathe, yet was obstinately determined to go on.

The following spring Denis's real war started, with his journey from Glasgow to Algiers, as a trained beachmaster, with 78 Division, for the invasion of Sicily. For the next two years we would be separated. We decided not to get married before he went. Who knew what tragedy the war might bring? He worried that he might come home crippled or blinded. So the second phase of our war life began.

Except for occasional raids on Bradford, the war seemed remote, and I felt guilty. Letters from Denis on the Italian war front reminded me how lucky I was. We took parties of girls potato-picking in the Dales, sleeping in empty schools and cooking them scanty meals. The enthusiasm we felt when a triumphant butcher announced a special treat for our meat-rationed kitchen rapidly diminished when we received a great tin bowl full of raw liver. I became a vegetarian for a while. Apart from that, we enjoyed the experience, learning more about the girls in a day spent thus than in weeks in the classroom. We even had some good theatre from the Shakespeare Company, evacuated to the north, and I joined the Green Room group of the Bradford Civic Theatre to learn stagecraft. I even learned to perform a dramatic stage curtsey — though when, in later years, I had occasion to use it, I was too embarrassed to try.

Eventually, the war came piercingly close to my own life. A succession of groups of soldiers were stationed in Keighley, for the moors with their scattered pot-holes were excellent training grounds. Among them the most popular were the Seaforth Highlanders. We learned to whirl with them in eightsome reels at dances in Keighley, and I marvelled at the seriousness with which these strapping lads took their delicate footwork. To my delight I found my much-loved cousin, Trafford, now a captain, stationed nearby.

We had kept in close touch all our lives. His parents, my dear Aunt Min and Uncle Hugh, had moved to Orpington, where they lived comfortably in a pleasant house with a tennis court and a maid. They had two children, Trafford (named after my grandmother Mary Ann Trafford) and Joy. Most summers they came down to stay for a week with us, though I do not know where we found room for them. When the war came, Joy was evacuated to us and attended my old school, wore our school uniform and adopted the protective colouring of a Forest accent. As we grew up, Traff — a year younger than me — became my dearest friend. We played tennis in Orpington, danced in Coleford, and walked together through the woods. Now, in 1942, he was in Yorkshire in uniform.

We met, rather as in *Brief Encounter*, in Keighley railway station buffet; and, over hard wartime rock cakes, we talked. "I know I shall be killed," he told me without emotion. "Don't worry, I really have accepted it." His mother had impossibly high aims for him which he knew he could never reach. He was not bookish, not

79

brilliant, but kind, wise and funny. In the chilly, blacked-out café we held hands. "Tomorrow night," he said, "we are exercising on Ilkley Moor and we shall be coming past your window on Skipton Road on the way back. Look out for me." The next morning I heard the troops approaching and saw Traff leading his wet and weary men along the grey street. When they reached my window, Traff barked, "Eyes left!" and saluted. The soldiers turned, smiled and saluted too. I never saw him again.

Aunt Min wrote that he had crossed on D-Day, and had been killed at Caen. His parents kept all the records carefully, including his superior officer's letter. Apparently one of his men had been wounded and Traff, crawling out of the foxhole to save him, was killed. His father, the old soldier, was heartbroken, and went to Caen to photograph the place where he was killed on the battlefield and his grave.

On the day I received the news, I had planned a reading of war poems with my class. It was with difficulty that I read the lines that constant repetition has not worn smooth. "They shall not grow old as we who are left grow old, / At the going down of the sun, we will remember them."

Whether it was my cousin's death or Denis's two-year absence in Italy, I do not know, but in 1944 I was restless. I had learned to love the wide skies of the Dales and the sweeps of heather over the moors, felt invigorated even by the wuthering wind. I was eternally grateful, too, for the inspiration of my colleagues, and have always remembered with affection the girls I taught, their blunt honesty and true friendship. When, many years later, I came to Haworth to give a lecture on Charlotte Brontë I was delighted to recognize in the back row of the audience some grey-haired matrons who called out: "Hallo, Miss Edmunds!" But then, in 1944, I wanted to move on. So I applied for a job teaching English and history at the Girls' Public Day School Trust school at Bromley, near London.

Bromley was on "bomb alley", the direct route from Germany to the capital, so there was no escaping the war here. I saw the devastation of London in the Blitz, sheltered in the Underground with families who cheerfully turned the platforms into their bedrooms, and was amazed at how quickly everyone adjusted to the life of blackouts and shortages.

The school maintained its reputation for high academic standards in spite of the war, and I learned from my colleagues a respect for the classics and for the relevance of Greek history and literature even in those desperate times. The girls cheerfully accepted the danger of the buzz bombs: "Sorry I'm late, Miss Edmunds, a buzz bomb cut out overhead and I had to get off my bike and lie in a ditch" was a frequent if not always accurate excuse. Buzz bombs were unmanned guided missiles that droned overhead and fell when the engine cut out. Worse still were the V2s, which gave no warning — if you heard the explosion you knew you were alive. Staff meetings were conducted with admirable British phlegm from under the staffroom table.

At first I lodged in a comfortable suburban house in Bromley. Then, for the last months of the war, I moved to Victoria to share a house with a bright New Zealand woman, a member of the GPO Film Unit and a friend of Dylan Thomas. She promised to introduce me, but alas never did: he had always "just left" the pub, or "been sick on the pub carpet" the night before. These were lonely times: a merciful amnesia blacks out my less admirable friendships, and I see no virtue in delving for the memories. Denis too, in Italy, had other affairs. Understanding, we had given each other freedom; and, as he wrote in his autobiography, "our love had only grown stronger as a result".

When peace finally came, Denis was still in Italy, so I joined the singing crowds outside Buckingham Palace alone, with a sad sense of anticlimax. However, he returned in August for the VJ-Day celebration of victory over Japan. He had been given leave from the army to come home to deliver his report on the Italian campaign. I went to Keighley to stay with him and his parents, and we all went by bus to Bradford for a celebration. On the way back to Riddlesden the bus stopped at every pub and, egged on by his proud father, Denis sang his whole repertoire of Italian songs, to much applause from all.

Denis was not out of the army yet: it took some months to bring the servicemen home, rig them up in their demob suits and pork pie hats, and find them jobs. Denis could have gone back to Oxford as a fellow of Merton College. I was with him when, during a spell home on leave, he was telephoned by a don who was to interview him: "Mr Healey," he said, "the weather is a trifle inclement [it was drizzling slightly]; would you care to postpone your interview?" This to a soldier who had so recently fought his way through Italian mud!

Denis decided that the cloisters were not for him. Like many returning soldiers, he came back with a strong desire to prevent another world war and to help build a better world out of the rubble left by the conflict. On that same home leave he spoke with passion at the pre-election Labour Party conference. As a handsome young major in uniform, he caused quite a stir, and was persuaded to stand as a Labour candidate in the Yorkshire constituency of Pudsey and Otley, near Keighley. A huge Conservative majority made it improbable that he would win it, but it would be good practice.

The hopeless seats are often the most enthusiastically contested, and this was an inspiring campaign; but it also showed him how little he knew about politics. I was present at a meeting in Riddlesden when the "polymath" met his comeuppance. During question time I heard with foreboding a familiar voice from the back of the hall. "What, Major Healey, is the Labour Party's solution for the Irish problem?" It was his father. Denis was flummoxed. As he later wrote, in his ignorance he was unaware that there was an Irish problem. But, knowing his father would puncture any pretence, he thought it better to admit ignorance — and it did him no harm. He did not win the seat, but he reduced the size of the Conservative majority.

I watched the astounding result of the election flashed on a big screen in Trafalgar Square, and cheered wildly with the rest — though I was sad that Denis was not one of the victors. Still, he had made his mark and was persuaded to apply for the job of International Secretary at Labour Party Headquarters. On 20 November 1945 the International Sub-Committee of the National Executive of the Labour Party appointed Major Denis Healey as its secretary — at the magnificent salary of £7 a week. (I had forgotten, until Denis reminded me years later, that as a teacher I earned £11 a week and he only £7 — and he an Oxford double first and a major in the army! It obviously rankled.)

So: the war was over, he had a job in London, and now could face the new world. Now it was the time for decision. When Denis had gone off to war we had decided not to get married, uncertain what the coming years would hold. Now he was back, and I would have been happy to marry right away. But, as we walked on Ilkley Moor and talked, I realized how difficult a decision this was for him. For the last years his life had been organized by the army in every detail, and sudden freedom was unsettling. I remember sitting on the rough grass and hearing him say, "I love you but I don't want to get married yet." At the time I was deeply wounded but, on reflection, I realized what a bewildering transformation life was for a young soldier returning home. Now, though, when he had a job and could see a future, he could face marriage. Characteristically, there was no romantic proposal on one knee. As we walked over the moorland road he suddenly turned and said, "I think we had better get it over with."

He had thought clearly and deeply before taking his decisions and, having taken them, would remain loyal. It was as true of his marriage proposal as it was of his dedication to the Labour Party.

CHAPTER
FOUR

MARRIAGE, WORK AND FAMILY: THE EARLY YEARS, 1945–1952

We were married that December — not, as Denis's biographer has said, in a register office but in the lovely church of St Peter's in Vere Street, London. Denis's parents were there; my family came up from Coleford, and we were joined by Uncle Hugh, Aunty Min and Joy. Uncle Hugh, now a distinguished official in the National Savings Movement, made a moving speech at the wedding breakfast in a restaurant in Soho. My elder brother, Bert, paid the bill: not only did he manage to disguise his horror at the size of it, he never complained or mentioned it thereafter!

Labour's National Executive, the party's governing body, met at that time at Transport House in Smith Square, near the House of Commons, sharing the building with the Transport and General Workers' Union. Though it was a quite separate body from the Labour government that had just taken office, there were a number of members of the Cabinet on the committee that appointed the new International Secretary: Aneurin Bevan, Minister of Health; Hugh

Dalton, Chancellor; Herbert Morrison, Lord President; and Ellen Wilkinson, Minister of Education. The General Secretary of the Labour Party, Morgan Phillips, was also present. (His daughter, Gwyneth Dunwoody, is now an outstanding Labour MP.) Professor Harold Laski was the chairman.

Denis's war record was impressive, and his academic qualifications also counted with the committee: a double first in Greats at Balliol; a senior scholarship at Merton; excellent linguistic skills, with fluent Italian and French, adequate German and Greek, and a facility for addressing any audience in at least a few sentences in the most difficult languages. But what had most impressed them was the radical speech he had made at the party conference in Blackpool that autumn, when, in his army uniform, he had roused the hall with a passionate attack on the "depraved, dissolute and decadent" European upper classes. He was appointed unanimously, and remained as International Secretary of the Labour Party for the next seven years.

Though some of his Oxford contemporaries had won seats in the 1945 Parliament and were now on their way up the political ladder — Christopher Mayhew, for example, became a minister of state at the Foreign Office — Denis never regretted those years as International Secretary of the party. They gave him an unrivalled expertise in foreign affairs that he could have gained from nowhere else; friendships were made then that would last all his life. Recently, when Lee Kwan Yew, the great architect of modern Singapore, was given a dinner in London to celebrate his eightieth birthday, while other guests addressed the "Chief Minister" reverentially, Denis joked and argued, as he had done fifty years ago, with "Harry". (In his Cambridge days he had been known as "Harry Lee".)

We spent the first night of our honeymoon in Denis's old home in Riddlesden, and then took the bus to an inn in the Dales, where we had walked with such pleasure for so many years. The Buck Inn at Buckden was full, and the only accommodation they could offer us was in a converted stable next door. We climbed through a trapdoor and found a room that looked comfortable enough. We were settling down in the candlelight when the trapdoor opened again and the head of a grey-haired old lady popped up. "Excuse me," she said, "but I am a poet and have written some poetry. Would you like to hear it?" Gently we rejected her kind offer and she disappeared, never to be seen again. I still wonder whether she really existed. The stable has now been converted to a hostel for young students working for the National Trust. I wonder whether her ghost ever recites poetry to them.

For the first months of our marriage we lived in a furnished attic flat in Manchester Square, overlooking the Wallace Collection and a few minutes' walk from Oxford Street and the bus to Victoria Station. Housekeeping was no problem — the flat was just one gaunt bed-sitting room and a gallery which combined bathroom and kitchen. It was primitive but convenient for Denis's work. I continued to teach at Bromley Girls' School, travelling by train to Victoria and then to

Bromley. I remember shelling peas for our supper on the train home and, I am ashamed to say, throwing the shells out of the train window. It was a happy life; we were both earning and could afford theatre visits and foreign holidays. In that postwar period the London stage was thriving, and for us it was an *embarras de richesse*.

When I became pregnant, I gave up teaching and we moved to an unfurnished flat in Kentish Town. Jenny was born in April 1948. At this time food, furniture and furnishings were still rationed. But I had been accustomed from childhood to be careful, and thoroughly enjoyed scouring the secondhand shops of Kentish Town where I bought for shillings some of my best-loved furniture — after a half century it still shines.

Gradually, Denis supplemented his income from the Labour Party with the proceeds of journalism. A weekly article, flogged out on an ancient typewriter, was translated into many languages and sent around the globe. The original sheets were indecipherable to me; rendered into Hungarian, German, French and Italian, they must have been incomprehensible. However, as he later learned, they had even been read with interest by the Dalai Lama.

A year after Jenny's arrival I was again pregnant and we were on the move once more. The Gaisford Street flat was too small for a growing family and, with the help of a mortgage and a loan from Denis's father, we were able to buy a small semi-detached house in Langbourne Avenue on the Holly Lodge Estate in

Highgate. Here Tim was born in 1949 and Cressida in 1951. Cressida's entrance caused some panic. A "placenta praevia" necessitated a rush to hospital and an urgent Caesarian operation. As I went under the anaesthetic, the nurse asked, "What name have you chosen?" "Cressida," I mumbled and to her puzzlement began chanting from Chaucer's *Troilus and Criseyde*: "O palace empty and disconsolate, O thou ring frae which hent is the stone!" Nevill Coghill's Oxford lectures had not been forgotten. Denis and Roy Jenkins exchanged worried reports — Roy's son was born on the same day.

For many years, first in Langbourne Avenue and then at the top of the hill in Holly Lodge Gardens, Highgate was to be our base, our much-loved home, and the inspiration for my first biography — the beginning of my writing career.

Holly Lodge Estate had been built in 1922 in the grounds of a country villa, Holly Lodge, which had been bought in the eighteenth century by the actress Harriet Mellon, with the help of the banker Thomas Coutts. She became his second wife and his heiress, and she in turn chose Angela Burdett, Thomas's granddaughter by his first wife, to inherit the Coutts fortune. Adding her grandfather's name to her father's, Angela Burdett-Coutts became, at the age of twenty-four, one of the richest women in England and the owner (among much else) of Holly Lodge, which was set in lovely grounds on the slope between Highgate West Hill and Highgate Cemetery. She went on to become one of the greatest Victorian philanthropists, and later I would unravel her extraordinary life.

Angela bequeathed Holly Lodge and the estate to her husband. After his death an estate of "stockbroker Tudor" houses was built on the site. Grassy avenues branch out from the central spine, on one of which, Langbourne Avenue, was our new home. It was an idyllic place for children. They played in what remained of Angela's lovely Holly Lodge gardens, with their lawns and crumbling summer houses, old stone urns, a hollow oak and a magnificent avenue of rhododendrons that led nowhere. Across the main road stretched Hampstead Heath with its swimming pool and ponds for brave swimmers and, within walking distance, the lovely eighteenth-century Kenwood House surrounded by flower-filled gardens. On the other side of the estate, the older and wilder part of Highgate Cemetery would provide all the ghoulish excitement that children love. Its mysteries were to be better enjoyed when we later moved to a larger house at the top of the hill where the cemetery was over our garden wall.

The estate was like a friendly village. In our first years on Langbourne Avenue, Francis and Margaret Boyd and their three children lived across the road. Francis, later Sir Francis, was the much respected parliamentary correspondent of the *Guardian*. After Denis became an MP he assured me that he would never misuse our friendship; and he never did. Serious and dedicated, he was a rare model of an incorruptible journalist. Nearby were Dr Fred Bell with his wife Margaret and their three children. He was a distinguished vet and lecturer, Margaret a maths teacher whose clear-minded intelligence and common sense made her a dear and valued friend. Their children, especially Paul, were friends for life.

Across the road lived Mrs MacAdoo, a dedicated piano teacher whose annual concerts were testing times for pupils — and their parents. Now, when I meet successful structural engineer Paul Bell, I remember the little redhead thumping away at Mrs MacAdoo's piano and weeping with frustration because he could not get it right; and I see Antony Gash — now a learned university professor — concentrating, eyes shut, a plump little boy lost in his music. Mrs MacAdoo discovered that Tim had "perfect pitch", and the memory of Jenny playing "Für Elise" still brings a tear. Cressida — the most accomplished pianist of our brood — was to enjoy these pleasures later. She went first to a little school on the estate and then to a church school in Highgate. Tim and the other boys took their music further at Highgate School, the excellent minor public school up the hill; here Mr Chapman, an exceptional music master, was a lasting influence on Tim, who sang with the Highgate Choir at La Scala in Italy in a memorable performance of Benjamin Britten's *War Requiem*. The little boys in their grey flannel suits were watched over with a friendly eye by another outstanding Highgate School master, Mr Mallinson, who gave us a quiet word if they got out of hand — as, for instance, he was once moved to do when they "regrettably were seen urinating on the avenue". Until he was over ninety, Mr Mallinson walked briskly to the school on the hill to which he continued to devote his life.

These years in a lovely setting with a supportive community, backed by the friendly neighbourhood shops at the bottom of the hill, gave me something I had sorely missed since my own childhood in the Forest of Dean. I was glad we could give it to our children.

It was also comforting to me in an odd and often lonely life, for in those first postwar years Denis was constantly travelling. It was during that period as International Secretary that he built a formidable knowledge of foreign affairs which, combined with his war years in Italy, gave him a breadth of experience in this field almost unrivalled in the Labour Party. Friendships made then in Poland, Czechoslovakia, Germany, Greece, America, Singapore and elsewhere have been of lasting value. Denis never forgot the knowledge he gained as a lowly functionary, meeting people at ground level. Sometimes I could travel with him, meeting officials with their families when we were all young, making friendships that endured as they rose to prominence in their own countries, giving international affairs a human face. Denis was also gaining the respect of the Labour Cabinet, and particularly of Hugh Dalton, the Chancellor, Ernie Bevin, the Foreign Secretary, and Philip Noel-Baker, Minister of Fuel and Power, for all of whom he wrote speeches.

★   ★   ★

In 1946 the Italian Socialist Party invited Harold Laski, Professor of Political Science at the London School of Economics and Chairman of the International Department of the Labour Party, on the first official visit by the British Labour Party to Italy since the war — a goodwill visit to Italian comrades. Denis, as the Secretary of the International Department, accompanied him, and Frieda Laski and I were included in the invitation.

Harold Laski's reputation abroad was at this time higher than in England, and we were welcomed royally. It was an unforgettable experience. Everything was novel, not yet familiarized by package tours: blue skies and lakes, green meadows and snow-capped mountains, men in blue overalls working in the fields: each new scene glimpsed through window or tunnel opening as the train chugged through Italy offered fresh delight.

There were unexpected excitements at stations en route. At one stop a group of men and women with bouquets ran along the platform calling for "*Dottore Laski*": "*Dove il dottore Laski?*" They were greeting not only the Labour Party, but Laski himself, who was well known in Italy. There were crowds to welcome him when I stood beside him on a balcony in Florence as he addressed an enthusiastic crowd in halting Italian. Denis had learned his fluent Italian in the war and was in his element, having come to love the language, the country and the people with a passion that he has never lost. Even now he will greet a surprised waiter in a restaurant with a flood of Italian — in dialects from Venice to Milan and from Florence to Naples. For me, too, the magic of that first visit has never faded: long meals with welcoming Italian hosts on flower-scented, vine-covered balconies, or in the mountains with anti-fascist partisans who had fought on our side during the war. We were warned that our car journey to Naples could be dangerous — there were still *banditti* along the rough road.

Above all, Rome rises eternally magnificent in my memory. Here the men of the party were to be received by the Pope. I sat on the steps and awaited their return and their reports. Apparently, they had been led by officials in medieval uniform into the presence. At the end of the interview, the Pope had turned to the trade union delegate and said, "I hope you know what a great influence you in the trade unions have?" To which Bob Openshaw, in his broad Lancashire voice, replied, "Aye, Pope, and so do you." Then the Pope opened a drawer containing rosaries, some black and some white, and asked Bob which one he would like for his Catholic friends — to which he replied, "I'll have one of each, thank you."

That visit was my introduction to a country I learned to love. It also gave me the chance to get to know one of the most remarkable characters of that time. Harold Laski inspired students from all over the world — years later I would meet some of his African students in Nigeria. They never forgot the welcome he gave them at his open house evenings and his genuine interest in them. A stimulating lecturer, he was also a brilliant raconteur — though I knew that many of his best stories were fantasies. "Edna," he would say, "did I ever tell you about the day FDR [Roosevelt] said to me, 'Harold, sit at my side in the White House for a day and you will understand my life'?" One day he told me how he flew into Brussels "crouched by the pilot's side". I never knew how much was true; but his fiction was more fascinating than most people's facts.

During that Italian visit I became very fond of him and his practical, intelligent wife. A small man with a little moustache, he was not impressive in appearance, but his large, dark eyes were warm and sympathetic, and he was generous and thoughtful. When we stayed for a weekend at their cottage, Harold would look out a quotation or a book that he thought might interest me, and I would find it in my place at the breakfast table with a note: "Good morning, Edna". Unusually among clever politicians, in a crowded room his eyes did not search over one's shoulder for someone more interesting to talk to, nor did he ask "and how are the children?" with obviously the least possible interest; nor "and what does Denis think about . . .?" Instead, he would switch the conversation to educational policy or something he knew I knew about, and ask what I thought. He was shocked when Denis once said: "Don't ask her, she knows nothing!" Fortunately, I could laugh, recognizing this as what we know in the family as "Willie humour", that inherited "brutal facetiousness".

Laski had an acute eye for talent. Not only had he supported my friend Leo Pliatzky through his years at Oxford, he had also encouraged a bright young trade union official in Maidstone. Impressed by Jim

Callaghan's presentation of a case, he urged him to study under him at the LSE — or at least to keep in touch with him.

Harold's end was to be tragic. He had been attacked by the Beaverbrook press as a revolutionary Communist, and decided to sue for libel. He had been so sure of success that, as he told me, he had planned to spend the award on a Beaverbrook scholarship for needy students. Alas! The Beaverbrook press made mincemeat of him, mocking him as a little man in a "band leader's suit". The loss of his case wounded him deeply, and he died soon after, in 1950.

We left the Laskis in Naples, and the rest of our visit was a second honeymoon. Some of Denis's army friends were still stationed in Naples, and they lent us a jeep in which Denis drove me to places he had known in the war. We drove to San Gimignano with its fabled towers and superb frescoes, still undiscovered by package tourists, and spent two nights in Gracie Fields' island of Capri, not yet spoiled by crowds.

On our return we were invited to lunch at the British Embassy in Paris. The ambassador's wife, Lady Diana Cooper, greeted us; dressed exquisitely in what I remember as flowing silk and wearing a large, elegant hat, she looked as beautiful as I remember seeing her on stage in her famous role as a nun. How graciously and skilfully she performed the introductions, how kindly she appeared to be interested even in me, how expertly she decanted the drawing room into the dining room for luncheon, and how wittily she engaged her neighbours in intelligent conversation. Watching, I learned the rule for a lady was to address your left-hand neighbour with the first course and your right-hand neighbour with the second course. In later years, I met her again at some reception, her beauty now fading, and the hostess brought a young man to be introduced. Abruptly, he said, "We have already met," and walked away. Her composure was unruffled but I felt wounded for her, a legend forgotten. It was a lesson not to be disregarded: "Golden lads and girls all must, as chimney sweepers, come to dust." Years later I would remember her again when, as wife of the Secretary of State for Defence, I lived as she had in Admiralty House, though I never aspired to her grandeur. She described in her autobiography how she had once expressed her delight with an opera singer: "I gave her a jewel from my person." I could not compete with that.

On this tour I had another taste of the embassy high life in Rome, where Sir Noel and Lady Charles received us at the British Embassy and gave a dinner for us. Lady Charles was an impressive lady, though I was rather reminded of Margaret Dumont in the Marx Brothers' films. At the end of the evening she took me aside to give me the advice she felt I needed on how to behave on official occasions. Apparently I had trailed awkwardly behind Denis. She felt I should have made my own way around the room. I think she would have liked me to make a dramatic entrance and dominate the room with brilliant conversation. I am afraid she was doomed to be disappointed. Even had I wished or been able to make the attempt, it would have been difficult to shine. I had only minimal Italian learned from gramophone records — and in any case, Denis, whether in full Italian flow or English, would always dominate.

For the first seven years of our marriage Denis was extremely busy, not only at his office in Transport House, but also travelling abroad and at home, entertaining foreign visitors, attending conferences, and reporting to Labour's International Committee and to Ernest Bevin, Foreign Secretary in the Labour government of 1945–51. In addition he was writing the pamphlets *Cards on the Table* and *Feet on the Ground*, designed to elucidate the Labour Party's policy on foreign affairs. In those years he not only gained a wide and deep knowledge of foreign affairs, but also closely watched the great political figures of the day and learned valuable lessons on the nature of power and its practitioners. Watching from the sidelines, I too saw history made flesh.

Denis developed a profound admiration for Bevin. In his early days as an MP he rarely made a speech without some touch of the hat to him, and in *The Time of My Life* drew a memorable picture:

Though short in stature, he was built like a battle tank, with the rolling gait and thick stumpy fingers typical of a stevedore. Slow and soft of speech in private, he could roar like any sucking-dove at a public meeting. He had shown a ruthless ambition in getting to the top of his union and could be brutally arrogant in debate . . . Except for the last five years as Minister of Labour in the coalition government under Churchill, he had spent his whole life as a trade unionist.

When King George V asked him where he had gained his extensive knowledge, he responded that he had picked it from "the hedgerows of life".

I always regret that, being much in the background in those days, I never had a chance to talk to Bevin at any length. "So this is your missus, Denis," he said when I was introduced, and thrust out a great welcoming paw. But I was impressed by the effect he had on the most surprising people. Suave and polished civil servants would talk to me of him with admiration and awe. They would delight in recounting his malapropisms and quirks of speech — but always with affection. When, on some tour, he was asked what he would like to drink, he replied, "Let's have them newts again" — having enjoyed a bottle of Nuits St George the night before. I understood his speeches better when I heard them than when I read them; whether or not you agreed with him, you knew you were in the presence of a great man. His wife, Florence, like most trade union wives, remained always in the background but was a great support to him.

Attlee I found more alarming. I was first introduced to him by Hugh Gaitskell who, with his wife Dora, was standing with him in a pool of silence in a crowded room, and called me over. Overcome by this unaccustomed attention, I joined them. Gratefully they withdrew, leaving me alone in the presence. Conversation with Attlee was notoriously difficult. The late Wilfred Fienburgh once said that conversation with most people was like a game of tennis, but with Clem it was like throwing biscuits to a dog: "Yup, yup," and the words were gone. In fact, I soon learned great admiration for the quiet little man who had managed to develop a rapport with Winston Churchill during their wartime partnership, and with King George VI, who also found speech difficult. In later years, when Denis was Defence Secretary, I sat next to Clem at a dinner. He was surprisingly chatty, so I was encouraged to ask: "Clem, what qualities would you look for in a minister of Defence?" I thought he replied, "Is Denis a warrior?" and was about to reel off his battle honours when I realized he had asked if was a "worrier". "No good if you are a worrier," he said; "Anthony [Eden] was a worrier — killed him . . . must make decisions and then sleep." On the day when India gained independence, I was sitting on the terrace of the House of Commons; I cannot recall why, nor what hour of the day or night it was, but I remember vividly Attlee stopping for a moment as he passed me and saying to me: "Great day!" His face shone. It was his long-awaited moment of triumph.

There were towering personalities in Attlee's 1945 government, and it is much to Attlee's credit that he held them in harness together. Someone once said of Nye Bevan, "He's his own worst enemy," to which Ernie Bevin replied, "Not while I'm alive he ain't." I learned to understand Nye better in later years, when

I went with him and Denis on a delegation to Moscow. But in the early days there were many clashes. Denis, Nye felt, was getting too cocky for a mere functionary from party headquarters. I remember one June night sitting after dinner on the terrace of the House of Commons with the distinguished American Helen Gahagan Douglas, wife of the actor Melvyn Douglas, quietly discussing the day's events, when an argument between Denis and Nye broke out. Denis, at his most infuriating, goaded Nye into stuttering fury: "I won't be preached to by a red-faced boy from Transport House!" I wish I could remember what sparked the flames, but they lit up the terrace.

It was as well that Nye had married Jennie Lee, who was more than his match, a politician in her own right and an eloquent and passionate public speaker. Her handsome figure, with flashing eyes and shining black hair, dominated any gathering. She was always incensed when, on diplomatic occasions, she was "dwindled into a wife". Once, after an embassy dinner, as was customary at that time, we ladies were ushered upstairs to powder our noses while the men stayed at the dinner table to discuss world affairs. Jennie was incandescent. I heard her furiously grumbling aloud in the bathroom, threatening to go home. I wish I could remember whether she did — she was certainly capable of so doing. Aggressive politician though she was, she always took pains with her appearance. When the pretty young wife of the MP Francis Noel-Baker asked if she should wear her plainest clothes when she went to the constituency, I heard Jennie tell her firmly, "Certainly not. Always give them your best." My last memory of Jennie was towards the end of her life when she was an influential arts minister in the Labour government. Standing on the stage at Covent Garden at the end of some special performance, dazzling in a glittering gown of gold, she made a long speech and held the audience captive. Though the raven hair was now snow-white, she never lost her power as an orator.

I have scarcely any recollections of Hugh Dalton. I never saw him as quite real. He seemed like a character in a play, booming from a stage; and I am sure that I was invisible to him. However, though I was always intimidated by Dalton, I had a great affection and admiration for his wife, Ruth, a remarkable lady. Prominent in local government in London, she was partly responsible for securing Hampstead Heath as a public space for the people's enjoyment. She was often hidden in the shadow of her booming husband. Their lives together were not easy. Their young daughter had died when they were both absent, and they had never forgiven themselves. With Cicely Mayhew, I often visited Ruth in her later years in her flat in Victoria. I was glad that I could thank her, at the end of her life, for the pleasure I took in walking on Hampstead Heath, and I treasure the gift — a lovely green glass vase — she gave me before she died.

I loved the walks on the Heath with the pram to Kenwood House, but in spite of my happiness I missed my teaching — especially with Denis so often away. Like many young mothers, I was losing the sense of my own identity and, as Denis grew in importance, I felt I was disappearing. So when I was asked to give a series of lectures for the Workers' Educational Association in Hemel Hempstead in the early 1950s I gladly agreed — though I warned them that I knew nothing about the subject they asked me to address, "Clear Thinking and the Press". I spent hours every week in Highgate Library reading all the newspapers, and learned some useful lessons. The first was that the newspapers that preached my own beliefs were not necessarily the most useful. The best were those, like the old *Manchester Guardian*, that separated news from views. To my surprise, it was often the *Telegraph* at that time that won my approval for its reporting, even when I disagreed with it.

I earned ten shillings for the hour's lecture, but by the time I had paid a babysitter and the Green Line coach fare to the suburbs, I was out of pocket. However, I went exhausted, and returned rejuvenated and refreshed. I discovered that I enjoyed the preparation of a lecture and creating a rapport with an audience. Lecturing, I found, was immensely challenging and rewarding; and it has remained so for me throughout the rest of my life. Married to so powerful a personality, I found it consoling to be visible in my own right. I am now amused to remember that I gave my WEA lectures under my maiden name and always took off my wedding ring. It seemed important at the time. So I began a lifetime of pleasure on various platforms, just as my mother had been renewed by her singing after a hard day's housework.

★　★　★

During these years when Denis was often away and always occupied with official work, the care of the children was mostly in my hands and, though he was devoted to them, he could give them little time or attention. So the family holidays were a joy for all of us.

The greatest excitement was the arrival of our first car — a Hillman Husky — which Denis drove up and down the Avenue in the pouring rain with a cargo of whooping children. Cars were still a novelty in our lives. When an MP friend, Geoffrey de Freitas, drove our children round London to see the Coronation decorations, and asked what they liked best, they said "the windscreen wipers" — a novelty that out-dazzled the lights.

The Husky made possible holidays further afield, and for many years it took us on magical trips in Cornwall and abroad. The magic was somewhat dimmed for me since it also made camping possible: I remember cooking on a Primus stove at a hole in a Cornish hedge, the wind whipping the sand into my teeth, and long night walks over wet grass to a smelly loo in the farm! It always rained in Cornwall. "Rain?" the children said. "What rain?" In and out of the sea at Treyarnon Bay, they were anyway always wet. They brought me baby crabs to cook for supper and a cook book with 100 recipes for seafood. I shall not forget those tiny crabs crawling out of the boiling water. I still hear their silent screams.

When Cressida was a year old, we drove to Yugoslavia with our first tiny tent. Tim and Jenny slept in the back of the Husky; Cressida slept with us in the tent in Denis's collapsible canvas army bath. On one unforgettable occasion we sealed ourselves and baby in the tent and then lit a mosquito killer capsule. It exploded, nearly suffocating us. Yugoslavia was desperately poor then and, badly bitten by mosquitoes, I bought a soothing powder from a dark little chemist's shop which was handed to me in a screw of paper.

The pattern of our holidays was often a week by the sea and then another in the mountains, usually in Italy where Denis was happily at home, wearing his wartime shorts, consulting his wartime maps and even trying to change his old currency. But for me, camping was a mixed pleasure. My heart often sank as we saw the camp site — crowded, hot and dusty under a flapping awning, or awash in mud in the mountains in Austria or the Swiss Alps. Often we sat glumly for days listening to rain on canvas, waiting for it to stop so that we could pack the tent and go.

As the years went by we acquired a remarkable orange tent we called "the igloo", which was blown up with a foot pump. Later, we bought an awning under which I cooked. It was designed by Denis and made by a tent maker in Switzerland. However, the roof needed propping up by a Nescafé tin at the top of the tent pole, otherwise rain would gather and descend on the cook's head. Our arrival at camping sites always attracted an interested audience, and I felt ashamed of our squalid equipment when we set up next to continental campers who could instantly whip a suite of chairs and tables out of a bundle of neat cylinders.

Then for me — a coward in high places — the chairlifts were agonizing trials, though magical in retrospect, as we swung over the silent forests, the children and Denis strung ahead strapped in their chairs and Jenny, always thoughtful, turning to ask, "Are you all right, Mum?" I never forget the shaming moment when, paralysed with fear, I could not jump out at the top of the mountain, or the anger of the attendant and the disgrace of stopping the whole chairlift to let me out.

On another occasion, fearing the chairlift, I walked up — only to find that, on the way down, my tired muscles could not cope: I slipped and broke my ankle. Jenny records the moment in her diary:

Friday 24th August. After lunch, and getting our breaths back we started walking down the way Mum had come up. Although beautifully covered in rich green grass and colourful flowers, it provided the exhausted Mum (before lunch and after lunch) with absolutely NO SHADE! About half way down I heard a sickening crunch, I looked behind me and saw Mum, sitting on the path with a look of excruciating agony on her face. "I've broken my ankle," she cried. "Mum's broken her ankle!" I echoed down to Dad and Tim and Cress. While Tim and co belted up to us, some very kind Swiss people made Mum comfortable and put an improvised cold-compress on her ankle.

Meanwhile, as I recall, Denis reached for his camera.

Then the Swiss people walked down to the nearest phone to call for a rescue jeep. In double quick time the doctor's jeep was up to us, containing Doctor and very pretty nurse. After giving Mum gallons of liquid into her ankle the doctor bandaged it up and put Mum onto the bed in the back of the jeep (which incidentally fell flat as soon as Mum sat on it). Then he drove her and Dad down the mountainside, while we started walking. When we reached the main road Dad picked us up and drove us to the Doctorhus, where we saw Mum just after having an x-ray. The x-ray showed that Mum's fibula had broken, or to put it plainly her ankle got broke. We left the Doctorhus to return next morning for Mum to have her leg put in plaster, in which she will spend a month. We drove home rather saddened and disappointed for Mum's sake.

My leg was tended by a doctor who showed me a piece of lightweight plaster which he said he had invented. However, it had been bought up by plaster manufacturers, who feared the competition, and was not marketed. With my plastered leg I went back to the tent, though Denis wanted me to retreat to a hotel.

When in 1964 Denis became Defence Secretary, I secretly told myself: "Thank God, we shan't be allowed to camp any more." But looking back, when all the holidays are mingled in the mind, the pains of camping are far outweighed by the pleasures: the warmth of the sun rising over the mountains and the flowering alpine meadows; the unforgettable aroma of bacon sizzling on the Primus; singing round the camp fire at sunset. Later there were weeks in Italy when we graduated to small rented villas, and we could sit in the evenings and sing on a comfortable balcony. A crackling tape remains of us singing in harmony the Italian songs newly learned; Cressida's clear young voice rises from the past in an achingly beautiful Norwegian song.

When Tim was a baby we took a little villa at Bocca de Magra, then a small fishing village near La Spezia, where the sea was still quiet and our elderly Italian hostess could swim upright in the clear water — wearing her sun hat. We even had a little Italian maid, Maresa, who milked the cow for our morning coffee outside our door. On one unforgettable day we left Tim in her charge and, Denis carrying Jenny, climbed up the mountain to meet Italian peasants who had been partisans during the war and who, over glasses of rough red wine, shared reminiscences with Denis and sang partisan songs with him. We returned to find Tim with a completely shaven head — all his golden curls gone. The village barber had made his regular summer round and Maresa had thought we should be glad of his attention. I have always maintained that Tim's lifelong reluctance to have his hair cut stems from this experience. Bocca de Magra is now a popular marina; I am glad to have known it in its simple state.

In due course Tim bought his own little pup tent, out of his earnings as a chorister, and the girls had a separate one. Soon we had quite a tent village — Healey-ville, the children called it. In those days, though camping in England was primitive, abroad camp sites were usually well equipped — some even had showers. Jenny's diary gives them marks for effort. Long journeys on holiday were enlivened by Tim reading aloud from the back of the car. There was the Hyman Kaplan holiday when Tim did the voices from Leo Rosten's book and reduced us all to hysterics. I felt sympathy with lecturer Mr Parkhill, who opened the session: "Tonight, class, let us devote ourselves to Recitation and speech." At Mr Parkhill's desk Mr Kaplan turned to face his peers. He placed one hand on the dictionary, as if posing for a statue, raised the other like a Roman reviewing his legions, broke into the sunniest of smiles, and in a ringing tenor declaimed: "Mr Pockheel, ladies an' gantleman, fallow mambers of beginnis' grate! for mine sobject I will tell about fife Prazidents fromm vundeful USA. Foist, Judge Vashington, de fodder of his contry. Naxt, James Medicine, a fine lidder. Den, Ted E. Roosevelt, who made de Spenish Var a soccess. Also, Voodenrow Vilson, he made de voild safe for democrats. An' lest, mine *favourite* prazident, a *great* human bean, a man mit de hot an' soul of an angel: Abram Lincohen! . . . Denk you." That holiday we all talked Kaplan-speak. Later, Tim's letter to Denis in Kaplan-speak during the Labour deputy leadership contest reminded us of those happy days.

As the years went by and the children grew up and Denis became a minister, these family holidays ceased, and to his regret he had less time and freedom to enjoy their company. "Was it all shining clear like gold, as I remember?" Tim once asked. Not quite. There were

110

times when he had an adolescent "shadow", as he called it, or when Cressida's alter ego — who I named "Maungy stamper" — took over in a black mood, or when Denis obstinately took us in search of a non-existent lake or waterfall that he remembered from the army, and refused to accept that it was no longer there.

He always insisted that, when travelling, our picnic halts should be perfection — off the road, with a view, on level ground and in sunshine. He would scan the sky ahead along a long French road and head for the blue. Once no suitable site appeared and, famished, we insisted on having our sandwiches in the car at the side of the road. Furious, he went alone into a muddy field, set up his table among thistles and cowpats and, watched by curious cows, ate his sandwiches there. Tim's camera recorded this scene. There were times when I thought I had two sons; as Jenny's diary once noted: "Dad and Tim lost their aeroplanes — and their tempers." However, when in later years, as a minister, Denis was called back from our holiday, the sun went out and we all realized how central he was to our enjoyment, the prime mover in all our expeditions. The holiday stood still until he came back.

CHAPTER FIVE

A COALITION OF COMMUNITIES: LEEDS, 1952–1964

My constituency, East Leeds, was typical of a Labour seat in any provincial city. It had one middle-class ward on the edge of the lovely countryside surrounding Leeds, two solid working-class wards based on council housing estates, and one ward of uncertain allegiance, composed mainly of two-room back-to-back houses of red brick which were rented from private landlords; its tenants therefore felt a cut above the council tenants, although their living conditions were often much worse.

Denis Healey, The Time of My Life

When the general election of 1951 came around Denis was not a candidate, having opted to remain for the time being a party functionary. He was not yet sure that he wanted to be an MP, and the in-fighting within the Cabinet was not doing much to attract him to a parliamentary career. As he told me, the view of the quarrelsome factions from below "was not a pretty sight".

However, his post as International Secretary had become increasingly stressful. Always the lone wolf, the least clubbable of men, it was only in the family that he could really relax. Working for a committee of exceptionally high-powered men and women with conflicting ideas and temperaments, his job was to present their policies in ways that they could use in their speeches; but he was increasingly unwilling to remain merely a backroom boy, and the views he expressed in articles and pamphlets were often his own and controversial. His two pamphlets had caused some argument, and after seven years he was ready to move on.

Contemporaries who had won seats in Parliament in the 1945 election were already ahead on the ladder. Christopher Mayhew, an old acquaintance from our Oxford days, was now minister of state under Hector McNeil at the Foreign Office — indeed, Denis reported to him. But Denis's own reputation was growing too, and when in 1951 it was suggested that he stand for Parliament in a by-election in South East Leeds, he decided to throw his hat into the ring. Major James Milner, the sitting MP and Deputy Speaker, had been offered a peerage. His main rival was a well-known local councillor, John Rafferty, who had many friends as well as some enemies; so some nerve-racking constituency selection meetings ensued before Denis was adopted as the Labour candidate. He was 34.

Here it is worth reminding the many critics of Members of Parliament that no other professionals have to be so tested by elections throughout their

113

careers. The first hurdle is the election by the political constituency party. Some demand to inspect the wife as well. Then, every five years at least, the whole constituency, membership average 26,000, votes in a general election. If, as in Denis's case, the candidate stands in a by-election — or if, again as in Denis's experience, a narrow majority in a general election necessitates a second soon afterwards — he may have to go through two elections in the five-year period. Even if the MP is content to be a good constituency member and climb no higher on the political ladder, he still has to submit to re-election every five years at the outside.

Two days before the Leeds by-election, campaigning was halted by the death of King George VI. There were no loudspeakers, no eve-of-poll meetings, and therefore turnout was low. However, on 8 February 1952 Denis won with a majority of 7,199, and remained a Leeds MP for the next forty years. In 1955 there were changes in constituency boundaries and South East Leeds became Leeds East, the development of the village of Seacroft with a council estate having created virtually a small new town within the borders of the old constituency. Officially opened by the Queen in 1965, Seacroft helped to solve Leeds's acute housing problem. Over the years it also produced its own problems.

Denis's fellow Labour members in Leeds — the fifth largest city in the country — were Hugh Gaitskell, Charles Pannell and Alice Bacon. Keith Joseph held the affluent Tory constituency in the north of the city. Charlie Pannell was a practical, down-to-earth engineer from Kent, who did not spend much time in Leeds. Alice Bacon was a doughty Yorkshire lass, an ex-schoolmistress who, with courage and intelligence, took on and defeated the extremists in her party. She was a devoted admirer of Gaitskell and supported him during his difficult times. Over the years we learned to understand and admire Hugh and Dora Gaitskell and, although Denis was never one of Hugh's devoted acolytes, I became very fond of them both.

In the Leeds years Denis fought and won ten general elections, steadily increasing his majority between the first in 1952 and the last in 1992. Looking back, I see those general elections as clear markers in the pattern of my life, periods when I learned more about the problems of life in a great city than at any other time. But I also see how separate a part of my life Leeds was, even though I made lifelong friends there. Denis, of course, himself a Yorkshireman, was completely at home. Even his accent changed back as the train chugged into Leeds station: grass (with a long ä) became grāss, cästles became cāstles. But for me, when I visited people at home and at work, this was a different world, with its own language, customs and traditions.

I had had my first Yorkshire lessons when I taught in Keighley. Then I had known Leeds only as an excellent shopping centre. But while Keighley was essentially a small country town on the edge of the moor, Leeds, especially in those early years of Denis's career, was quintessentially urban, marshalled into monotonous

115

streets and courtyards. There were rows of back-to-back houses, built in the 1880s to accommodate the population explosion when workers were drawn from the countryside into this throbbing centre of industry.

Much of the housing hastily erected in the Victorian period to house workers near the new industries was of dreadful quality: poorly constructed, bleak, crowded and insanitary. But it was not thus everywhere; there were some more enlightened spirits who met the challenge in various ways. In Parkend, in the Forest of Dean, my grandfather was allocated a house in a terrace built for workers in the iron foundry industry; it was solidly built, with gardens, and set amid lovely woods. In Letchworth and Welwyn, Ebenezer Howard created the first garden cities, designed specifically to make a pleasant environment in which to work and live. In Yorkshire, the idealist Titus Salt built a model village for his workers on the River Aire near Leeds, calling it Saltaire. Leeds itself also had men of vision. Quarry Hill flats in the centre of Leeds, built between the world wars, were considered models for their time; and in 1952, when Denis became MP for South East Leeds, the city council was still engaged in imaginative housing schemes, notably in the new suburb of Seacroft.

But all of this took time and money, and there were still areas of appalling poverty which horrified me on those early visits. Here I made my first acquaintance with the "back to backs": small houses joined to their neighbours on three sides by party walls. It was a close and mostly supportive community, though always open to critical eyes and ears. Poor though the housing was,

116

the women kept the Yorkshire housewifely standard which their great-grandparents had brought from their country villages. On weekdays the streets were often silent and canvassing was fruitless, for most of the women worked all week, many of them in clothing factories like Burton's; but every Saturday the front steps were scrubbed and whitened and even the street itself was swept. In our first years in Leeds, before the Clean Air Act of 1956, even on Sundays the factories belched out an acrid yellow smog, blackening the houses and choking the lungs. Nevertheless, when we visited the constituents at the weekend, there was also the smell of good Yorkshire baking — buns, biscuits, bread and cakes — and on Monday the washing was strung across the narrow streets on lines hung from lamp-posts.

In 1957, Brian Thompson could write: "From any high window in the city centre, the encircling skyline bristles with new tower blocks. In a few years the red city of the Victorian working classes will have disappeared. The most infamous areas have been no more than memories for many years." But in 1952 there were still "infamous areas". The men and women of Leeds City Council were energetic and imaginative and were transforming the city; but for housewives there remained the constant battle against the smoke-filled air, and the dust of demolition and rebuilding.

The suburb of Hunslet is engraved on my memories of that 1952 by-election. I had grown up in a house without sanitation indoors, but in the back-to-back housing in Leeds, "down the garden" was "down the street". Our first Labour Party office shared with neighbours an overflowing unflushable lavatory at the end of the street. Our second had once been a butcher's shop, and hungry mice and rats still roamed. In these mean streets, men and women of distinction were brought up — and some of them recorded their early experiences. In his great 1957 book *The Uses of Literacy*, Richard Hoggart, who became Director-General of UNESCO, brilliantly described Hunslet, where the novelist Keith Waterhouse and the playwright Willis Hall were born. Hoggart himself was a child of the Leeds streets; they were his landscape, his whole environment. His upbringing here left in him a profound sense of locality, and a feeling for the physical immediacy of a working-class environment where the streets interconnect in a pattern that cannot be understood by driving round them in a car. Over the years I have walked those streets for many hours, visiting and canvassing and becoming so absorbed in the sense of close community that sometimes I became lost in the new housing estates.

Over the forty years when Denis was one of the city's MPs, I watched the growth of Leeds and saw the tremendous efforts made by a powerful city council to improve the population's housing, health, education, transport and cultural life. Having seen it in the early fifties, I can appreciate how great was their task; it is not easy to build a new Jerusalem. The "dark satanic mills" may have gone, the old back-to-backs may have been replaced by new housing; today, great motorways

118

sweep through and round the city, and new schools, colleges and university are lifting Leeds's status in the academic world. But, as I was to see, the new world has brought new problems, some of them shared throughout the nation. In the early fifties Denis had only one drug problem brought to his monthly surgery — now it is a constant battle. The sword cannot yet sleep in the hand.

New fashions and new needs have changed the face of Leeds as an industrial city. In 1952 Burton's was the world's biggest multiple tailor, with over six hundred outlets, and the biggest factory was in Denis's constituency. In the early days, during general election campaigns, the great workrooms were a sea of red. Huge photographs of Denis beamed from the ceilings, rosettes adorned the sewing machines and the girls wore fancy garters of red ribbon. Here and there a brave lady put up her blue banner and wore outsize blue rosettes. I always stopped to talk to these stalwarts. I admired their courage! Montagu Burton, the founder, was not only a successful businessman, he was also an idealist. His son, Stanley, a quiet, gentle man, collected watches and continued his father's philanthropic work. The older women working in the factory told me how old Montagu knew them all and listened to their troubles and complaints. Stanley and his wife, Audrey, became close friends of ours and were often kind hosts to us in their lovely house near Harrogate.

Now the factory has gone, along with so much of the other industry — primarily engineering — that generated employment in the first decades after the war. Occasionally in those early years I had to address an election meeting outside the gates of the Royal Ordnance factory at Barnbow to fill a gap in the schedule before Denis arrived — an alarming experience for me. But eventually that too was sold off by the Conservative government. So unemployment on the council estates in East Leeds became exceptionally high; the service industries which took up some of the slack created by the decline of manufacturing did not require the old skills which the government had made redundant, and there was no provision for retraining. The challenges for all who had the interests of the city's inhabitants at heart were immense.

Through all the great changes in the constituency during our time, we enjoyed the constant, steady friendship, support and counsel of our Leeds friends.

I early realized that Leeds was a coalition of communities, and since Denis had friends in all of them my visits to Leeds opened many windows on a wider world. In the nineteenth century, drawn by the prospect of work in the expanding city, Irish immigrants had come to work on roads and railways; Jews had arrived from Russia and the Baltic states, fleeing the pogroms that followed the assassination of Tsar Alexander II in 1881 and bringing with them skills in tailoring, shoemaking and commerce — Marks & Spencer, Burton's and other famous firms were born here — and also their love of music and the arts. Later, West Indians came and brought dance and vitality; Indians and Pakistanis, too, brought new colour to the

120

grey streets. Each wave of immigrants, with their different traditions, religions and cultures, came first to the poor areas of Leeds and then, as they prospered, moved up to more affluent districts like Roundhay and built their mosques and temples.

We had decided to make our home in London, and though on some of our visits to the constituency we stayed in hotels, or sometimes with Stanley and Audrey Burton, usually Bernard and Rose Gillinson were our kind hosts. It was they who first introduced me to the Jewish community in Leeds. This remarkable couple, who made an immense contribution to the life of Leeds, made us at home in their comfortable house near Roundhay Park. Hugh Gaitskell and Charlie Pannell also stayed with them. Their home was, for us all, a welcoming haven of peace and comfort, especially in the whirl of electioneering. Bernard and Rose remained our close friends until their deaths.

Rose's family had left St Petersburg after the Revolution and moved to Palestine, where she moved in government circles and became secretary to Ben-Gurion. Though she spoke many languages fluently — Russian, French, Italian, German and Hebrew, as well as English — she still kept an accent and a turn of phrase that were unmistakably Russian. She kept her good looks until the end and carried herself with the style of one who had been a great beauty. Generous, warm and affectionate, she loved bringing interesting people together for a splendid meal. Through Rose and Bernard we met artists and sculptors — Harry Thubron, Terry Frost, Reg Butler —

and professors from the university. Always self-deprecating, the Gillinsons nevertheless did much to encourage young artists, buying their paintings and sending them food and bedding when they were penniless.

Bernard was a small, reserved man in whom one sensed a profound sadness. A Hebrew scholar and intellectual of wide learning, out of filial loyalty he spent his working days running the warehouse business his father had founded as an immigrant from eastern Europe. Even here Bernard encouraged art by allowing young art students to hang their paintings in the warehouse, where the workers could enjoy and buy them. I had always admired a portrait that hung in their kitchen of a simple old man I thought was Bernard's father. It was in fact the eighteen-year-old David Hockney's famous 1955 *Portrait of my Father*, which Bernard had bought for ten pounds to encourage him. Hockney remembered being amazed: "It was a great deal of money, and as my father had bought the canvas I thought, it's really his painting, it's his canvas — I'd just done the marks on it. So I phoned him up and said: 'There's a man who'd like to buy this picture, can I sell it?' And he said, 'Ooh, yes.' He thought it was because of him, you see, and he said: 'You can do another.'"

Other Jewish immigrants brought their skills — artistic and commercial — to Leeds, and their descendants profoundly enriched the business and cultural life not only of Leeds but of the wider country and the world beyond. Marks & Spencer started out as

122

a penny stall in Leeds market. I remember once sitting next to old Israel Sieff at some function and babbling about my love of M&S. "Stop it," he said. "I know what's good about us — tell me what's wrong." Israel — thou shouldst be living at this hour! Our other friends included Dame Fanny Waterman, the vital little piano teacher who inspired great musicians and founded and ran the internationally famous Leeds Piano Competition.

Looking back, it rather surprises me to realize that, until I went to Leeds, the Jewish community was almost totally unknown to me; so it was for me a new world discovered. Its music and ritual I found strangely moving; perhaps they appealed to memories of the Old Testament of my Baptist childhood.

Among our friends in the Anglican church quite the most remarkable was Ernie Southcott, victor of Halton church. A tall, black-haired Canadian, he swept through Leeds in his long black cassock, his dark eyes glowing with intensity. Later he moved to a London parish but, out of his Yorkshire element, he withered and died. I have rarely met anyone in whom the divine fire burned more fiercely. He became one of Denis's closest friends and inspired the house meetings which Denis held on his visits to Leeds. Ernie had solved the problem of housebound wives who could not get to church by taking the church to them, conducting services in their houses — even sometimes making the kitchen table the altar. Douglas Gabb, Denis's agent, initiated a similar system of home visits for Denis on his weekends in Leeds, so that he could meet people in

123

their own surroundings and quietly listen to their troubles. In that domestic setting even the shyest could manage to speak.

However, in Denis's constituency by far the largest religious community were the Catholics, descendants of the Irish who had flocked to Leeds in the Victorian era; as they flourished, they established churches and convents, and brought priests and nuns to the city. In my childhood there was only one tiny Catholic church among a myriad Nonconformist ones, and the black-robed nuns were terrifying to me. Here in Leeds there were huge Catholic families on the estates and the Catholic schools were full to overflowing. Many of Denis's loyal party workers were Catholic — notable among them Eamon McGee and his pretty young wife, who seemed effortlessly to produce a new baby every year and still canvass energetically during every election.

Two particular friends were the Moynihans, who used to give Denis a huge lunch in the interval between surgeries. Mary worked in Burton's, so it was Joe who guided me round their area, introducing me in his soft Irish voice to the priests and nuns we met on our rounds. One of my great pleasures during electioneering was the ritual visit to the nuns at the convent. There I, the old lapsed Baptist, would kneel gratefully while the gentle nuns prayed for me. Afterwards, in a room filled with the scent of beeswax, there would be a quiet glass of sherry and questions, not about politics, but about our family.

Although they were not politically partisan, many of the priests and schoolmasters were friends, and Denis managed to get larger premises for an overcrowded Catholic school. Perhaps he had vestigial race memories of Catholic grandparents in old Ireland. During our first election, nervously canvassing in a narrow street, I was greeted by a huge Irishman at one doorway with "And which is t'Oirishman?" I could only point on our leaflet to the name "Healey" and say, "With a name like that, what do you think?"

There were times when Ireland seemed very close. On Saturday mornings, Denis held his surgery in the Catholic church hall where the children were practising their Irish dancing. I sat with the fond mothers and admired the ornate costumes, some of them heirlooms, all of them horrifyingly expensive. Serious, concentrated, the little boys and girls danced the old jigs as their forefathers had done in the narrow confines of their Irish huts.

On Saturday evenings, too, when we visited the Irish club, I realized how deep the Irish roots went in Leeds. Even Denis's accent acquired a touch of the brogue of his grandfather. There was a small man who from time to time would come over and, white-faced, whisper to me, "Get him out of here, Edna, there's going to be trouble!" Denis and Douglas would laugh, but I always caught his fear.

As the years went by, new communities settled in the constituency. For many years Denis's party secretary was a brilliant Bengali electrical engineer, Ashoke Banerjea, who lectured at the university. Driven by a restless energy, he would dazzle me with descriptions of his latest invention. At a time when Seacroft was a new development, Ashoke was full of ideas for its improvement. I remember particularly his insistence on having a bowling green outside the Labour Club to which the members could escape from the noisy, smoke-filled room inside. His wife, Yvonne, a domestic science teacher, balanced his enthusiasm with her Geordie common sense and dry wit. "Aye," she said when I once admired a pretty girl in the club, "fur coat and nae knickers!" I often welcomed the respite from my rounds in her comfortable, well-organized home. Alas, their marriage ended sadly. As with Ernie Southcott, the bright sword outwore its sheath and Ashoke died young.

He had introduced me to another of the exotic worlds that made Leeds such a community of nations. He once asked me to talk to a group of Pakistani ladies and I was taken to their meeting by a local councillor who left me at the door, saying wryly, "Men not welcomed." This was another of the occasions when, listening to their problems, I learned more than I taught. One professional lady explained that at that time progress for women was sometimes more easily achieved in Pakistan than in their community in Leeds. It must be remembered that this was some decades ago — the world has changed since then, and so has Leeds.

However, the core of Leeds is, as it always was, still stoutly Yorkshire. Here were people whom Mrs Gaskell and Charlotte Brontë would have recognized, the true Yorkshire characters whose ancestors had brought to the city the breath of the moors and the customs of their villages. They were tough, sturdy, laconic — in that climate you did not open your mouth too long or too wide. It was "two coats colder than in the south", we always said. Wary of strangers they are, but friends once made are for life. They are not given to extravagant praise — so a word from them is all the more precious — and criticism comes straight from the shoulder.

Douglas Gabb, Denis's party agent for forty years, symbolizes for me Yorkshire at its best. He had a more profound influence on Denis than any other single person in the constituency, and was throughout these decades one of Denis's best friends. Douglas came from a poor home; his father, a soldier, was often away and his mother worked as an usher in the local theatre. After a spell selling theatre programmes and another in a racing stable in Newmarket he trained as an engineer at the Yorkshire Copper Works, and remained an engineer the rest of his life. Every spare hour was devoted to voluntary work for the Labour Party, as a city councillor and as Denis's agent. He refused to draw daily expenses as a councillor when they finally became available, and took only £50 at general elections, all of which he spent on his party work. For a time he earned a little extra as a milkman, getting up at five o'clock every morning, and with his wife, Ivy, ran a small newsagent's shop.

The support of his wife and family was an essential element for Doug, and life was often not easy for them. When I first knew Ivy she was a harassed mother with young children, taking little part in her husband's political activities. His work as a city councillor, alderman and later as Lord Mayor dominated his life, so Ivy had to deal with all the domestic problems and the care of the children, and it was not until the end of his career that she blossomed. She had dreaded the prospect of being Lady Mayoress, but although she remained shy on public platforms she proved a great success and, because she was always her natural self and genuinely interested in the community projects of the city, she put others at ease. When the children were older she and Doug took up ballroom dancing and this gave her new poise and grace. She took great pride and pleasure in making pretty dance frocks.

Harry and Gertie Bray were two more typical tough Yorkshire friends. Harry was not so tough when we knew them — his cough shook the walls — but he was a great reader with a surprising taste for the occult. Gertie was a remarkable lady. When quite young she had run a building company, building a solid housing estate to her own design with modern appliances, including refrigerators and central heating, some of it with her own capable hands. Builders told me, with admiration, that it was a pleasure to watch Gertie, wearing her dusty red beret, laying a line of bricks. But those rough hands could also play a spinet with delicacy. She worked on equal terms with Lord Harewood to foster the musical life of Leeds, and in her comfortable home she held musical evenings and poetry readings.

128

It was during campaigning for all those general elections Denis fought that I learned most about this multi-racial constituency. Through all those forty years I never ceased to feel that Leeds was a foreign country; but I learned a great deal there and made wonderful friends. Denis's understanding of his coalition of communities was all part of his abiding belief in the brotherhood of man — one of the mainsprings of his political creed.

Denis went up to Leeds for a weekend at least once a month and held surgeries in different parts of the constituency. He always considered these the most important part of his work as an MP, especially later when he was a Cabinet minister. Not many Chancellors of the Exchequer would have walked round shopping centres immediately after a Budget, invited comment and taken the outspoken criticisms in good part. There were times in his career, too, when he was deeply unpopular with the left wing and had to put up with shouts of "Hitler Healey" from students and heckling at public meetings — but he was usually greeted with a smile, though sometimes, when he was Chancellor, also with hands held protectively over wallet pockets.

In cold little offices in public libraries or church halls, windows opened into other people's lives. These surgeries kept him in touch with real life. In some countries government ministers have no constituency duties; but in Denis's view, as he has memorably put it, "Every MP should act as a Miss Lonelyhearts." It was salutary to come from the chandeliers of Buckingham Palace to the broken glass on streets in the worst areas and "take physic, pomp," as Shakespeare wrote. I once watched an irate man slap a jamjar full of slugs on Denis's surgery desk with "And how would you like to find these on your kitchen wall?" A poem from a distraught young woman moved him to tears. The problems of power were put into perspective when compared with the desperate human tragedies brought to him on these visits. In the forty years since Denis first went to Leeds, he dealt with at least twenty thousand individual cases and in perhaps six thousand had some success. It was as worthwhile for him as it was for them.

On the rare occasions when Denis was unable to attend his surgeries, I stood in for him, supported by Douglas Gabb or another councillor. Then I realized that, in a great city like Leeds, the councillors not only understood the problems better than MPs but frequently were responsible for solving them. To a troubled constituent I always explained that I myself could not do anything but would faithfully report the problem to my husband. Sometimes they would have a cry and then say, "You needn't bother to tell him, love, I feel better now." On these occasions Douglas was invaluable, a fount of knowledge and wisdom. He knew his city, its streets, schools, hospitals and history, and since the majority of problems concerned transport, education, health and housing, his advice was all-important. He had a shrewd eye for the fraudulent, but a kindly heart for the genuinely distressed.

I went to Leeds as often as I could; but at the beginning of Denis's parliamentary career, when

Cressida was a baby and Jenny and Tim were still young, I was needed at home, and the Leeds constituents understood this. Later, when Cressida was a student at Leeds University, I enjoyed the chance to see her and have a meal together on my visits.

I do not think I was ever a good constituency wife, unlike many who live in the constituency and daily face the questioning and sometimes the anger of constituents. They are accessible and vulnerable when their husbands are in remote Westminster, especially when the member's party is unpopular and simply going shopping means facing the critics. There is, too, the problem of separation when the husband is in London during the week: some marriages have fallen apart as a result. We were lucky in always having our home in London. Husbands of women MPs have their own problems, although in my day they were fewer in number. Occasionally an MP solved these dilemmas by marrying a fellow member: Nye Bevan and Jennie Lee, for example.

Nevertheless, throughout the years Douglas Gabb and the party chairman made sure that I was used as much as possible, and Denis's mother was a willing surrogate mother for our children from time to time. So I opened bazaars and garden parties, even made speeches. Often I learned the hard way. My first disastrous experience was opening a garden party at a hospital. I wore high heels, a large hat and white gloves, and carried a handbag and a sheaf of notes on "Labour's plan for public health". I was greeted at the entrance by a band and was marched behind it around the grounds. There was a high wind and the promise of rain, and to cap it all I was presented with a large bouquet. I should have been wheeling a trolley! My speech was flapping in the wind so, quickly discarding it, I mentally noted what would henceforth be my rules for opening garden parties: a small hat, skewered securely with hatpins wound round a lock of hair (hats are a nuisance but they hide wind-blown hair); a bright-coloured mac (it will rain); flat shoes (there will be mud); no note, except a postcard for the important names (which will be forgotten); the briefest of speeches (it won't be heard anyway through the cries of babies and happy shouts of children); smile throughout, though your feet are killing you as you walk round the stalls, and make sure you buy something, however unwanted, from each stall (you can always give them to the next bring-and-buy).

I visited schools and presented prizes, and over the years watched the work of the Leeds education committee with great interest. Here I was on home ground. I rightly prophesied that the experiment with open-plan classrooms would not work. To me this was regressive. I remembered the problems in the mixed classes in the "big room" in my childhood, and noticed on later visits that the teachers made their own barriers by putting bookcases between the classes. My guide on these occasions was our good friend Councillor Doreen Hamilton, the wife of a distinguished professor of psychiatry at Leeds University, Max Hamilton. Max had introduced the "Hamilton Scale", which became accepted as the measure of depression. He helped me

132

greatly with advice on the psychology of genius when I was researching my book on the wives of great men. Doreen, herself a teacher by profession, had worked on the Leeds City Council to promote nursery education and had been responsible for introducing a nursery class into every school in the Leeds area. This was made possible, as she told me, by the "grant from Councillor George Mudie of £1.5 million in one year to build and equip nurseries — and in those days millionaires weren't two-a-penny". (George Mudie later succeeded Denis as Member for Leeds East and became Deputy Chief Whip, thus fulfilling my prophecy in his early days that he would one day become an MP.) Warm, caring and tireless, Doreen made a great contribution to education in Leeds, and, now in her nineties, still follows the city's affairs with interest.

Routine constituency visits were one thing; election campaigns, of course, quite another. The electioneering pattern remained more or less the same. I would go to the constituency for some days before the election; but the work began before this. First there was my contribution to the manifesto, which traditionally contains a few moving words from the candidate's wife about how good a husband and father the prospective MP is. I doubt whether many people read it, but they usually liked to see the photograph of a happy family, and might stick it up in their window. Our first manifesto carried a lovely photograph of Denis with our baby Cressida. Then there were long days in party headquarters folding the manifestos into envelopes to be sent freepost to every household in the constituency — a lengthy task and always a good chance for me to chat to party workers over innumerable mugs of tea. Among them were always some mysterious strangers who appeared, worked silently and then disappeared, not to be seen again until the next election. Some were admirers of Denis; some busy people who made this sole political effort every five years or so.

Then came the canvassing, dreaded in prospect but usually rather enjoyed at the time in spite of ravening dogs and fierce men in houses on mean streets, where windows were boarded up and pavements bristled with broken glass. There were also comfortable little houses with coal fires in burnished grates, kettles bubbling and home-made buns offered. But, as I early learned, I was not meant to sit and gossip; my job was to register yes or no, take the request for a car on election day and move on.

My first tutor in electioneering was Major Milner, the retiring MP, in the by-election of 1952. He showed me the ropes, walking with me round shopping centres. "Smile over to there," he would urge, "one of ours." A day with the major and my face would ache with smiling. He was tall and good-looking with a brisk military stride, and he had developed the canvassing technique to a fine, though not always convincing, art. Experienced canvassers like Douglas Gabb quickly sensed the mood but, good or bad, remained unflappable. If my smile was not returned or the eyes were carefully averted, I immediately despaired, to

134

Doug's amusement. "There are many thousands who will vote for Denis and fewer thousands who will not — cheer up!"

In those days there were many public meetings, later to be replaced by the inaccessible face on television. My job was to make a short speech at one base, holding the fort until my husband replaced me, then move on to the next schoolroom and repeat the performance. After my first embarrassingly sycophantic wifely speech, to my dismay Milner said fiercely: "You are not wearing your wedding ring; never do that again!" After Cressida's difficult birth my hands had swollen badly, so my ring was cut off, and I was still waiting to replace it. Mrs Milner, a quiet, elegant lady, kept a beautiful house adorned with delicate flower arrangements, and held garden parties in her pretty garden. I felt I could never reach the Milners' standard.

Polling day had its traditions. Certain Labour Party members offered their houses for the day as committee rooms strategically placed near polling stations; these were good places for a halt, a cup of tea and a progress report. The state of the poll was marked on large sheets of paper, and cars to be requested for the old and lame were also marked. Traditionally, a heavy poll in the morning might mean a Tory victory, because that was when "they" voted. "Ours" flocked in after work if we were in luck. A very good sign was when workers bothered to vote *before* work. I was never sure how efficient the marking-off system was, but it kept people happy and in touch. Certainly many wicked old ladies took rides in the cars of our opponents, then voted for

135

us. Or so they said. Some of the importance and social pleasure of the occasion vanished with the introduction of general postal voting in the election of 2005.

Our duty on election day was to go round all the polling stations in turn, shake hands with the poll officials, commiserate on their draughty polling booths, enquire about the tea situation, smile at the policeman on duty and then move on. This would take all day. Then there was a short break and a quick meal, and the next stop was at the count at Leeds Town Hall where, in a tense hush, invigilators wearing blue or yellow or red rosettes walked up and down scrutinizing the piles of voting papers as they were heaped up, estimating by the growing piles which way the vote was moving. I always felt our opponent's pile was terrifyingly large.

Then the presiding officer would stand on the platform flanked by the candidates and announce the result. Denis, who was on each occasion the winner, would make a short speech, and his opponent would follow — to cheers and boos. In 1952, wishing our crestfallen Conservative opponent goodbye, I tactlessly wished him "better luck next time". By this time the first national results were out and we could begin to see which way the pendulum was swinging. After the count we always joined friends and opponents, usually at Yorkshire Television Headquarters, to follow the results on the big screen. So it was that, over the years, to groans and cheers, we watched Labour's fortunes wax, wane, wax again and wane again. Then it was a weary return to our hotel as the sun rose over the city.

136

The morning after the count we always drove back to London, listening to the car radio as the country results came in. Generally there was hope from the cities but little from the country; indeed, some years we had lost hope before midnight and listened sadly as one after another of the country seats were taken by the Tories. Indeed, for Denis's first twelve years in Parliament each election brought in a Tory victory; for these were the years of opposition.

CHAPTER
SIX

WESTMINSTER WIFE: OPPOSITION, 1952–1964

Even though we had decided to live in London rather than Leeds, the Westminster life meant frequent separation. Denis was often away travelling the world, keeping up his wide knowledge of international affairs and representing the Labour Party at overseas conferences. At that time, too, MPs' hours were not family-friendly. The House of Commons sat from 1.30 until 10 p.m. — and often much later, sometimes right through the night. So I was often alone with our three young children.

However, there were compensations. In June 1953 we were lucky in the parliamentary ballot for seats in Westminster Abbey for the Coronation. We walked from the Commons on a chill grey morning among other MPs, some unfamiliar in top hats and morning suits; I was frozen in my new yellow silk dress. Since the invitation had ruled out large hats, I wore a confection of black net with a yellow rose. Outside the Abbey huge crowds waited, wet but cheerful — some had camped on the pavements all night. Inside, we found our numbered blue velvet chairs, high up in the gallery.

As Big Ben struck eleven, we heard the jingling of carriages; and now memory is reinforced by the oft-repeated television pictures, of the splendid procession — ancient knights in heraldic costume — and then the lovely young Queen, her long train held by little pages, slowly moving up the aisle to Handel's triumphant *Zadok the Priest*. I remember vividly being moved by the powerful symbolism of the ancient ritual, the removal of the splendid robes, the slight figure in simple white now burdened by the symbols of majesty — orb, sword, ring — the anointing, and finally the coronation itself to the repeated shouts from the four corners of the Abbey: *Vivat Regina!* This was ceremony at its most moving, the dedication of a single lovely young woman in the midst of all the magnificent trappings of state.

Occasions like this were welcome breaks in what was, in those early years, often a lonely life. I recall being invited to a grand dinner at which the late Richard Dimbleby was host. Instead of after-dinner speeches he called on distinguished guests at random for off-the-cuff comments. Dozing in post-prandial contentment, I was horrified to hear the great man announcing, "Now I call on Mrs Healey to tell us what it's like to be an MP's wife." I stood, frozen, then said: "To be an MP's wife? It is to be bereft of speech," and sat down!

The years between 1951 and 1964, when the Tories were in power, are usually described in Labour records

139

as the "Thirteen Wasted Years". Attlee's victorious government of 1945 had swept through massive projects: founding the National Health Service, rebuilding shattered cities, reclothing and resettling huge armies. But by 1950 he and his ministers — many of whom had also served in the wartime coalition government — were exhausted. They won that election, but by only four seats. When Attlee called another in 1951, he lost and Churchill returned to Downing Street.

I often watched debates from the gallery of the House of Commons, and, seeing Churchill slumped, waxen-faced, on the front bench, often with his eyes closed, wondered how long he would keep his crown prince, the Foreign Secretary Anthony Eden, waiting. There were flashes of the old wicked humour. I once saw him scrabbling on the floor, interrupting Attlee as the opposition leader moved to the peroration of his speech. "It's all right," he explained with a cherubic smile, "I'm just looking for my jujube."

When Churchill did finally resign in 1955 and the debonair Eden led the Conservatives to another victory, his reign was short, ill-health and the debacle of Suez combining to destroy him. In 1957 Macmillan became prime minister, and his government was returned to power in October 1959 on a wave of confidence that sustained it until the Profumo scandal in 1963. It is an indication of the change in press behaviour since then that no hint of the scandal in his own life ever reached the newspapers. I certainly knew nothing of it. Lady Dorothy Macmillan, with all the assurance of her

140

Devonshire background, conducted a long affair with MP Sir Robert Boothby, yet made Macmillan a perfectly effective political wife. I remember that she invited me to meet Indira Gandhi when she was in London and I took tea with them both in the drawing room at Admiralty House, where the Macmillans were living while No. 10 Downing Street was being repaired. Indira Gandhi had been at Oxford before me and remembered her time there with great pleasure. Quiet and self-deprecating, she laughed at her own "hopelessly poor public speaking voice". I little thought at that time that I should one day be the hostess in that great drawing room, or that the bright gentle lady I met that day would meet so tragic an end. I watched her funeral pyre on television with the deepest horror.

In 1963 Macmillan resigned through ill-health. While in hospital he had taken advice on his successor from the "magic circle" of senior Tories and had asked the Queen's consent for the appointment of Sir Alec Douglas-Home. In order to serve in the Commons, Sir Alec had to sacrifice his peerage as the Earl of Home. Though the gentlest and most charming of Tory leaders, he was not the most effective. Given to self-mockery, he claimed to solve economic problems with the help of matches, and laughed that his head looked like a skull on television. He had not been the unanimous choice of the Tories: there were many who preferred the brilliant, but somewhat opaque, Rab Butler.

It happened that on the day of decision I was with Denis at 10 Downing Street as a guest at a lunch given for some foreign dignitary. Gradually, from conversation with Lady Douglas-Home, I realized that she was to become mistress of No. 10. After lunch, as I stood drinking coffee by the window with Mrs Rab Butler, I was startled by her fierce anger: "I will never forgive the Tories," she exploded, "for what they have done to Rab!"

For his first seven years in parliament Denis was a backbench MP, rapidly establishing himself as a formidable expert on international affairs, mounting effective attacks on the succession of Tory governments and regarded with respect on all sides of the House. The Tories received his maiden speech with traditional courtesy. They said that, having for so long heard his words through the mouths of Cabinet ministers, they were glad he could now speak for himself. Listening from the gallery, I was surprised at the quiet, even dull, academic tone of those early speeches. It would be some years before he found his real parliamentary voice — vigorous, humorous, powerful. But whatever the tone, the content was always well-informed and based on extensive first-hand knowledge of the world, gained in war and during his seven years as International Secretary of the Labour Party, and constantly replenished by frequent travels.

In 1959 Denis was elected to the Shadow Cabinet by the parliamentary party and was therefore in the running for a ministry if Labour gained power. Foreign ambassadors, interested to know a possible foreign minister, invited Denis to their embassies in London and I was often included. Diplomatic life was a world of its own. Ambassadors represented their countries in London in beautiful houses: the Russians and others in a private gated road in Kensington, the Americans in a splendid mansion in Regent's Park, where Walter Annenberg later displayed his wonderful collection of art treasures. (On leaving London in 1974 he also generously donated a swimming pool to Chequers.) Dinner parties in these establishments were grand affairs with superb flower arrangements and delicious food elegantly served, and called for handsome evening dresses.

I learned diplomatic rituals at the dining table. *Placement* was of the greatest importance. The most important guest was seated at the right-hand side of the hostess, the second most important on her left; similarly, the chief lady was seated at the right and the second lady at the left of mine host. Among the British, royal guests took precedence. The Communist countries were usually the keenest sticklers for precedence — I have known an east European wife leave an official dinner because she felt her country had been downgraded — though the aristocracy were also vigilant: I once heard a duchess complain that she had been placed below her rank. I also learned the established pattern for diplomatic dinner conversation. The host speaks to the lady on his right during the first course and the lady on his left during the second. At the end of the meal, ladies would be taken upstairs to "powder their noses", while gentlemen smoked their cigars and discussed world politics. In the old days

143

screens would hide the chamber-pot cupboard at either end of the sideboard.

There were other traditions, too — some of which we learned the hard way. When one diplomatic evening trailed on and everyone was obviously dying to go home, it was not until a whisper from a Foreign Office official that we realized that since we were the guests of honour no one could leave until we did!

During this period, not only were we entertained by many ambassadors in London, but Denis was also invited to visit their countries — and I was often welcomed too. We also accompanied Hugh Gaitskell, Attlee's successor as Labour leader, on official visits to Yugoslavia and Russia. Hugh, who valued Denis's wide-ranging knowledge of foreign affairs and often sought his advice, was glad to have him with him on these occasions.

I came to know Hugh and his wife Dora very well and had a great deal of affection for them both. I admired Dora's brisk common sense and intelligence: she was a loyal, loving, though not uncritical wife, who kept him in touch with real life. As a Leeds MP, Hugh shared many of our Yorkshire friends, and he and Dora, like us, were frequent guests at the Gillinsons' hospitable home. We always shared too, the nerve-wracking election nights at the count in the Leeds Town Hall.

Like many former public-school boys of my acquaintance, Hugh tended to keep his female friends in separate compartments. Once he asked me if I had ever wanted to be an MP. When I replied, "Only for the

Forest of Dean, and that was long ago," he said, "Good. If you had become an MP I should have had to think differently about you." To Hugh, women in politics were a different breed. Educated as I had been in the sex equality of a co-educational school, I found this puzzling.

On the visit to Yugoslavia I began to understand the complexities of Yugoslav politics and the bitter, deep-rooted hatred between Serb and Croat, and marvelled that Tito managed to unite the country. Our guides and interpreters had bitter memories of atrocities, passed down from generation to generation. The persisting enmity recalled the perpetual problem of Ireland, where feuds lasted from the days of King Billy and earlier. The most intractable problems the world over are caused by old wounds festering for generations. One day, as we travelled through mountainous country, our guide told us that he and his brothers as boys had gone into hiding there with the partisans. "And your mother?" I asked. "Oh, she came too," he said.

One evening on this tour, after an official meeting, Hugh insisted on finding somewhere to dance. Though I was fond of Hugh I dreaded his invitations to dance, for he had both a surprising passion for dancing and absolutely no sense of rhythm. It was the only time when I agreed with Nye Bevan's description of him as a "calculating machine" — "one, two, three, one, two three", we plodded. On this occasion our puzzled hosts finally found us a dusty, seedy hall at the top of a high building. This seemed to satisfy Hugh. So Denis and

145

Sam Watson, the trade union delegate, sat miserably watching us shuffle around. Suddenly Sam muttered, "I don't know about you, Denis, but my pants are full of little flies."

In 1959 we visited Moscow as guests of the Soviet government, this time travelling with Nye Bevan as well as Hugh and Dora Gaitskell. We were greeted at Moscow airport by a welcoming party of officials who placed us in our correct order of precedence in the waiting cars. Gaitskells in No. 1; Bevan in No. 2; Healeys in No. 3. (Jennie Lee, Bevan's wife, had declined the invitation. As an authority on Russia, Nye told me, who had bravely walked alone over the Tatra Hills on an earlier visit, Jennie would have considered it an insult to be lumped in the baggage van with the wives.)

One bizarre incident at the beginning of our visit must have puzzled our hosts. When our bags were taken to our rooms, the Gaitskells sent to our room a hamper which did not belong to them. It did not belong to us either; since we knew the Gaitskells were bringing a large Wedgwood china bull as a gift to the Khrushchevs, we assumed the hamper must be for them. When we opened it, to our astonishment we found only dirty linen — it was the Gaitskells' laundry basket, which the chauffeur who took them to the airport had picked up by mistake with their luggage!

To the surprise of our hosts, Nye had insisted on bringing a Polish journalist friend, K. S. Karol, to act as his personal adviser and interpreter in Jennie's place. He had even persuaded Malik, the Soviet ambassador in London, to authorize Karol to stay in the same apartment as us, away from the other journalists. In fact, as Michael Foot explains in his biography of Bevan, Karol's principal duty "was to discover ways and means, by the use of his expert Russian, to find relief from the oppressive proximity of the rest of the delegation. It was not such an easy task . . . ; but they did escape to the Indian Embassy and to the Polish Embassy, and all the while Nye sighed for other escapades like a would-be truant schoolboy."

One unexpected schoolboy moment occurred at a football match to which we had been invited, at which Moscow Dynamo were playing. Sitting between Hugh and Nye, while they shouted in unison, I suddenly saw two little boys in their different school caps. "Fair play!" the Welsh approval came in one ear, and "Well done!" the Wykehamist voice in the other. And they were both shouting for the same side. There were many times on that trip when Nye enjoyed being a wicked little boy. When the Russians, always insistent on protocol, placed us in our cars, Nye delighted in getting their order confused, saying to me, "Come on, girl, you and Denis get in my car!"

Wives were not invited to the political discussions, so when we were asked what we would like to do or see, I always asked to be allowed to visit some ordinary home. I found this a better way of understanding a country than reading the briefs — excellent though they were. Accordingly, in Moscow, when my guide said, "You will say, 'They only let you see what they want you to see,' so choose a flat, and we'll call," and drove me through streets lined with high blocks of flats, I pointed to one and we duly went up and knocked. An alarmed lady came out, and it was explained that we came from England and wanted to see a typical Muscovite. She immediately burst into tears, shut the door and a moment later reappeared wearing her best jersey — proof that she had not expected us. This friendly greeting was repeated again and again during our visit when I was received by women in their homes. The flat itself was a single room which housed a family: beds were stowed away in the day — very much as they were in England and Scotland in the nineteenth century. When a young man later showed me his poems, the theme of one being "I am only alone in the street", I understood.

The most memorable visit of all on this trip was the one Dora Gaitskell and I paid to the Khrushchev home on the Lenin Hills. It was unusual for foreign visitors to be invited to a Soviet leader's home, but this was just before Khrushchev's first expedition to America and Mrs Khrushchev wanted to get some experience of western customs. Also, Dora was to present the Wedgwood china bull to her. The world's press, eager for photographs, followed us to the gates of the villa; however, we insisted that this was a private visit and they were not allowed any further.

The villa was small, surrounded by unkempt grass. Inside, we were ushered into a sitting room which, with neat lace cloths over velvet, reminded me more of Tolstoy and Dostoevsky than of Marx or Lenin. We were brought trays of sweet cakes and coffee by an

148

elderly waiter who might well have been a character from a Russian novel reporting cherry trees chopped down. We were warmly received by Mrs Khrushchev and her daughter, who spoke good English, and by Mrs Gromyko, whose husband was at that time the Russian foreign minister. Mrs Khrushchev laughingly compared her own buxom figure to her mental image of slim American girls, and the Russian ladies joked about their need to take a slimming course.

Mrs Gromyko's English was fluent and both she and Mrs Khrushchev were clearly highly intelligent. Mrs Khrushchev was, I believe, a trained engineer. They asked many questions about America, and in turn I asked about the role of women in Russia. Towards the end, Mrs Khrushchev said what a pity it was that we had no camera to record this friendly meeting. "As it happens . . ." said I, and took out Denis's little camera, which he had slipped into my pocket. I set the camera, then we all held hands and were photographed by the secretary. Then we went out into the sunshine to be taken again. I hoped I had set the camera properly, but had absolutely no confidence in my skill. However, we left with, as I thought, two or three immortal scoops. As we drove away, pursued by photographers, I was offered large sums of money for the negatives — all of which I firmly refused. This was a private occasion.

We were taken by train for a brief visit to Leningrad, travelling all night in a sleeping carriage while stout ladies in starched white pinafores sat on guard along the corridor. We marvelled at the Hermitage Museum, but modern art was still only represented by worthy examples of Soviet realism. The dazzling beauty of gilded palaces and the robust humour of the joke fountains and waterfalls were all another world away from sober Moscow. At this time the Russians were taking great care of their heritage, renewing gilding, restoring gardens.

On returning to Moscow we heard that Macmillan had called an election for 8 October — five weeks ahead — with the leader of the opposition caught in Russia. Khrushchev got the message before we did! The press immediately called for comments from Gaitskell, who had disappeared after our farewell dinner. Nye and Denis finally found him dead to the world in his room, having been completely knocked out by the endless succession of toasts. Nye quietly took the press conference and never once mentioned the real cause of Hugh's "illness". As Denis recorded in his autobiography, "such magnanimity is not universal in politics".

Indeed, throughout that visit the relationship between Nye and Hugh was easier than I remembered it previously. I was constantly aware that Nye was in an odd frame of mind, unusually careful of his health, enjoying talk of philosophy and poetry with Denis, and generally in a valedictory mood, as though subconsciously aware of the cancer that would kill him the following year. It gave Denis great satisfaction to know that, on the Moscow tour, he and Nye had come to a final understanding and acknowledged their shared love of something beyond politics. I was glad to have known something of one of the most charismatic leaders of the Labour Party.

150

★ ★ ★

The sudden declaration of the election date changed our plans. The Russian tour had been intended to finish with an official visit to Poland. At first Hugh thought of fulfilling that engagement, but Nye saw that we must immediately get back.

On the way home Denis looked forward with excitement to developing my Moscow film. Knowing my own fatal hamfistedness, I dreaded the moment. But I was saved. Back in his darkroom he made a mistake he had never made before — he put in the fixer first, wiping the film clean. Ashen-faced, he confessed; generously I forgave him: first, since I doubted whether I had set the camera properly; second, because I was never sure I would not succumb to journalists' bribes — which I would have felt to be a betrayal; and third, there was a certain satisfaction in watching the infallible Healey making such a monumental mistake.

Barbara Castle and members of the Shadow Cabinet had given us an enthusiastic welcome at the airport to kick off the election campaign; but despite the energy and unity of this beginning, the 1959 election ended in failure. Macmillan's theme of "You've never had it so good" touched a chord on the housing estates where the chance of home ownership was to prove a great attraction.

On election night, Hugh Gaitskell strode into Leeds Town Hall for the count with arms raised triumphantly: this time we really felt we were winning. But it was not to be. I sat beside him as the first results came in — it was the first time we had portable radios with us to monitor events — and after the first few results Hugh turned to me and said, "We've had it. We've lost!" I wondered then how he could possibly tell, but in later counts I, too, could read the pattern in those early results, when the country moved like a flock of birds.

As the results poured in, Hugh sat by me, deflated, his supporters not meeting his eyes. When we left the town hall at the end of the count we knew that while our seats were safe, nationally we had lost. My last sad image of that election is of Hugh sitting on the stairs among discarded leaflets. Was he waiting for his car? I do not remember, but he was an unforgettable picture of lost hope. At 3a.m., back in his party rooms as Tredegar, Nye Bevan watched the television cameras focus on Hugh's face as he conceded victory to the Tories. Nye spluttered with rage: "Hugh should not have given up until the last minute!" But Hugh had correctly done his sums.

In the week after the election, commiseration came from an unexpected source. I met Selwyn Lloyd, the Tory foreign minister at the time, at a party. He said, "I really am sorry — I truly believe in alternate government, and besides I left a lot of difficult problems on the desk thinking that it was Denis who would have to deal with them!"

Neither Hugh nor Nye would see the fruit of all their years of hard labour. Nye was dead within months, and less than three years later, after a short illness, Hugh followed him.

The unexpected sudden death of Hugh Gaitskell on 18 January 1963, at the age of fifty-six, stunned the

Labour Party and shattered his friends. We heard the news first in a call from the BBC asking for an immediate comment. I will never forget how quickly Denis was able to pull himself together and, though deeply shaken, pay a warm tribute to the man who was not only his leader but his friend.

Roy Jenkins, who knew him well, and loved him this side of idolatry, described him with justice in his book *A Life at the Centre*: "He would not have been a perfect Prime Minister. He was stubborn, rash, and . . . only a moderately good judge of people. Yet when these faults are put in the scales and weighed against his qualities they shrivel away . . . He was that very rare phenomenon, a great politician who was also an unusually agreeable man."

Gaitskell's death in 1963 was a defining moment in Labour Party history, sowing the seeds which would later ripen into a split in the party and the formation of the SDP. His closest supporters would find it difficult to adjust to the new leader, Harold Wilson.

CHAPTER
SEVEN

DEFENCE: A VIEW FROM THE BAGGAGE TRAIN, 1964–1970

The unexpected early death of Hugh Gaitskell struck at the heart of his circle of friends. Roy Jenkins and Tony Crosland, his closest allies in the Labour Party, were devastated. With Nye Bevan's death in 1960 the Bevanites had lost their leader; now the right-wing standard-bearer had fallen too.

Fortunately for the Labour Party, a competent successor was at hand. Harold Wilson was talented and energetic; on his appointment as President of the Board of Trade in 1947, he had become the youngest Cabinet minister since 1806. In 1951 he had belonged to the Bevanite faction, resigning from Attlee's Shadow Cabinet with Bevan over the policy of charging for false teeth and spectacles on the NHS, so in the election for a new party leader he could count on left-wing support. He won with ease.

After a passionate speech at the 1963 Scarborough conference foreseeing "the white heat of the technological revolution", Wilson led the party to a narrow victory in the 1964 general election. As we drove down the motorway from Leeds to London the morning after the count, we listened to the last results from the country constituencies coming in on the radio, and heard the majority Labour appeared to have the night before whittled away. Not until the last moment could we be sure of success — and then it was without an overall majority, which was achieved only with the general election of 1966.

In these years I knew Harold Wilson only by repute, and in all the time that Denis was his colleague I scarcely ever held a conversation with him — indeed, I doubt whether he ever addressed more than five sentences to me — yet I felt I understood his background and the traditions and values that shaped him. His family, like mine, was rooted in Nonconformist traditions, in his case in the Congregational Chapel. His route to university had been, as mine had been, through elementary and grammar schools. I had collected my badges in the Girl Guides, he in the Scouts. To the end of his life he was exceedingly proud that he had reached the dizzy height of a King's Scout, and his fondness for the Queen owed something to this interest which he shared with her father. At Oxford — where our paths may have crossed at Nonconformist tea parties, though I do not recall a meeting — Harold would have been more at home with the Welsh undergraduates at Keble than with the arrogant intellectuals at Balliol or New College. His commitment to hard work and self-improvement was rewarded by an excellent first-class degree. King's Scout Harold would go on collecting badges to the moment he

155

retired from the premiership — with the badge of the longest-serving prime minister.

On 1 January 1940 Harold married Mary, the daughter of a Congregational minister, in Mansfield College chapel, Oxford. For the first years of their marriage Mary stayed out of the limelight, bringing up their three children and making a comfortable home. Later, her own talents were recognized when she published her books of poetry. Her mother was a weaver, and Mary was proud that she was skilled enough to manage three looms. "Betty Boothroyd's mother only had one," she told me once, triumphing in her victory over the Speaker of the House of Commons. Late in life Mary and I shared memories of the hymns we had sung in Sunday school as little children and, over coffee in the House of Lords, we sang together (in low voices) the words that have always been embedded in my mind as an example of the Nonconformist drive:

> Just as I am, young, strong and free,
> To be the best that I can be,
> Lord of my Life, I come.

Wilson's main aim in choosing his first Cabinet was to balance the left and right wings of the Labour Party. He could select his team from a vintage generation. In this parliament, on all sides of the House, there were men and women of exceptional ability, perhaps uniquely qualified to lead the country. It was a generation tested in the fire of war: they had no illusions, they had known its horrible reality. Denis never forgot the experience of being dive-bombed on the Italian beaches; as Minister of Defence he later refused to allow aerial bombardment during the war of Confrontation when British troops faced Indonesian invaders in Borneo. He and his contemporaries could bring to politics qualities that later generations lacked.

One notable appointment was Barbara Castle, whom Wilson made Minister of Overseas Development in 1964 and Minister of Transport in 1965. This represented an advance for women, hitherto confined to the "caring" ministries. Wilson wanted, he said, "a tiger in his tank", though this "tiger", who opened the spectacularly beautiful Severn Bridge and introduced seatbelts and the breathalyser, never learned to drive a car.

Barbara Betts had, like me, taken the road from grammar school to St Hugh's College, Oxford, but, unlike me, had been soaked in politics from childhood. She had been fighting mock elections at Bradford Girls' Grammar School when Denis was at Bradford Boys' Grammar School. She had not enjoyed academic life at Oxford and her results had been disappointing. Elected for Blackburn in 1944, at the age of thirty-four, she blazed a trail in Parliament until 1976 when Callaghan, as Prime Minister, felt his Cabinet would be more comfortable without her.

I had never known her well, but greatly admired her fierce dedication and her vitality, though I was somewhat intimidated by her blazing honesty. When our children were young I did some freelance lecturing, and was thoroughly put down when Barbara, asked by a journalist what she disliked in life, said — among other things — "pin money lecturers". I did not dare confess that I was one. When the Labour Party gave a celebration dinner for Denis's eightieth birthday, Barbara's speech, unlike the others, was uncomfortably direct and uncompromisingly honest.

Wilson had called Denis straight away offering him the Ministry of Defence, and the permanent secretary, Sir Henry Hardman, came up to Highgate to brief him. Next day an official car with driver appeared at our Highgate home, and so did security men with a safe to be bolted in — both, incidentally, were removed just as rapidly when we lost the election of 1970.

Having assembled a talented Cabinet, it was Wilson's constant aim to keep it in balance and united: he had seen at first hand how Attlee had managed his similar collection of big beasts. His own technique throughout his period of office as Prime Minister was to ensure that no single minister became too powerful. In the first years after 1964 this was easier, for the men and women who were new to office were too occupied in learning the job and running their departments to threaten his position. As far as Denis was concerned, the difficult problems of defence were more than enough to keep him occupied. I do not believe Wilson ever wanted to put Denis in his natural place — the Foreign Office — where he would have been uncomfortably dominant. As it was, during his period as Minister of Defence it was said that half the officials at the Foreign Office thought Healey ought to be

Foreign Minister, the other half thought he was. So when in 1968 Foreign Minister George Brown blew his top once too often, as he often did, and gave in his resignation, Wilson accepted it and settled for a quiet life, appointing in his place the quiet and gentle Michael Stewart — a safe pair of hands, and an unthreatening one.

Defence is perhaps the most demanding of all the ministries. A defence minister has to look ahead in time and around the world in space. He must have the strength, indeed, sometimes the ruthlessness, to make major changes in defence planning that bring in their wake cancellation charges and job losses. It is not surprising that Denis's predecessors had not lasted long, as I realized when paying my first visit to his office in the headquarters of the ministry in Whitehall. Around the walls were portraits of previous ministers with their brief dates of service. Denis would survive there for six years.

For many years he had managed without a permanent private secretary, with the help of part-time typists or secretaries from a Westminster agency, often writing his constituency letters in his own indecipherable handwriting, or typing them on his aged typewriter. Now he had three offices — one in the Ministry of Defence, with an army of civil servants, one in the House of Commons where he did his constituency work, and one in Leeds. Party work and ministry work had to be kept strictly separate, so he needed a full-time personal secretary — and this is where Harriet Shackman came into his life. Harriet

Shackman loved people and is remembered with affection by all who knew her. We could never discover her age, and it was only serious illness that made her retire after twenty-five years with Denis. She had wanted, she said, to "die at my desk".

Harriet was both a bridge and a barrier to the outside world, understanding and often dealing with the affairs of the constituency. Dedicated not only to Denis but to the Labour Party, she became also a friend and confidant to me and indeed the whole family. To the end of her working life she remained vital and keenly interested in life, music and books, working loyally for the Labour Party in her spare time. The House of Commons was her life, especially after the death of her beloved husband, David. When Harriet finally retired she was overwhelmed by the scores of letters wishing her well, among them a long hand-written letter from Neil Kinnock. It was a tribute well deserved, and typical of Neil's good relationship with the workers at the coal face.

In every top job there are often difficult choices to be made of which the general public is unaware; frequently the interests of the family conflict with the demands of the job, and the children often suffer. Thus it was for us when, after some months at Highgate, we reluctantly decided that we must move to Admiralty House in Whitehall, where Denis could be both immediately accessible and secure. So we packed up, let the house in Highgate to American friends and moved into Admiralty House — complete with dart boards and

160

Cressida's hamster in its cage. It was not an easy decision. It would mean disruption of our family life.

Admiralty House, standing immediately opposite the Banqueting House in Whitehall, is best seen from St James's Park, on to which its great first-floor windows open. Through the graceful stone screen on the Whitehall side, the impressive Palladian entrance leads to the main Admiralty building, constructed in 1625. Here the First Lord of the Admiralty shared his residence with other Admiralty lords. When the second Earl of Chatham became First Lord in 1788, he used his influence with his brother William Pitt, the Prime Minister, to have built "a few rooms of his own where he might dwell in privacy". Parliament accepted the estimate of £13,000, "to be exceeded ... by only £310", and so Admiralty House — one of the loveliest of government residences — was built. The entrance to the house itself is almost invisible — through a simple black door in the left corner of the cobbled courtyard. An exceptionally elegant double spiral staircase leads from the hall to the first floor and the apartment now allotted to the Minister of Defence.

When Duff Cooper was First Lord of the Admiralty, he and the beautiful Lady Diana had lived grandly in the whole of A.H. (as she always called it). On the ground floor were the main state rooms. The first floor — the *piano nobile* — contained a splendid library, the state bedroom of the First Lord, a dressing room and a large boudoir for his wife. On the floors above were guest bedrooms, family bedrooms, rooms for servants, and nurseries. A navy yacht was also at their disposal

161

and their children could travel with them, wearing their own sailors' uniforms. After Macmillan's time at the defence ministry in the 1950s, when Admiralty House needed repair it was decided it would be more in keeping with modern living to divide the house into separate apartments. The ground floor was taken over by government hospitality, to be used by any department for official entertainment. The first floor became a separate apartment for the Minister of Defence, with a drawing room, dining room, grand bedroom and bathroom, and guest bedroom and bathroom. Above this, another apartment was allocated to the Commonwealth Secretary, Arthur Bottomley and his wife Bess, later to George and Grace Thomson and their children. Our children had their rooms on the top floor, separated from us by a dark stairway. Here there were also flatlets for the use of other ministers.

This was to be our base in Westminster until 1970. It was very grand, very clean and very new. Chandeliers sparkled above an enormous drawing room with an immense lacquered Chinese screen. The doorman was surprised to see us immediately waltzing across the acres of blond carpet. But it was a long way from Highgate, and home it was not. We missed the garden, too; and while St James's Park was lovely, it was no substitute for Hampstead Heath and Highgate ponds.

Luckily, Denis's wise private secretary, Patrick (later Sir Patrick) Nairne, perfectly understood the stress of running the Ministry of Defence. He knew that the minister would need somewhere to relax, and suggested I look for a bolt-hole in the country. So I found a coachman's cottage in the grounds of a big house at Withyham near the Ashdown Forest in Sussex. Here we spent weekends whenever possible, and this refuge became essential for Denis's health and the family happiness. How wise Pat Nairne was, understanding the human as well as the intellectual demands of the minister's job: the British civil servant at his best. Denis wrote: "Without my rural oasis at Windleshaw Lodge I doubt if I could have survived the whole six years as Defence Secretary." During precious weekends here he took up the piano again and renewed his passion for opera. Had it not been for the cottage, Denis would have seen little of either me or the children, and the importance of family is clear from his diary: "played chess with Tim" . . . "walked with Jenny" . . . "took Cressida riding in Ashdown Forest".

The cottage was quite primitive when we bought it, with two empty coach-houses and a little living room downstairs, and upstairs tiny bedrooms and bathroom. Gradually, with the help of an imaginative architect, we transformed it. The coach-houses became two sitting rooms, one of which took our second-hand grand piano, a huge Erard (bought from a ballet school) that gave Denis the greatest pleasure. Throughout his ministerial life stress could always be relieved by what he called "a burst on my banjo" — fragments of Bach or Mozart played with spirit on this sonorous old instrument.

During these first years of Denis's ministerial career there were many changes in the family. Jenny left Camden School and went to train as a teacher at

163

Roehampton, then taught at Gospel Oak Primary School for some years. After school Tim spent a year in Paris preparing to take up his scholarship at Balliol College, Oxford, to study French and History. I had mistakenly imagined that a spell of ordered French education would complement Highgate's classical schooling: instead, his arrival coincided with "Les Événements", the student revolt of 1968. I should not have been so happy had I realized at the time that he was observing and taking part in modern French history, learning how to run from smoke attacks by the dreaded riot police, the CRS, how to avoid the flying paving stones, and how to survive on a diet of baked beans. He kindly protected me from the full horror of that year. But it certainly improved his French and gave a new depth to his study of French history.

As Jenny and Tim moved away from home, Cressida became very isolated at Admiralty House. We did not realize, until she told us many years later, how lonely she felt at this time. She had even considered asking to be sent to boarding school. I remember once finding her in her room on the top floor of Admiralty House singing sadly to her guitar in the dusk and looking out over Whitehall: "Here I sit in this old window / watching all the folk go by."

Cressida had hated moving away from her friends in Highgate. There were some compensations — the Thomsons had friendly daughters — but her old friends found the address too overwhelming. Even for herself, as an eleven-year-old, it must have been daunting enough to come in through the great black

164

door past the guardian doorman. For Tim and Jenny, too, it was hardly the place to hold teenage parties.

All of us hankered after dear old Holly Lodge. Cressida brought her pet hamster, which promptly died of shock. She insisted it was hibernating; when finally she agreed it could be buried, it had to be taken up to Holly Lodge and buried under the hollow oak "where my heart is". Solemnly, Jenny and Tim created a suitable coffin and carried it up to the gardens and buried it with due ceremony.

Years later, as a surprise present for our golden wedding anniversary, Jenny and her husband, Derek, produced a wonderful "Golden Book", a collection of photographs accompanied by reminiscences from family, friends and colleagues. Cressida recorded her impressions of Admiralty House:

What a great mausoleum of a place it was. The guards . . . I remember being told they were there to protect us and feeling duped — all of them were pensioners . . . not reassuring at all. How could any of them tackle a burly intruder. And when I asked one what the initials on his badge stood for he said "Ministry of Public Works" with a look that said "this is not your home and I shall be here long after you've left it".

When later I wrote a book on the wives of famous men, I felt I should write a sequel on the children of famous men and women. They have never had an easy row to hoe — Dickens's son, Charley, at Eton, was constantly reminded, "Consider what name you bear"; Livingstone's son changed his surname and went to America to fight in the Civil War and was buried at Gettysburg — but it is infinitely worse now. We have been lucky that our children were not caught in the blinding glare of intrusive publicity or in danger of kidnapping, a threat that Colleen Rees had to face when Merlyn was Secretary of State for Northern Ireland: one of their sons had the shame of a police guard to and from school. Nevertheless, they too have found things difficult at times. Cressida later found it easier to make her life in America where, with courage and hard work, she has become a doctor of clinical psychology, entirely under her own steam.

For Cressida, as for Denis, the cottage was salvation. I arranged riding lessons for her in Ashdown Forest; she took part in village life; and at weekends Jenny came down to join us, as did Tim when he was in England. For all of us the cottage brought fresh air and inspiration. We had good and interesting friends as neighbours: Sir Denys Lasdun, the distinguished architect, and his wife, who had a cottage in the woods nearby; Frank Giles — then the editor of the *Sunday Times* — and his wife Lady Kitty, a daughter of the late Lord Buckhurst, whose family owned much of the area. Their daughter Belinda became a great friend for Cressida and they rode together over the forest. We enjoyed enormously our visits to Dione and Pat Gibson, later Sir Patrick Gibson, at their house "Penns in the Rocks" with its lovely gardens and collection of pre-Raphaelite paintings. These friends helped to make the weekends times of real relaxation for Denis. All his life in times of stress he has needed the refreshment of art, music and poetry — and here, in the country, he found it.

It was a great bonus when our old friends Jack and Frankie Donaldson came to live in Sussex. Jack had been Denis's colonel during the war in Italy and together they had brought music, and especially opera, into army life. Denis had written to me from Naples of Jack's remarkable wife, who had bought a farm in his absence and run it almost single-handedly, then written excellent books on farming. Subsequently she became a distinguished author, writing, among other biographies, a brilliant life of her father, the actor and playwright Frederick Lonsdale. Later, her much-praised life of the Duke of Windsor was made into a popular television drama.

After the war, Jack had founded with his own money and helped to run a remarkable family settlement, a health and social centre in Peckham. The Labour government made him Minister for the Arts and a peer, an honour he deserved and enjoyed. I think he was simply the most honourable man I ever knew; the *chevalier sans peur et sans reproche*. During Denis's most stressful days as Minister of Defence, Jack often took us to the opera at Covent Garden, and even though Denis often had to leave before the end to vote — or deal with a crisis — these evenings lifted the pressure and kept him sane. Gradually I lost my old prejudices about opera. It's "a bastard art", I used to claim. In fact I had never heard an opera in Coleford

PART OF THE PATTERN

and understood neither the language nor the traditions, so I would sit listening with awe to Jack's Etonian "Bravo! Bravo!" I tried a "Bravo!" myself once, but it did not sound in the least convincing.

Frankie came from another world. As a girl she had accompanied her father to grand parties at the Café Royal where admirers drank champagne from her slipper. I realized how far apart our childhoods had been when she once said, with genuine surprise, on being invited to supper with friends, "How odd to be invited to dine with one's grocer." In anyone else this would have been snobbery; in her it was an honest reflection on her own different background. I loved and admired her greatly, and later welcomed her sharp assessments of my own books; her clear direct mind cut through my meanderings. Now both Jack and Frankie are dead we realize how much we miss them and what these country friendships meant to us — and especially to Denis in the grinding years of government stress.

In Admiralty House the navy was ever-present. Pictures of Captain Cook's voyages round the world hung in the state rooms on the ground floor. Here Nelson had dined — and here had cruelly shown his irritation with his wife. She had shelled a dish of walnuts for her one-armed husband, who had awkwardly upset it. Tears followed, and an infuriated Nelson had paced the streets all night. His marble bust stood on our drawing-room chimney-piece, opposite one of Wellington. I often looked at these two different faces, wondering what it is that makes a man of genius. Later, these

168

musings provided the theme of one of my books, *Wives of Fame*.

I was myself to have one particular personal link with the navy. In 1967 I was invited to launch the Polaris submarine *Renown*. It was an honour I viewed with mixed feelings. I had never been a nuclear disarmer, believing that if war was inescapable it had better be as swift and efficient as possible. So I countered the argument "How could a priest bless such a ship?" with "How could you send young men to war without a blessing?", and in my short speech after the launch I said, "Let her existence be enough."

It had seemed frivolous on such an occasion to be concerned about what to wear. But I had an uneasy feeling about sailors' superstitions, so nervously consulted the Navy Department in the Ministry of Defence. I had proposed to wear a green coat for the launch — "was it true that green was considered unlucky?" There was an embarrassed silence, then: "Do you have an alternative, Mrs Healey?" I did, and wore it.

I followed the *Renown*'s career over the years with great interest (though I found it more and more difficult to descend the steep ladder for the official dinner — the hole seemed to get smaller as years went by!), becoming fond of the captains and their wives — and one particular mother. On special occasions, as after refits, we exchanged presents. Once I was given a crystal vase and gave in return a painting by Chris Osborne of my Sussex countryside in summer. This proved a most welcome reminder of England when the submariners were out in the depths of the sea for weeks at a time. I felt great sympathy for the women whose husbands were out of reach for so long and who have to resist the temptation to burden them with news of problems about which they can do nothing. Finally came the day of decommissioning, when I stood with the captains and ship's company and was ceremonially presented with the *Renown*'s flag. It was a heart-tugging moment: an old admiral beside me confessed that he was near to tears — as I was.

At that time security was not so tight or so visible for the Defence Secretary as it was for the Foreign Minister, Prime Minister and the Minister for Northern Ireland, but there were occasions in Admiralty House when sniffer dogs appeared on their investigating rounds, especially when American ministers visited. Great dogs silently padded through the rooms, terrifying me.

I grew accustomed to other sudden appearances. There was the man who cleaned the pictures. He only used the finest silk on the oil paintings, so Hartnell's offcuts cleaned the faces of the great. Then there were the strange men who came regularly, on their rounds of government buildings, to wind the clocks. Responsible for all the clocks in Whitehall, they disappeared as silently as they came. Cressida later remembered in the "Golden Book" the lack of privacy at Admiralty House:

> playing the piano in the hall and suddenly the man
> who wound up the clock coming silently in, fixing
> the innards of the grandfather clock, then leaving

again. Mum in her nightie ducking and hiding behind the sofa having heard one of Dad's officials calling out "Minister, Minister". He'd entered silently, striding over the noiseless dense carpets. How silent it was there with plush carpets, noiseless doors, so you never knew who would be about.

There was another visitor who came even more silently. One morning, Vera, my very sensible cleaning lady, suddenly saw the face of a lady appearing in my bed — blue-eyed, high-cheekboned and beautiful. As Vera retreated in alarm, the face vanished. Who could she be? John Julius Norwich, Lord Norwich, to whom I told the story, said, "Mamma, of course [Lady Diana Cooper] — beautiful, blue-eyed and in bed at eleven in the morning." She had lived there and slept in that room when Duff Cooper was Minister for the Navy.

My ghost, however, I decided, was Martha Ray, whose portrait hung over the fireplace. A famous actress and opera singer, she had been the mistress of the Earl of Sandwich and for many years had lived quite publicly with him at Admiralty House, bearing him many children. She was shot outside Covent Garden Opera House by a clergyman — the Reverend Hackman — not because he disapproved of her morals but because he was passionately and jealously in love with her. The night before my ghost appeared I had held a dinner party at which the Bishop of London was a guest. Perhaps, I decided, he had disturbed her. When next an official from the Ministry of Works called, I told him — expecting to be mocked. However, he said, "Would you like us to do something about it? Strange things happen in these old houses." I always regret that I did not witness a "bell, book and candle" exorcism. Vera consulted a friend, a medium, who advised her that should the lady appear again, she should stand quite still and say, "Hello. How can I help you?"

Many other interesting, if less mysterious, guests came to Admiralty House. Official dinners were provided by government hospitality in the rooms on the ground floor. But for private discussions Denis liked to give small informal lunches, cooked by me, at which I would leave them alone to talk.

A frequent visitor was the retired Field Marshal Montgomery, who would sometimes drop in for lunch on his way to the House of Lords. I think perhaps he was lonely — he didn't seem to mind our simple family lunches, indeed, he said he enjoyed my home cooking. He was also anxious to persuade the minister to create no more field marshals after him. On his first visit he looked at the two marble heads of Nelson and Wellington on the drawing-room mantelpiece and, pointing to the great soldier, rapped, "Shouldn't have meddled with politics!"

It was more than twenty years since Major Healey had stood on the desert sands of North Africa with the First Army, while a charismatic Monty condescendingly welcomed them. "Proud they must be," he said, "to be joining the great Eighth Army." They had cheered through gritted teeth. Now he was a frail old man and smaller than I expected. Surprisingly, he enjoyed talking to Cressida, then barely in her teens. "Where is she?" he asked one day when she was at school, his hand behind his back holding a box of chocolates. "Tell her," he said, "that there are *two* layers." When Cressida came home I told her to keep the wooden box he had inscribed for her, to remind her in later years of a very great man. "He may be a great man to you, Mum," she said perceptively, "but to me he is just a lonely old man."

"People are always writing," he once told me sadly, "asking if I am dead yet!"

One day he told me a strange story. He was being driven home in his official car and, passing a small red-haired boy waiting at his bus stop in the pouring rain, stopped and offered him a lift. Then, unwilling that the child should be unaware of the honour, he asked, "Do you know who I am?"

"No, sir."

"I'll give you a clue — it has to do with fields."

"Good, sir, I like fields, what do you do there?"

"I am a field marshal, I kill people in fields."

A horrified silence, then: "Please, sir, I'd like to get out now." And the little boy scuttled away.

Monty told me this in his clipped, brisk voice, completely unaware of any insensitivity towards an impressionable child.

Life at Admiralty House was never dull. We had many visits from the family. My sister, Doreen, often came and took care of the children when I travelled with Denis. She once brought my elder brother, Bert, who could rarely be persuaded to leave Coleford, but

173

thoroughly enjoyed watching Trooping the Colour from our huge windows. On these occasions Aunt Min and Uncle Hugh and our much-loved cousin Joy came, bringing her children too. Uncle Hugh, hearing the bagpipes below, was moved to tears, the old Seaforth Highlander remembering his long marching days in the First World War when the pipes had revived the troops' flagging spirits. Aunt Min, who in her Forest of Dean girlhood had always dreamed of a life like this, loved the swank of it.

But the visitor I most wanted to see was my mother. What would she make of it all? True to character, she steadily refused to be impressed. On her first visit, after using the cloakroom outside the drawing room, she found a comfortable seat, surrounded herself with cushions, as she always did at home, then said, "There's a nasty great fly in your lavatory, you had better go and deal with it." And I did, immediately. Throughout her visit she repeated, "Now, don't let this go to your head." She came to the Royal Tournament with us and sat in the Royal Box, where evening dress was expected which she did not have. Unfazed, she said, "I'll wear my best and they'll have to do with that." The little figure in her "best" had true dignity, and the brown eyes watched the navy manoeuvres below with unembarrassed approval. It was, she said, "All shipshape and Bristol fashion."

Over the course of these years there were many grand occasions to which we were invited: royal garden parties, receptions and banquets. The palace dining room on such occasions never ceased to amaze me: the gleaming long table, the gold plate and exquisite dinner services, and, at the end, the startling contrast of the entrance of the enormous kilted Highlanders, playing their barbaric bagpipes as they circled the table. "Never have I seen so frightening a vision," a German diplomat once said to me. Once we were invited to spend a night at Windsor Castle, and after dinner the Queen and Prince Philip guided us round the castle. We finished in the library, where each guest found some book of interest to them laid out on the table. To my embarrassment, I was asked to sign my first book, *Lady Unknown* — what does one write in a book for a queen? On this occasion I had a long and surprisingly easy chat with Princess Margaret. I had shared a book launch with Group Captain Townsend, whose memoir had come out at the same time, and she wanted to hear about it. When a flunkey came to say that the Queen had moved on, she said sharply, "Go away, I'm talking to Mrs Healey."

On these palace occasions there was usually one familiar face in the royal procession: that of Earl Mountbatten. At the time Denis became defence minister he was Chief of the Defence Staff — not the easiest of colleagues, demanding royal protocol on all occasions. Philip Ziegler, Mountbatten's biographer, kept on his desk a notice: "Remember, in spite of everything, he was a great man." In the end, Denis had to tell him it was time to resign, yet he thought Denis "brilliant, charming and nice". He was too polite to say ". . . and also could be brutal and ruthless". But he was unfailingly charming to me — "the boss's wife", as he

175

called me. Tall and handsome, he would come across the palace floor to greet me. He had a combination of royal presence and ease of manner that is not common in royalty. On one occasion in the first days of office, I stood in line with Denis at a reception to receive four hundred military attachés and their wives from the embassies. After eight hundred handshakes I turned to Lord Mountbatten and said, "There must be a royal trick to protect your hands." Looking down at me, he said, "My dear, my great-aunt, the Empress of Russia, on Easter Day received hundreds of peasants to kiss her hand. She would never wear a glove but at the end of the day had a lump on her hand the size of pigeon's egg." So I squared my peasant shoulders and carried on.

On another occasion, at a celebration on Horse Guards Parade for the 150th anniversary of Waterloo, he called me to stand beside him to watch the parade. He told me that they had been uncertain whether to invite the French ambassador and that he had privately told him so. "Don't worry, I'll come," said the ambassador; "the celebration for the Battle of Hastings is coming and we will invite you too."

I heard of Lord Mountbatten's assassination with the greatest sadness.

Every year in June, Trooping the Colour took place outside the windows of Admiralty House and, since it often coincided with my birthday, I usually made it the occasion for a party. The week beforehand, early morning rehearsals much disturbed our old friend Roy Jenkins when, as Chancellor of the Exchequer, he lived nearby at No. 11 Downing Street. Early one morning he telephoned: "For goodness' sake, Edna, tell Denis to make his soldiers belt up — I'm trying to sleep!"

It was strange to think that the young students Roy Jenkins and Denis Healey I had known so long ago were now neighbours in such elevated positions. Now each was so immersed in his own department that we saw little of each other, though once Jennifer sent her son round to borrow bread because they had an unexpected influx of trade union leaders for beer and sandwiches. There were many such moments worthy of inclusion in the television series *Yes, Minister*.

Tony Crosland, one of our other old acquaintances, was now minister of state in the Department of Economic Affairs. We had known Tony since our Oxford days and I had then regarded him with awed affection in spite of his notorious arrogance, though I always reckoned that as far as he was concerned I was invisible. Later I was surprised to discover that, in spite of what he himself called his "la-di-da" accent and his upper-middle-class family, his religious background was Nonconformist like my own, though he was brought up in the stricter Plymouth Brethren. I believe this partly explains the puzzling mixture of elements in his character. Behind the wild behaviour and the heavy drinking were always an innate seriousness, an idealism and a compulsion to serve, combined with a powerful mind. He had a physical courage that was tested to the limit as a paratrooper in the war. He had enjoyed the camaraderie of battle and had an ability to accept and even to enjoy the rough life of the army. After the war he returned to Oxford, gaining a first in PPE, then became a Fellow of Trinity College and taught economics. Among his students was the young Tony Benn, whom he affectionately called Jimmy. There was nothing wrong about Jimmy, he once said, "except that he was a bit cracked". Later, as neighbours, they kept up this odd friendship to the end of Tony's life.

Tony's brief first marriage was a failure. His second, to Susan Barnes, transformed him. A successful journalist from a family of successful journalists, Susan had come from America to London in 1956 with her Anglo-Irish journalist husband and two young daughters. Tall, blonde, with stunning good looks and a wide and gentle smile, she captivated Tony and they married in 1963. Susan was the perfect match for him. Loving him deeply, she could accept him as he was, and by allowing him his freedom secured his deep and permanent love. She was always prepared to put aside her own absorbing work when he was free; never bored when he was not, she would stay awake for his late-night arrival from Parliament so that he could unwind by chatting about the day's business — unlike Denis, who was never given to chatting at the best of times, and certainly not at night. Whatever burden it was that Tony had carried for so long, Susan helped to lift it, releasing him to concentrate his formidable intellect on the political problems he cared about so deeply. Susan freed him from Vanity Fair.

It is not surprising that, again and again in those years at Defence, Denis's diary entries often end: "To bed —

178

dog tired." As he wrote in *The Time of My Life*, "Throughout my six years as Secretary of State for Defence, I worked harder than I had ever imagined I could . . . It was not easy to squeeze in my monthly weekends in Leeds, and more difficult still to find time with my family."

Yet he "loved every minute of it". He was in a world that he understood from his wartime experience, a world he had studied and on which he had lectured at service colleges and elsewhere. And though some of the service chiefs had on the whole been less than enthusiastic about working with a Labour government, Denis won their respect. Although he had no previous experience as a government minister, at forty-seven he was still young, with immense energy, a powerful mind capable of marshalling the floods of information that poured in from all over the world at all times, and an enormous appetite for understanding its complexities. Above all, he was capable of the ruthlessness that was demanded by the present situation.

His immediate problem was that, as a member of the Labour Cabinet, he was committed to saving millions on the defence budget, but as Minister of Defence he was pledged to secure the safety of the nation: twin demands not easy to reconcile. It was inevitable that in wielding the knife he should leave pain, but at the end of his time as defence minister he could claim with some pride that as a nation we now spent more on education than on defence, whereas until then we had spent a greater proportion of our national budget on defence than any of our NATO colleagues. It has now been generally agreed that he was one of the best defence ministers on record.

With Denis so completely absorbed in his work, I might have felt isolated. But the service chiefs and the civil servants I had to deal with were unfailingly kind and helpful, and, best of all, I was encouraged to accompany Denis whenever he travelled abroad and there was room for me on the plane. I was even led to believe that my presence on these tours was helpful. I could visit schools and hospitals and talk to service wives. I doubt whether I did much good, though I always remembered from constituency work in Leeds how troubled wives found it a relief to air their worries. Service wives often have to deal with husbands under stress and children who, uprooted from home and friends, find it hard to cope with different climates and foreign customs. Also, civil servants who had watched successive ministers come and go knew how stressful the defence job was, and understood that the presence of a wife on these official tours helped to make the pressure bearable. Thus, in those first years of office when Denis travelled the world, I was immediately made to feel part of a team. This was not so in other ministries; but the services understood the importance of wives and families, and whether I was actually of use or not they made me feel so.

I was also most grateful during Denis's time at Defence for the wisdom of the service chiefs' wives on the matter of dress — which could be a conundrum, given the wide variations in the degree of formality required. When on tour, they advised me, "Look out of

180

the window of the descending plane and take your cue from the dress of the ladies in the reception line below." For Hong Kong the accessories were long white gloves, hat and stockings; other hosts were more relaxed.

I was fortunate, too, in that I could leave my children for brief periods in safe hands. Denis's spry little Aunty Dolly would willingly come up from Newnham. Since her parents had died she had made her living caring for other people, so she was a most competent homemaker. In Highgate, too, she was near her beloved sister, Denis's mother. After finishing his career at the technical college in Keighley, Will Healey had spent some time with Win in Barbados as an adviser on technical education. On their return to England they bought a little house at Highams Park near Epping Forest, where they lived until Will's death. Both Win and Dolly adored the children as did my own sister, Doreen. What an immense debt wives have always owed to the self-sacrifice of single women!

The peregrinations began with a visit to Norway in April 1965. It was my first experience of long flights, and — although I am normally a craven coward in high mountains and suffer vertigo — I found flying exhilarating. The magic of skies at sunrise and sunset, the timelessness of days when there were two sunrises or no sunsets, never ceased to thrill me. I often found myself humming, "Up above the world so high, like a tea tray in the sky," as we "rode secure the cruel skies".

Wherever we went in the world, there was always someone Denis had known in his earlier life working for the Labour Party. In Norway it was the Minister of

Defence, "Gubbi" Harlem, whose guests we were. His daughter, then an attractive girl, was to become Prime Minister of Norway as Gro Harlem Brundtland. Gubbi was an old friend from Denis's days as International Secretary, and Denis liked to call himself an old Norwegian journalist from the same period, having tapped out his weekly articles for *Arbeiderbladet*.

This was Denis's first official overseas visit and he was not yet accustomed to ceremony. Our plane landed in northern Norway to a scene of startling beauty. A welcoming party, with a scarlet-clad band, waited to greet the distinguished guest. As he surveyed the magical vision of birch trees in a snowy landscape from the top of the plane steps, Denis's immediate reaction was to turn to Pat Nairne, his private secretary, for his camera. Quietly and firmly, Pat whispered, "Not now, Secretary of State, not now!"

Our hosts, however, were friendly and informal, the simple house warm and wood-scented. While Denis toured Norway's border with Russia, I was given my first glimpse of life in the land of the eternal sun; I learned of the problems of getting to sleep in perpetual daylight and the high incidence of mental disturbance in the months of perpetual night. A tour like this was for me sheer pleasure, though exhausting; but for Denis, though pleasurable, it was merely the background to continuous work, hard thinking and relentless discussions about major military and political problems with the government of whatever country we were in.

After sampling the snows of northern Norway, in June 1965 I was allowed to accompany the minister to

182

the deserts of Arabia, where the Federation of South Arabia, which included the old Crown Colony of Aden, was in a state of turmoil: rebellious tribesmen in the hinterland were fighting among themselves and against the Adenis. Since Aden was an important staging post to the Far East and East Africa its stability was important, and our troops were fighting there. No leisurely welcome with a band here: on landing we were greeted by an armed escort and driven at high speed through dangerous territory to our army hosts' residence on the hill. Here Admiral and Lady LeFanu maintained an establishment of ordered calm. In the cool of the evening I watched the men playing bowls as though they were on some English village green. Lady LeFanu, confined to a wheelchair but unruffled alike by her lameness or the heat, was towed out daily by her husband for her swim within the shark barrier. My respect and admiration for service wives was mounting fast.

One day, we flew up to the interior to see the chief of one of the troublesome tribes — the Sharif of Beihan. Upset by the bumpy flight, on seeing the reception party armed and fierce on the sands below us before the whitewashed palace I feared I should disgrace myself by being physically sick as we landed. However, fear also gave me control — much needed during the splendid meal of curried goat from which our host offered us the choicest unidentifiable portions. We sat cross-legged on the floor — with some difficulty: watching Denis twisting himself into a knot, I was near hysteria until, quite rightly, the British official in charge quietly brought me to order. It was an early, and important, lesson in being a guest abroad: other peoples' customs should not be the subject of giggles. I never made that mistake again.

When, with difficulty, we had hoisted ourselves up after the banquet, Denis was taken for discussions with the Sharif and I was led to the harem, where the ladies of his household were waiting to welcome me. At first they were completely invisible, except for their dark-rimmed eyes shining over the veils. Then, when all the doors were closed, they discarded their black robes and were revealed in the most elegant Western dresses, down to their immaculately painted nails. I felt shabby in comparison. We talked of visits they had paid to the wider world. Some of them would have liked professional careers; one wanted to be a doctor. Never have I felt so intense a combined frustration in a little room. Nor was that the only shared emotion: when the newest wife, who was not there, was mentioned, the air was sharp with jealousy.

Later, the Sharif presented me with a heavy silver belt, made of Austrian Maria Theresa coins — alas, it was for a slimmer waist than mine! It had no clasp, so the Sherif called his camel driver who produced a rusty nail to link the coins.

I was allowed to go with Denis deep into the desert to a rarely visited area, the Hadhramaut, where a group of villages had been built round an oasis. The houses were skyscrapers constructed entirely of mud. The small house where we stayed had a large, cool pool in the basement, infinitely refreshing after the sandy drive across the desert. This was my first entrance into the real Arab world: others were to follow.

In the Hadhramaut we were invited by the local sheikh to one of the most unforgettable evenings of my life. For a while before the meal we sat on huge cushions on the terrace outside his palace under a sky so deeply velvet and in a silence so profound that we could hear the faint sounds of camels in the far distance. No one spoke — or needed to speak — until our souls had caught up with us. We were then invited to a quiet feast inside, during which our host asked me if the neighbouring sheikh had served our meal on the floor or on a table. I think he was proud to have given us the comfort of seats at a table.

That night we slept under the stars on the roof of the house, and in the morning I looked down to watch an Arab family at breakfast. Once again I was impressed by the dignity of the elders and the sense of order. The vastness and stillness of the desert seemed to have an effect on all — nurses, doctors and voluntary workers alike. When I see on television screaming hordes of angry Arabs I think of these quiet desert scenes and hold them in balance.

On 19 January 1966 we were off on our travels again. This time we put a girdle round the Earth in ten days, often sleeping on bunk beds in the Comet. The reason for this whirlwind tour was that at this stage Denis was still hoping to keep a British military presence in the Far East after withdrawal from Malaysia, Borneo and Singapore, and was considering a possible base in Australia. He needed to consult the Australian government, and also to consider an alternative stop-over to Gan — the small island in the Indian Ocean where we had a base. He was considering the little island of Aldabra, uninhabited save for wild birds and animals. On top of this, he also needed discussions with the American government. So we flew west to Washington, where he had talks, then to San Francisco, where we spent the night after our plane broke down. It had earlier made a difficult landing on a snowy airfield, having to use reverse thrust, and this, I was told by Air Vice-Marshal Elworthy who travelled with us, had caused the trouble. My only moment of fear during the whole journey had come when I had watched the Air Vice-Marshal's face as he listened to the sound of the engine during the flight to San Francisco.

We transferred to a commercial flight for the next leg of the journey, to Fiji. Here we had a brief stop in what seemed a wild and barbarous country and then, in our repaired plane, went on to Canberra, where we spent three days.

Here we had many old friends, particularly Gough Whitlam, leader of the Labour opposition, and his wife — a couple who towered above their fellow politicians in physical height as well as in personality. Mrs Whitlam was a distinguished writer and we were old friends. At the White House we called on the Liberal Senator (later Prime Minister), John Gorton. On the table beside him was a photograph in a silver frame — face down. He picked it up and showed it to me. "That's what I once looked like," he said. It was an extremely handsome

186

face, unlike his present war-damaged, crumpled features. It was a profoundly sad moment.

We were invited to a dinner at the Governor-General's residence, which was unexpectedly formal; the Governor was, after all, the Queen's representative in Australia. I was told that on leaving I must curtsey — I thought they said three times, so for good measure I curtseyed once on taking my leave and again at the door, remembering my lessons at the Bradford Civic Theatre. I began to have sympathy with the republicans.

We flew back over the Indian Ocean, making a brief stop at Gan, where some of our party snorkelled in the crystal-clear waters, and a Pakistani airman gave me a coconut in its shell, painted to look like a strange sea beast. It still stands on our bookcase, a wonderful reminder of that remarkable tour.

Aldabra, incidentally, was never adopted as a staging post. Environmentalists, led by the redoubtable Tam Dalyell, objected, since the island was a sanctuary for some of the world's rarest birds. Once, at an official dinner, when we lifted our plates we found drawings of wild birds and "Save Aldabra" slogans — our hosts' children had been busy. Later, when Aldabra was found not to be suitable anyway, and was not used, Denis wrote to the children to tell them he had listened to their appeal. They were delighted.

In July 1966, in preparation for his important Defence Review of that year, Denis spent a fortnight in the Far East, in order to inform himself before deciding whether to spend on or to cut our military bases east of Suez. This was another of the unforgettable periods of

187

my life in the "baggage train", taking us to Singapore, Malaysia, Sabah and Borneo, Brunei and Hong Kong. Denis had inherited from the Conservatives two conflicts: that in Aden and one in Borneo. The dispute in Aden was finally settled. Borneo, however, was a greater problem and one which, had it been handled badly, might have well blown up into a long and bloody conflict.

Borneo was to be of particular interest to me when later I wrote the life of Angela Burdett-Coutts, the granddaughter and heiress of the banker Thomas Coutts. She had been the patron of Rajah Brooke, the first White Rajah of Sarawak at the end of his life, and he bequeathed Sarawak to her in the first draft of his will. Later, almost reluctantly, the British government took it over, with Sabah and a duty of protection to the little state of Brunei. I wish I had known in 1966 that I was later to write about Rajah Brooke: I would have looked more carefully at his magnificent portrait there.

The Federation of Malaysia had been formed in 1963, comprising Malaya and Singapore and the part of Borneo under British protection. Singapore had left in 1965. The other part of Borneo belonged to Indonesia, whose President, Sukarno, had ambitions to take over a large part of south-east Asia, including Malaysia. The Indonesian island of Sumatra was only 100 miles off Malaya, and Sukarno was trying to infiltrate his troops across the narrow Malacca Strait, as well as from bases in Kalimantan across the border into Malaysian Borneo. At the time Denis became defence minister, British troops were involved in "confronting" the Indonesian invaders, and this episode therefore came to be known as the period of "Confrontation". It was necessary to secure the cooperation of local Borneo and Malay troops, and at this time the British forces under General Templer in Malaysia were waging a highly successful but slow battle for the "hearts and minds" of the local population, fighting along a marshy jungle border, with the invaluable help of Gurkhas.

Essential to British interests in this conflict were the helicopters used by the SAS and its sister service the SBS — the Special Boat Service. I am glad I was not expected to join Denis on his day at sea with the SBS, which involved being winched into a helicopter from a submarine. But I was sorry to have missed a spectacular demonstration of the skills of the SBS, when a handsome young officer with a group of Marines parachuted from an aircraft into the sea and swam to meet Denis on the submarine. This was Paddy Ashdown, later to reappear in the pattern of our lives as leader of the Liberal Democrat Party.

For part of our time in south-east Asia we were based in Singapore as guests of Sir John Grandy, Air Vice-Marshal and Commander-in-Chief in the Far East, and Lady Grandy. They were lively and amusing hosts. Lady Grandy was lame, but nevertheless accompanied us on a tough tour with great fortitude and energy. She advised me on my dress for our visit to Borneo: a hat to keep off the burning sun; trousers tied at the ankles to stop snakes slithering up my legs; army rig on top, tight at the wrist to keep out the leeches. We spent a hilarious evening preparing Denis for taking the

189

salute. A hat was needed to hold on his heart, so John ransacked his wardrobe and found a wild assortment of headgear, which Denis tried on, in his inimitable way, accompanying the exhibition with suitable song.

Occasionally I was even made to feel that I was some help. In Kuala Lumpur the army had set up a rehabilitation centre for lepers where they could earn their keep by farming, rearing chickens, and selling eggs and vegetables in the villages. However, the local population were afraid of infection and were reluctant to buy their merchandise. I was asked therefore if I would go to see a small group of Gurkhas in the camp and shake hands with them to prove that leprosy was now not infectious. It was the most moving visit of my tour. The members of the little Gurkha company were so smartly lined up in front of their tent, their salutes were so crisp, their smiles so broad — I could have wept. So I shook the lepers' maimed hands with the best will in the world. I hope it made some difference.

But perhaps my most unforgettable day was that we spent in the remote jungle up the Limbang river in Borneo, visiting the chief Dayak headsman in his long-house. These people had been head-hunters in the old days; now it was important to have them onside in the Confrontation with Indonesia, so the army was using all the charm of its "hearts and minds" campaign to secure their friendship.

We were taken part of the way by helicopter, then by hollowed-out tree-trunk canoe, paddled up the river by Dayaks. Fascinated by the sight of their long, pierced ears, I forgot my usual fear of boats. Landing at a

190

muddy bank deep in the jungle, we were greeted by a troop of boys playing bugles and drums and climbed up a slippery rope ladder to the long-house, raised on stilts above the forest — a long, low, wooden building within which small rooms were ranged on each side of a central corridor. A cockerel was ceremoniously beheaded and its bleeding corpse waved above us as we were paraded down the corridor.

Then the ceremonies began. We sat cross-legged in the centre of the room and were served a potent native drink, a mixture of rice-gin and honey. ("Keep your hand over the glass," my army guide had advised. "It looks like Aunt Mary's home-made wine — but it packs a punch.") The chief's daughters, exquisitely dressed, danced a welcome, every movement graceful, delicate. I felt shabby in my army rig. Then they took a heavy leather belt and sword and one of them handed it to a soldier, a Scot, who danced a Highland sword dance to great applause. To my horror, I saw the belt and sword coming to me. I was glad I had taken my guide's advice and kept my hand over my glass. I did my best and danced, hoping to win "hearts and minds"; I did genuinely want to reach out to these lovely girls in their remote jungle. I must have succeeded, because before we left the chief clapped his hands and pointed to the rafters. A rope basket was let down from which he took with great ceremony a grisly, greenish, shrunken human head and presented it to me. The heads were family heirlooms from a past war — he was giving me their family treasure. "Look pleased," whispered my officer adviser. "This is a great honour — they never do this."

I remembered the Foreign Office ruling on gifts, but what could I possibly give in exchange? I gave the only thing of value I was wearing: my watch. Then I remembered that my host had many wives, and hoped it went to his old chief wife, to whom I was later presented. She had watched the proceedings from the shadow of the forest, remembering perhaps when she too had danced for the foreigners.

Meanwhile, the head had been packed for me in a brightly coloured plastic shopping bag. I had hoped to astonish the customs officer on the way home — but he was unimpressed. "Archaeological specimen, I presume," he said. Still, when workmen painting our bedroom in Admiralty House found it packed in a box hidden behind a sofa, I believe they were suitably surprised — and puzzled. I sent it over to the Ministry of Defence, hoping they would welcome an extra head. It has since disappeared; perhaps it may one day be rediscovered to perplex future historians.

After this Far East tour, in August 1966, the Indonesians retreated from Confrontation and the crisis was past. Denis records the conclusion of that war with some pride. A four-year campaign, in circumstances that threatened a British Vietnam, had been waged with fewer casualties than occur on the roads on a Bank Holiday weekend at home. Remembering his own wartime experience, he had steadily refused to allow air bombardment. The British forces had relied on the SAS and the skill of the Gurkhas, and the brilliant "hearts and minds" campaign conducted under Field Marshal Sir Gerald Templer. Lady Templer, too, had done remarkable service, learning the language and working for the health of the local community.

The army was rightly proud of its conduct of the campaign and felt our subsequent withdrawal from the Far East as a betrayal. Field Marshal Templer never forgave Denis. Some years later he reappeared in the pattern of our lives. Now retired, he and Lady Templer lived in the flat next to ours, in a block opposite the Chelsea Pensioners' Hospital. When I first met him on the stairs, he said curtly: "Hello — I can do with you, but I can't forgive him." He died one night, having the evening before received a friend for a farewell drink. We were unaware of his departure: he had been moved to the Chelsea Hospital as silently as his soldiers had moved in the jungle.

"The end of Confrontation made it possible to reduce commitments: 1967 devaluation made it essential," Denis noted in his autobiography. This was a time when cruel decisions had to be made and old friends offended. The Minister for the Navy at this time was a friend from our Oxford days, Christopher Mayhew. He and his wife Cicely had in recent years become close friends; we had seen a great deal of them and their families and I had a great deal of affection for them both. Chris had always had a diamond-hard integrity: given a choice he would, in any difficult situation, always take the hard option. I always saw him as the boy plugging the hole in the Dutch dyke, or the one who stood on the burning deck "whence all but he had fled". Cicely was a brilliant civil servant, handsome, clear-eyed and direct. Had she not married

Chris she would have made an excellent ambassadress. Chris had opposed the withdrawal from east of Suez and the loss of the promised aircraft carrier. He felt the navy had been let down. So he resigned, and with him went the gentle, kindly Admiral Luce, the Navy Chief of Staff. Cicely wrote that perhaps we should let the dust settle before we met again. Alas, I never saw Chris again — and heard of his sudden death in 1997 with great sadness.

Lee Kwan Yew, the charismatic Prime Minister of Singapore, was also a very old friend who did not want us to leave the Far East. We had known him and his wife, Choo, when we were all young and Harry Lee, as we knew him then, was a rising young politician. Later he was to become very authoritarian, but I never lost my admiration for them both or for his great achievement in the creation of the new Singapore. He and his wife had met in Cambridge as law students and secretly married there. "Why should I tell people?" she asked me briskly. "It was nobody else's business." She was as brilliant as he, and both got double firsts. When he became a politician she managed the family law firm. Though I always found her warm and compassionate by nature, nevertheless I should not like to have been a malefactor confronted by those keen eyes.

In later years, whenever they came to England, Harry brought me orchids from Singapore, carefully packed with detailed instructions for their care, which I religiously followed, knowing that he would always ask about their condition on his arrival. To our son, Tim, and other students of his generation, he was something of a dictator.

194

Tim met the great man once in Admiralty House and, pointing to his own long hair, said, "You would have this cut off, wouldn't you?" Harry smilingly agreed.

When I visited Singapore with Denis in July 1966, I told Lee Kwan Yew how impressed I was with his new reclamation schemes, schools and hospitals. "But," I said, "I should like to see the worst of your problems." So he arranged that after I had finished my programme as minister's wife, I should be taken down to his slums. Accordingly, to my British army guide's surprise and a little alarm, at the end of one day's engagements a white van suddenly appeared to take me, at the Prime Minister's request, to a marshy area where whole families were living in hovels. In one, an old man lay dying on a kind of shelf on the wall. Then two schoolgirls — his granddaughters — arrived, dressed in immaculate white school uniforms, and proudly demonstrated their good English. I have never forgotten that visit. Incidentally, on that occasion I was aware for the first time of the Singapore security officer I had been given. She was a delicate, dainty little lady who packed a dainty pistol into her dainty little handbag. I was told she could use it with deadly accuracy. Apparently she practised every day.

The British army's presence had been welcomed in Singapore, and Lee Kwan Yew was deeply disappointed that Denis's White Paper of July 1966 announced that half the British forces in Singapore and Malaysia were to leave in 1970 and the rest by 1971. It says much for the strength of their friendship that no rankling wounds were left after so painful an operation.

CHAPTER
EIGHT

DEFEAT AND OPPOSITION, 1970–1974

During the years 1964–1970, members of the Labour government had been absorbed in the work of their ministries, ploughing their separate but parallel roads through swamps and thickets, with Wilson desperately trying to keep them together. But for many members of the Labour Party this period was a time to study maps, to decide where they were going — and, indeed, whether their journey was really necessary. With Gaitskell's death in 1963 the latent divisions in the party had begun to become more evident, and this split in the party would widen over the following years until some of the centre and right wing left to form the SDP.

To understand the Labour Party that has determined the pattern of my life since my marriage, it is necessary to look back over the years. What was remarkable, in fact, was not that the Labour Party was divided in these years but that it had held together for so long. For, more than any other British political party, Labour has from the beginning brought together people from totally different backgrounds and with markedly different shades of political belief. This variety was, indeed, why in my first year at Oxford I chose to join the Labour Party. At that time I was influenced by Attlee's *Labour Party in Perspective*. Much of that book, still vivid to me in its memorable orange cover, is dated — it was first published in 1937 — but much is still relevant. Attlee noted the composition of the Labour Party in the House of Commons at that time: "nearly 300 men and women comprising individuals of differing social backgrounds but united in their support of Socialism". He also remarked that, during all the party's years of existence, "there has never been a time when there were not questionings in the ranks and suggestions of breakaway movements. There has never been a lack of candid criticism of the policy and achievement of the Party."

Attlee also noted — to my mind a highly significant point — that "leaving aside Owen and the early pioneers . . . the first place in the influences that built up the Socialist movement [in Britain] must be given to religion . . . there are probably more texts from the Bible enunciated from Socialist platforms than from those of all other parties . . . not only from dissenting bodies but also many clergy of the established church." This has certainly been true throughout politics in my lifetime. Nonconformist religion was the foundation of my own political belief and was the background of many Labour leaders and their wives: Harold and Mary Wilson, James and Audrey Callaghan, Tony Crosland. On the other side of the party divide, too, Margaret Thatcher was partly the product of the Congregational chapel and Sunday School.

Attlee had noted that class differences in the Labour Party were more marked than in any other party. His postwar government included not only products of public schools like Hugh Dalton and Hugh Gaitskell but also Ernest Bevin, who, poor and illegitimate, had left school at eleven, and Nye Bevan from the Welsh mining valleys. In my time at Oxford, from 1936 to 1940, I had seen in the Labour Club the same wide spectrum of background and political belief, the same juxtaposition of distinct and different accents, traditions and cultures.

Chris Mayhew was typical of the public-school rebel who joined the Labour Party, as he wrote, to "cast down the mighty from their seats". As he remembered in his memoirs, "inequality, injustice, imperialism, fascism and war were all to be abolished". But, as he admitted, he had no understanding of working people:

> The working class was an abstraction, a trump card in the political debate. My only personal contacts with working-class people had been made at my mother's club in North Kensington or at the holiday camps she organised for them each year at the seaside; and here social class proved an insuperable barrier . . . we had no subject of conversation in common . . . We read different newspapers, frequented different parts of London, ate different foods and knew different kinds of people . . . It required a long period in the Labour movement and . . . in the British Expeditionary

Force in France [during the war] before I felt completely at ease in working-class company.

There were many at Oxford like Mayhew who inserted a glottal stop into their cut-glass speech in order to mask their origins — so that the Labour Party became "the Par'y of the workers". Others, like Roy Jenkins — later to be called "one of nature's old Etonians" — adopted the accents of the upper class. At this time, regional accents clearly marked one's position in the layered class structure; Margaret Thatcher and Ted Heath discarded their regional accents.

Then there were the grammar-school students like me, who had made our way to Oxford through competitive exams, impelled by what Roy Hattersley has called "the obligation to succeed". Many of us came from ordinary, or even deprived, backgrounds, bringing a totally different pattern of life and language. (It is interesting that, after the public-school boys Attlee and Gaitskell, leaders of both Labour and Tory parties came from grammar-school backgrounds, Wilson and Callaghan being followed by Heath, Thatcher and Major.) There were others who had left school early and won their way from the world of work in mines or factories to scholarships at Ruskin College.

We all sat in meetings together and danced together at Ruskin dances, where the children of aristocrats, meritocrats, workers, conservatives, liberals, socialists and communists would all swing around to the beat of Denis Rattle and his Bandits, the future father of the great conductor, Sir Simon Rattle. Many of these

199

strange bedfellows found themselves uneasy in at least some of the political company they kept, but for a while were held together in a common cause — the fight against fascism. Later we would go our separate ways.

Before and since my political birth at Oxford in 1936, there have been many such alliances and separations. In 1931, faced with a world financial crisis, the Labour Prime Minister, Ramsay MacDonald, led some of his party to join with Conservatives and Liberals to form a National Government. The Spanish Civil War also drew together many of differing political persuasions. In those days Denis Healey and Ted Heath could march shoulder to shoulder in the fight against fascism. During the Second World War, Attlee and his colleagues joined Churchill in a coalition government. Later still, there were cross-party alliances in opposition to the Suez campaign: I watched Denis and his friend, the Tory MP Nigel Nicolson, who fiercely opposed it, fuming with anger together in the Commons.

During the Wilson government there were deep differences over political theory and the aims of socialism, over the Labour Party constitution, and, most of all, over whether Britain should join the Common Market. However, the real divide in the Labour Party was between those who wanted instantly to destroy the old and to build again on the rubble, and those more pragmatic spirits who had learned the realities of political life from work experience, or in war, in local government as councillors, or in national government as ministers. Denis often quoted a young Polish exile, Leszek Kolakowski:

Democratic Socialism requires, in addition to commitment to a number of basic values, hard knowledge and rational calculation . . . It is an obstinate will to erode by inches the conditions which produce avoidable suffering, oppression, hunger, wars, racial and national hatred, insatiable greed and vindictive envy.

It will do far more to help real people living in the real world today and tomorrow than all the cloudy rhetoric of systematic ideologies, or the tidy blueprints of academic theories.

These were the values that inspired many like me across the left, right and centre of the Labour Party — and, indeed, across the political spectrum. But there were destructive forces on the extreme left of the Labour Party whose fire was fuelled by hate and envy.

After Gaitskell's death, his acolytes found it difficult to accept the new leadership. Forming the 1963 Dining Club (from which the SDP would eventually emerge), they began to lay plans to replace Wilson. At this time the three obvious right-wing heirs to the leadership were thought to be Tony Crosland, Denis Healey and Roy Jenkins. Tony had little support in the party and Denis was totally occupied by his work at the defence ministry, but Roy was making a great impression as an orator in the Commons; and, at the same time, he was approachable and attracted younger acolytes.

So Chris Mayhew set out to replace Harold with Roy — with the objective, as he says in his memoir, *Time to*

Explain, of halting the drift to the extreme left and restoring morale in the party. Using with great relish his wartime experience in SOE, he organized a campaign so secret that even Tony Crosland, who attended some 1963 Club dinners, was unaware of it. Chris was the chairman, and this group became the nucleus of an organization which would later help to make Roy Jenkins the leader of the Social Democrats.

I followed Chris Mayhew's career with particular interest because I had known him at Oxford. He was typical of those who were essentially Liberal, but had been drawn into the Labour Party during the Popular Front anti-fascist period.

By 1969 Wilson was becoming increasingly unpopular and opinion polls showed Labour losing ground in the country; so in May that year Mayhew decided it was time to strike. However, after careful canvassing he found that there was not enough reliable support in the parliamentary party — and the plot fizzled out. Eventually, in July 1974, Chris finally abandoned hope of reforming the party and "decided instead", as he wrote, "to leave it and denounce it". Roy Jenkins tried to dissuade him: "wait for us," he said. When Chris met Jeremy Thorpe by chance in a Commons corridor he stopped him. "Jeremy," he said, "I can't take the Labour Party any longer. I want to join your lot." Wilson had picked up the rumours of disaffection and scheming; jumping to quite the wrong conclusion, thinking at first that Denis was the villain and for a while treating him with great suspicion.

202

Denis, in fact, had been so absorbed in the work of the Ministry of Defence that he had been fully aware neither of the strength of the plotters nor of the Labour Party's loss of popularity in the country. During this period Cecil King, chairman of the Mirror Group, tried in vain to persuade him to lead the plot against Wilson. I sometimes received telephone calls from his wife, Ruth, which I later realized were attempts to involve me in the campaign. However, I too remained blissfully unaware of what was going on, since her whispered conspiratorial telephone calls always came at times when I was busy with the children or my own work.

The growing rumour of disaffection in the leadership of the Labour Party was one of the reasons why the party was losing support in the country. On visits to the constituency during the general election campaign of 1970, I felt disillusion in the air, increased by a ridiculous story that there was a shortage of salt! Old friends were not meeting my eyes; new Jerusalem was still far away. In this election, Denis was busier than usual, electioneering across the country and still running the Ministry of Defence; he had not noticed the signs.

The election came on a long, hot June day. The cloudless skies were good omens for us — "ours" always walked; "they" had more cars to take "theirs" to the polls. After the count in the town hall we knew that Denis was safe with a comfortable majority. However, back at the Gillinsons' house, I listened to the early results on the radio while Denis went upstairs to his desk to write the victory speech. After the first few were

203

declared I called up to him, "You had better come and listen — we are out!" Like a flock of birds, many of our supporters were flying away.

As we drove down the A1 to London and heard the last results on the radio, our fears were confirmed and I began to panic. We had not expected to lose the election. We had been embedded in Admiralty House for six years. In that time a family accumulates a great deal. Now all our possessions there had to be cleared out — immediately. It was Friday, and impossible to find a removal van that would take a piano. Finally, we hired a big yellow self-drive van and the ex-Minister of Defence drove us triumphantly out of the courtyard into Whitehall and down to the cottage — hamster cage and all, as in a Cockney flitting. We sang, "My old man said follow the van, and don't dilly dally on the way." It was a political disaster, but we were happy. We were going home.

The change from government to opposition was abrupt, and it took some time to adjust to the new life. Although in opposition much of the burden of power vanished, so did the support. Ex-ministers missed their official drivers. On the day of defeat, Roy Jenkins had asked for his car to pick him up at 4p.m. — only to be told apologetically by his driver that it, and he, were no longer available. Fortunately Denis, the least pompous of men, had always had his feet firmly on the ground; but he missed his driver and office staff.

★ ★ ★

In opposition Denis was busier than ever. He was popular in the country and for the first time was elected to the National Executive of the Labour Party — almost a unique privilege for a right-winger. Not the most patient of listeners, he endured hours of impatient boredom: "NEC wittering" is a frequent note in his diary. He loathed wasting time and did not endear himself to his colleagues by obviously carrying on with other work during committee meetings.

His diary seemed as full as before. There were some engagements made when Minister of Defence that he was still expected to keep as a member of the Shadow Cabinet and a possible future Foreign Secretary, so much of the diplomatic round and travels continued. The entry for an American visit in January 1972 is typical. After a full round of lectures in New York he wrote: "5th January. Off to Washington, lecture and questions. Then State Department for Ron Spiers on SALT Agreement. Dinner at National War College; lecture went very well. Back to hotel, very tired, BUT wrote diary before bed. Friday: talks on Defence. Saw Peterson at White House and Laird." Fortunately, in Washington, he could relax with our dear friends Dave and Ann Linebaugh, so it was "lovely dinner and chat". Dave had been a great friend when he was at the US Embassy in London and Ann, his clever and dynamic wife, was a particular friend of mine. I think as a couple they were the closest friends Denis ever had in his life. Denis was away when Tim was born and it was Dave who drove me to the hospital. On the way we hit a dog; but Dave's love of dogs was outweighed by his fear that

I would give birth in the car. Typically, he later rang the police to enquire after the dog. Dave had gone on to serve at the American Embassy in India and had suffered terrible injuries in a car accident. He was flown back to Washington, where the President and his wife made sure he had the finest treatment, but for many years his hold on life was tenuous. However, strapped together early every morning by the devoted Ann, he continued to work in the American government and looked forward with great joy to Denis's visits. Whenever Denis was in Washington he stayed with them and learned a great deal from Dave's wise comments on the state of the nations. On this particular visit Denis found time for art galleries: not for nothing had his officials in the Ministry of Defence called him "Maximum Extraction Healey".

This January diary continued: "Off on Pan Am Jumbo. Home 2–3a.m. Friday 14th, read the newspapers, 100 letters. Saturday, to Leeds." However busy he was, he never lost touch with his constituency and would slip easily from banquets in New York or Washington to fish and chips in the Seacroft Centre in Leeds and his regular Saturday lunch with his councillor friends, Joe and Mary Moynihan, in their little house on a council estate. Joe kept Denis in touch with the Irish Catholics in his constituency; Mary, who worked in a clothing factory, kept his eyes firmly fixed on the realities of working life, besides making him enormous comforting meals. On this occasion, while he was starting on the roast beef, he "took a call from Tom McNally in Luxembourg about Malta", followed by "full surgery at Cross Gates. Sunday, great discussion Harehills Club. Trouble with Trots [Trotskyists]. Home late, worked in train. Very tired. Monday, African service broadcast on Rhodesia. Tuesday, Memorial service for King Frederick of Denmark in Abbey. Lime Grove for Panorama on Rhodesia, votes 10 and 11pm. Wednesday, TV for BBC, saw Maudling [Reggie Maudling, the Tory Chancellor], Swiss Ambassador." Not surprisingly, "dog tired".

Those words — "dog tired", "exhausted" — had repeated themselves too often in his diary over the previous six years in government. I am amused to hear ministers discussing a forty-eight-hour week for workers when they themselves frequently work non-stop both in and out of office! At Defence, Denis had worked at high pressure often for ninety hours a week. After long years watching politicians from the sidelines, I am firmly convinced that five years running any of the great ministries is enough. Sabbaticals should be made available for such ministers — though not necessarily through a change of government.

Even in opposition, then, there was little time for wife and family; so we valued as much as ever the times we had together, over weekends at the cottage or on holiday.

Fortunately, at this time I had my own excitements. I was invited by the English Speaking Union to make a month's lecture tour in the USA in February 1971. Looking back, I am amazed that I left Jenny, Tim and Cressida, then little children, with their adoring

207

grandmother, Win Healey, and flew off for a month with a wad of air tickets to New York, Chicago, Santa Fe, Richmond and Pittsburgh. Win was concerned, not for herself, but for her son: as she complained to Aunty Dolly, "What about Denis, who will make his meals?" I replied: "Who makes mine when he is away for a month?" Nevertheless, halfway across America I was unbearably sick for him and the children, and wanted to go home.

It was an invaluable experience. I asked to stay in private houses rather than in hotels. I have always learned more about a country sitting at someone's kitchen table than in the corridors of power or an impersonal hotel, however luxurious. I learned how emigration had often strengthened ties with the parent country. The Irish in New York wore their shamrocks on St Patrick's Day; the farmers' wives in the midwest welcomed me with Swedish accents and served great plates of beef. There were French nursery songs on the piano in a house where my hostess told me her grandparents had come from France. "How would you like your egg?" she asked. "Boiled — in an egg cup," I said. Puzzled, she asked what an egg cup was, and was amazed when I pointed to one on her mantelpiece. "So that's what it is!" she said with surprise.

In Santa Fe the setting was Spanish with Indian overtones. I went to see the Navajo reservation near an atomic research station and read a moving poem by an Indian schoolboy called "This is America" — contrasting their Indian wagons with the power of scientific advance. In Chicago, my audience jingled with expensive jewellery. A young man showed me his watch. "Look," he said, "Cartier; I've got two more in a drawer at home." Far outside New York, I sat on the steps of a wooden hut shelling peas with an old Jewish couple. He was immensely rich. Looking for a present for the wife who had everything, he had, as a surprise, bought a plot of land in the wilderness and built a log cabin for her. Here she could enjoy the one thing she did not now have: simplicity. In Richmond, Virginia, I stayed with descendants of Robert E. Lee and felt as never before the tragedy of a civil war that to them seemed like yesterday. Had I not stayed in private homes, I should never have understood so keenly how America is a "melting pot" of nations, nor why, when Americans sing their national anthem, they so solemnly place hand on heart. I also learned that American is a language with many roots and English is only one of them.

Most of all, I had valuable lessons in the art of public speaking. I had had a good grounding back in the Forest of Dean, where my history teacher, Bobby Noble, had taught me how to amass necessary information, then to reduce it to what would fit on a postcard, then to put the postcard aside and speak directly to the audience. "Eye contact is essential — otherwise they fall asleep." In America I also learned the importance of understanding the culture of one's audience and the subtle differences in how language is used. The first time I described myself as a "socialist" in America the shocked horror on the faces of my audience showed me that for the next ten minutes they were stunned deaf. It was a useful lesson when later I spoke, as president of the Dickens Fellowship, in Japan and in Boulogne in France. There is sometimes a latent hostility in an audience — I found it sometimes in all-male societies, such as the Rotarians — which has to be overcome immediately. Usually it can be done by jokes at one's own expense. "Charity" in Japan had a different connotation, and my French host explained the chill I sometimes felt in France with, "We never forget what you did to Joan of Arc". Folk memories are durable, and can infect relations for many generations.

These were the years of marriages and departures. In August 1971 Jenny married Derek. Characteristically, Jenny wanted "no fuss": so the wedding was a simple ceremony at St Pancras Town Hall followed by a buffet arranged by me at Holly Lodge with their closest friends. It was the happiest of days, though I shed a tear as I watched them driving off in Jenny's red mini, the car covered in streamers and clattering with strings of tins. Denis's diary recorded: "A lovely day but very tired."

Cressida, working in a restaurant in Collioure in the south of France, was sad to be absent. After taking her degree at Leeds University she had worked for a while in the Citizens' Advice Bureau in Leeds and then in a children's home in Harpenden. However, she was back in time for Tim and Jo's wedding on 22 April 1972 — a grander affair. She forsook her customary jeans and, dressed in white lace dress with hat and white gloves, was an unfamiliar but fetching sight. Greater love had no sister for a brother. The London wedding, in a beautiful Kensington church exquisitely decorated by Jo's mother, Val, was followed by a grand reception at the Belgian Embassy. It was a splendid affair with a witty speech by Tim's Langbourne Avenue friend Tony Gash, now a university professor. We had all the traditional confetti ritual — Jo radiant in an elegant green velvet going-away suit — and Denis again briefly records: "a lovely day".

So our birds had left the nest; but they continued to come home — particularly to the cottage — and we visited them when we could: Denis found time to buy Cressida a gramophone and drive it out to her at the children's home at Harpenden. His diary also records chess with Tim, chats with Jenny and pleasant family meals at the cottage.

Through the years in government the cottage had been Denis's salvation; and so it remained in opposition. Whenever possible we drove down at the end of the week. A diary entry records a typical weekend: "cut grass — very tired — machine gave out . . . started making new fence . . . weeding and cleaning pool." We had enlarged the coachman's cottage and built on a sun room with a balcony, with great doors that opened wide on to the apple trees in the paddock. On one unforgettable warm summer evening we were all sitting in the gloaming with the doors wide open, listening to a record of Rita Streich singing "The Nightingale Song". Suddenly, from across the paddock, we heard the unmistakable piercing notes of a real nightingale. I held my breath as there came a reply —

liquid, urgent — from another in the orchard before us. We listened to the magical trio with tears in our eyes.

At times like these I knew that, however much we loved our Highgate home, one day we would move our base from London and settle in the real country. Meanwhile, the cottage on the edge of Ashdown Forest was our refuge, with pleasant expeditions to Tunbridge Wells, where Denis made for Halls, his favourite secondhand bookshop, and I explored the antique and junk shops. Here Denis could forget the problems of the Labour Party, the row over the Common Market, and the warring factions and disillusionment that came with opposition.

In April 1972 the crisis in the Labour Party over the Common Market came to a head. The party, like the country, was divided on whether or not Britain should join. In 1967, when Labour had been in power, there was a majority in the party in favour, and Wilson had applied to join. However, De Gaulle replied "Non, messieurs" and vetoed the application. Had Labour won the election in 1970, George Thomson would have become the negotiator; instead, he was relegated to the Shadow Cabinet as Minister for Europe as Ted Heath took over in No. 10. An enthusiast for the Common Market, Heath reapplied to join and put Geoffrey Rippon in charge of negotiations for entry. Enthusiastic Labour pro-marketeers like Roy Jenkins, Bill Rodgers, Shirley Williams and Chris Mayhew organized support for entry, and one hundred Labour members signed a *Guardian* letter in favour of joining. However, at a

212

special conference on 7 July the Labour Party voted 5–1 against entry; so Harold Wilson, who had no strong feelings either way, accepted the majority view, and when on 21 October 1971 the Conservative government introduced the Common Market Bill, the Labour Party opposed it.

For pro-marketeers like Roy Jenkins, the vote was a matter of principle: having supported entry when Labour was in power, they considered it dishonest to oppose it now. But while Heath treated the issue as a matter of conscience and allowed Tory MPs a free vote, Wilson put on a three-line whip. Chris and the pro-marketeers organized, realizing that if Labour succeeded in defeating the government, the chance to join would be gone, perhaps for ever. On the other hand, if enough Labour MPs could be persuaded to vote with the government or abstain, Heath would get his bill through. The pro-marketeers saw this as an historic moment — a time when the national interest was more important than party discipline. It was, however, with great reluctance that they followed the Tories into the "Yes" voting lobby, or abstained.

Their campaign succeeded. The bill to join the Common Market was passed with an overall majority of 112. Sixty-nine Labour MPs had voted in favour and another twenty abstained. The pro-marketeers pronounced themselves "very satisfied", though some of them lost favour with Wilson.

Immersed in his departmental affairs as Shadow Foreign Secretary, Denis had not taken much part in the in-fighting over the Common Market. Unlike Roy

Jenkins, for whom joining the Common Market was not only an intellectual but also an emotional cause, Denis and Tony Crosland had both taken the view that to join was right, if the time was right; and both were unwilling to dig themselves into either of the opposing trenches. An article Denis had written for the *Mirror* was treated by both pro- and anti-marketeers as indicating unconditional support for entry. This was not so. Denis's main point was: "If our economy is strong when we go in we should reap a splendid harvest. If it is weak, the shock would be fatal ... in any case, everything would depend on the terms." The pro-marketeers assumed he was more enthusiastic than he was, and his later ambivalence, which was shared by Tony Crosland, made both of them deeply unpopular with the market enthusiasts. This was to be an important element in the future contest for the party leadership.

As for Roy Jenkins, he saw ahead a long period of wrangling as the bill progressed through Parliament, and although at that time he was deputy leader and the favourite to succeed Wilson, his ambition to be Prime Minister in waiting faded. Besides, there was now a better prospect on the horizon. Wilson had already offered him the nomination as President of the EEC Commission. From that time, as he wrote himself, his "eyes were towards Brussels". In April 1972 he resigned as Shadow Chancellor and deputy leader. Wilson moved Callaghan to shadow Foreign Affairs as he requested, and offered Denis the position of Shadow Chancellor.

On 10 April Denis recorded in his diary: "Harry Nicholas warned me of pending departure of Jenkins, Thomson and Harold Lever. Harold asked me if I would like Shadow Chancellor. If not, Tony for a year. I said would it work, would think it over. David Owen advised me to take it and I decided to." Young Dr Owen was confidently prescribing for the older warrior! On 11 April Denis's diary continues: "Slept badly, saw Harold and fixed Chancellor's job with Jim as Foreign Secretary." On 12 April, once again he slept badly — as well he might. This was a turning point in his career. He was taking on a job for which he had little training and, perfectionist as always, was determined to master it.

At the same time, there were difficult Shadow Cabinets to endure: the deep rift over the Common Market was getting ever wider, and Harold was becoming neurotic about leaks from Cabinet meetings, obsessed by the fear of plots to oust him and replace him with Roy Jenkins, while Roy, suspected by Wilson of responsibility for the leaks, was increasingly exasperated. "Roy barely contained himself," Denis noted of one Shadow Cabinet meeting, and "Roy emotional" of another.

Did Wilson, quite wrongly thinking Denis was plotting against him, relish the idea that battling with high finance would keep his rival quiet for a while? Certainly for the next two years Denis would be preoccupied studying economics at home and abroad.

★ ★ ★

215

There were some compensations in the limbo of opposition. Denis had time to reflect on his period as defence minister. I, too, was well into my first book, the life of the philanthropist Angela Burdett-Coutts. So instead of a holiday, we welcomed the opportunity to spend some time at the Rockefeller Study Centre at Bellagio on Lake Como. Denis was accredited as a resident scholar in order to write a major work on defence, and I was admitted as an accompanying wife. On our next visit, I was the resident scholar — writing a new book, *Wives of Fame* — and Denis was the "accompanying spouse"!

That first visit was one of the most enjoyable months of my life. Here I could write in peace in an incomparable setting, in company with interesting men and women from different worlds studying different subjects. Denis was given a study in a monkish little hut on a terrace above the lake, and I could work in the library or out on the terrace. On our next visit I was allotted my own study with a wonderful view of Lake Como.

This had been the site of the estate of the Roman writer Pliny, whose bust now surveyed the terraced gardens. I remembered enjoying his treatise on gardens when I was a student at Oxford, and now made a daily pilgrimage up to him. I remembered, too, the gentle voice of Marcus Todd, the professor lecturing on Pliny at Oriel College: "Underneath this humble sod," we used to say, "lie the bones of Marcus Todd. Now he's up among the gods, pushing cherubs through Pass

Mods." I hope he is able to spend time up there with his adored Pliny in the garden of the Villa Serbelloni.

In the autumn of 1972 we were able to take up the invitation made a year earlier by the Chinese government to visit the country for a fortnight as their guests. By this time Denis was Shadow Chancellor, no longer Shadow Foreign Secretary, but nevertheless the Chinese were glad to welcome one who would certainly hold high office in a future Labour government — and in 1972 the parties were evenly balanced. The Chinese were coming out of the period of isolation in which they had been immured during the Cultural Revolution and wanted to renew contacts with the Western world. Denis had been fascinated by China ever since 1935, when he had visited the famous Chinese exhibition in London, and I was very glad to be included in the invitation. I had caught the excitement of that 1935 exhibition from newspaper reports — but at that time the prospect of visiting London from the Forest of Dean was as remote as the prospect of visiting China. I was furious that one of the two essay subjects in the Oxford scholarship paper was "The Chinese Exhibition" — I had even considered calling my essay "On *Not* Seeing the Chinese Exhibition". In my childhood, China had seemed to me a magical land of delicate, willow-pattern landscapes, and at Bell's Grammar School I had read Arthur Waley's translations of Chinese poetry. At Oxford, too, I had been enthralled by Edgar Snow's *Red Star over China* and Mao's epic Long March. But then came the Cultural Revolution and the shattering of poetry and romance in a dark

217

period when realism was the order and a rigid discipline forced children to betray parents; when scholarship, beauty and culture were dirty words; when Mao's words in the "Little Red Book" — waved by all as a symbol of allegiance — were holy writ.

But now the Cultural Revolution was over; the *chargé d'affaires* and his officials at the Chinese Embassy had become friends and had visited us at the cottage, although strictly speaking at that distance from London we were out of bounds. Their driver loved the country and insisted on digging up a root of primroses to take back to London. I served them a disastrous meal of duck that had shrunk to a sparrow and blackberries still half frozen, which they sucked in courteous silence. In return they gave us splendid, exquisite Chinese meals at their embassy, where the ambassador himself served us exotic delicacies and I learned to use chopsticks.

So now, in the autumn of 1972, we set out for China with great enthusiasm. Our plane landed for a short while in Moscow, where we were slightly perturbed to have our passports examined with suspicion and then removed. At that time there was deep hostility between Russia and China. Finally we landed in Peking, beginning the most fascinating foreign visit we have ever made. From our first moments at the airport, decorated with huge portraits of Mao surmounting the elegant calligraphy of one of his poems — which our hosts could not translate — all was strange and exotic. The cyclists who thronged the wide streets through which we were driven wore muslin masks since, as we

218

were to discover, the proximity of the Gobi Desert meant that the whole of Peking was covered in a fine sandy dust. Our hosts explained that, at this stage in their economic recovery, vacuum cleaners were luxuries they could not afford. However, the little schoolchildren we saw from our hotel window, swinging along, smart in their red scarves, looked rosy and healthy. As we were later to discover, this generation were escaping the suffocation and sterility of the Cultural Revolution, during the period when China was cut off from the world. We were overwhelmed by the charm and intelligence of the children as they danced and sang for us, and by the musical virtuosity of the young prodigies who would later enthral the musical world.

Our programme was full, and the young men and women who were our guides and interpreters could not have been more helpful, though awkward questions were always met by official patter.

The pattern of our visits, whether to farms, schools or hospitals, was always the same. First we were settled with mugs of tea poured from large, brightly coloured vacuum flasks — and then the lecture would begin. After a while we needed no translation. Drooped shoulders, lowered heads, meant that we were in the poverty and depression of the pre-Mao days; then the heads came up as we were told of the transformation under Mao — but — and here the squared shoulders of the body language said: "We have achieved much, but there is much to be done and we welcome your questions and comments and criticisms." Difficult political questions produced stony faces and replies

219

reeled off from the official machine. I usually asked about the position of women and their need to control the birth rate. They explained their historic fear of starvation. At a farm I asked why, when their agricultural machines were painted in such bright colours, the people were dressed in such drab uniformity. At that time the Mao suit was obligatory, the only variation being a better cut and material for high officials. They smiled politely but noted the comment. The ritual questions encouraged change. Nowadays, Chinese women are as elegant as Westerners.

The most fascinating visit was to a hospital in Peking where we watched three operations at which acupuncture was used as an anaesthetic. Denis photographed me, eyes wide with horror over my mask, watching a thyroidectomy being performed on an elderly lady. The surgeons assured me that they had conventional anaesthetics at hand but were using only acupuncture. The patient had a screen before her face so that she did not see when the knife cut her throat: she did not flinch — though I did! The next operation was on a young woman who was having her fallopian tubes tied. After this major invasive procedure the patient shook hands with the surgeon and took herself back to her bed. Then came a young man who had an operation on his knee — he was not as stalwart as the ladies and showed his discomfort. At the end of our visit, when the surgeon asked for our comments and criticisms, we were speechless. Should I have suggested a different handling of the knife?

220

Perhaps our most moving encounters were with gentle, elderly professors who had suffered during the Cultural Revolution, when an interest in Western culture was considered dangerous and when intellectuals were regarded with suspicion and degraded and humiliated. Those who lived through this ghastly experience were scarred for life by it. This was illustrated recently at a lecture given in Peking by the American violinist Isaac Stern, who, after praising the remarkable performances of very young Chinese prodigies in his audience, asked why, in contrast, the young men and women performers so lacked spirit. Immediately elderly men in the audience spoke up, bitterly attacking the Cultural Revolution which had killed spontaneity and soul in that whole generation.

In our visit to a literature class at Peking University, we met a mild-mannered old professor who was expounding *Wuthering Heights* most sensitively. Denis immediately explained to the class that the Brontës were born in Haworth, near his Yorkshire home, and then — to my horror — offered to sing to them a song of the Yorkshire proletariat. The professor welcomed this, obviously politically correct, contribution. He did not know what they were in for. In his typically robust way, Denis blasted them with:

We're all down in t'cellaroyle [cellar hole]
wi' muck slats at t'winders
Bum bailiff cum arter us but he'll never find us
'Cos we're all down in t'cellaroyle
wi' muck slats at t'winders.

221

I tried to explain that this was about the Yorkshire proletariat hiding in the cellars from the rent collectors, but I think they were too shattered to comprehend and too polite to comment.

The Cultural Revolution was now officially over and only once did we see the "Little Red Book" waved in unison — by the actors on stage at the end of a play. But there was still suspicion of intellectuals, and scholars and administrators were still being sent for brainwashing to collective farms, where they were compelled to work with their hands. At the "May 7th Cadre School" near Peking, we watched the attempts to make high-ranking officials understand the realities of peasant life. Teachers who were deemed to have got "out of touch" were condemned to six months of corrective treatment, bureaucrats to three months. We were introduced to a headmistress who had apparently become "too proud". Now she fed the hens, and we watched her calling them to order with her school whistle.

In the customary preliminary ritual of explanation, the reformed intellectuals told of their initial horror when they were made to clean the latrines. Again, we needed no translation; their shame at menial tasks, their disgust at handling ordure, was obvious. We were shown great cartloads of superb vegetables to be taken to "our comrades in the city". As they explained, they now realized that without what they translated as "the stuff", vegetables would not grow and they would starve. I thought of this when later I was taken by the young women to the smelly latrines — trenches dug in

222

the field. I was amazed but embarrassed at their undisguised curiosity as they watched me take down my knickers. But then I realized that I was the first Westerner they had seen. I hoped my underwear did not disappoint them.

I found the collective farm curiously similar to my own experience during the war, when I had taken the schoolgirls for weeks potato-picking on a farm in Yorkshire — a salutary experience for pupils and teachers alike. Denis too, was reminded of the Chinese visit when, as Chancellor, he "had to listen to officials who had never done a day's manual labour in their lives, pontificating on the pay scales appropriate for dustmen and miners". The Cultural Revolution undoubtedly did terrible damage, with much real suffering and painful humiliation caused to musicians, intellectuals and high-ranking officials; but I felt there was perhaps something to be learned from the collective farm experience.

However, it must be remembered that this visit took place more than thirty years ago. China today is a very different country, and the ancient elegance has been allowed to reappear as a background to a very modern and successful nation.

Our hosts could not have been more courteous. Since the end of the Cultural Revolution much of China had become more open to visitors, though generally official guides remained obligatory. Westerners, with our round eyes and white skins, still mesmerized little children, and we in turn were bowled over by the enchanting boys and girls who sang and

223

danced for us in schools or at crèches, although I was uncomfortably aware that they were the property of the state rather than their parents. In a country haunted by the memory of the famines that had swept it in the old days, population control had become a political necessity. Marriage was generally discouraged before the age of twenty-five, and the behaviour of the young until then was strictly governed. When we visited China again fourteen years later, we found that only one child was allowed to each couple, though rules were relaxed on the collective farms in the countryside where more hands were needed.

Although the harshest measures of the Cultural Revolution were now over — the imprisonments and dismissals, when children were encouraged to report on their parents and cultured academics were shamed and degraded — there was still rigid state control of expression. We were taken on a conducted tour of Shanghai, Hanchow and Nanking by friendly guides and interpreters, who, though generally relaxed and humorous, repeated the official line and clammed up immediately we asked difficult questions. But at least now they were allowed to take some pride in the achievements of the past. We climbed the Great Wall; we toured the Museum of the Ming Tombs and marvelled. At that time only two of the tombs had been excavated, revealing exquisite works in jade and ivory. The miraculous army of clay soldiers was still to astonish the Western world. There was no hurry to excavate the rest, they told us — "China had a long past and a long future." I asked the young woman

224

curator of the museum why she had chosen this job. She replied that she had not chosen, she had been directed. Supposing she wished to leave for another town? "Why would I want to do that? I wouldn't know anyone." The idea was genuinely astonishing to her.

A confusion of images remains of that tour: muddy villages, streets of ramshackle little houses, poverty and elegant pagodas; curious crowds, drably dressed; delicate calligraphy in windows of old shops; in the parks, old men carrying their caged birds for an airing or exercising in controlled slow motion. It was a country still remote and unchanged. Only in Shanghai was there a memory of a cosmopolitan past, with hotels and shops retaining something of the old Western influence.

In Peking I had one unforgettable morning with an old woman in a tiny little home in a dusty courtyard. On these official tours I have always asked if I could visit an ordinary woman at home, and on this occasion, although I was perfectly aware that my "ordinary woman" would be carefully chosen, nevertheless I learned more in an hour with her than from volumes of official briefs and speeches.

She told me of her starving childhood, when they ate the leaves of trees; how she married to escape and was bullied by her mother-in-law. She showed me her tiny feet — because they had been bound, she could not run away. "And now," she said in triumph, "look at me. How well I live." It was just one whitewashed room: her luxuries were a sewing machine and a brightly coloured vacuum flask, a chest and a mirror. Compared with a council flat on a housing estate in Leeds, it was poverty. For her, it was heaven. Again, it must be remembered that I am describing a scene from thirty years ago — China is a different country now.

The most remarkable event of many on that Chinese tour was our visit to Chou En-lai. He had been Prime Minister for many years and had come through the Cultural Revolution because of his old loyalty to Chairman Mao, who was at this time too physically frail to see visitors, although he was apparently still mentally active. Denis had not expected to meet so eminent a member of the government, since Labour was at this time in opposition; but Chou, at seventy-five, though also frail, was well informed on British politics: he knew that the Conservative and Labour parties at this time were evenly balanced and that Denis was a possible Foreign Secretary, or even Prime Minister. He would also have been briefed by our friends at the Chinese Embassy in London that Healey was a man to watch. Moreover, the Chinese were expecting visits from the British Foreign Secretary, Alec Douglas-Home, and Henry Kissinger, adviser to the US President. Denis's opinion on these individuals and their governments would be useful.

We were told that, since he did not sleep well, Chou conducted many interviews late at night. So our guides told us to wait in our hotel for a call from him. Apparently I would be welcome too. One night at eleven an official car took us to the Great Hall of the People, where a horseshoe of chairs waited — each with a small table bearing tea and biscuits. On one side sat the British ambassador and two members of his staff; on the other sat the Chinese officials. I was placed in the middle next to Denis, Chou En-lai and his famous interpreter, Nancy Tăng. The son of a mandarin, Chou was well educated and spoke English, Japanese, French and German. As a leading Communist he had become Mao's right-hand man in the civil war against Chiang Kai-shek, and had suffered with him during the legendary Long March across China.

The interview lasted for four hours, and no one spoke during that time except Denis, Chou En-lai and the interpreter. Occasionally our teacups were refilled. After two hours, Chou said: "Mr Healey, I am enjoying this, may we have a short break and then continue?" And they did — until well into the early hours of the morning. All this time I dared not move in case I broke the spell.

The conversation began slowly, with Chou En-lai making enquiries about the state of politics in Britain. Well informed, he had obviously read the latest English papers. He talked of Chinese relations with Japan, and of the present Sino–Soviet hostility. As they relaxed, Denis asked him questions about China's present problems. The dialogue was frank but friendly. Chou remarked that President Nixon had "opened the door for the Conservative government to outpace the Labour government on the finalization of normal relations between Britain and China". Denis replied that "the Chinese had made it much more difficult" for his party. When Chou asked if this was a reference to Hong Kong, Denis said he was thinking of the burning of the

British Mission. Chou said that the two were related. There had been ultra-left tendencies in China which had been exploited by bad elements. Lin Piao was one of these. He had apologized, and the Chinese had rebuilt the Mission at their own expense. Then Denis encouraged Chou En-lai to talk of the past and of the Long March. "Ah, I was young then," Chou sighed, and indicated his crippled arm. He was clearly very conscious of his age, referring to it several times. Gradually both men became at ease and eventually joked like old friends.

Denis obviously made an excellent impression on Chou. When at 2 a.m. he rose and bade us farewell, our host turned at the door as he stood upright in the doorway, though small and slight and wearing the usual Mao blue suit, in memory I see him tall and straight in the dress of a mandarin. He was one of the most charismatic politicians I have ever met.

In the light of the fascination and challenge of this visit, it is not surprising that it was with some sadness that Denis had given up shadowing foreign affairs and returned to the grinding battle with high finance.

CHAPTER
NINE

11 DOWNING STREET: THE WILSON YEARS, 1974–1976

Labour had lost the 1970 election unexpectedly. In 1974 there was an equally unexpected victory. That February, embroiled in a miners' strike, Heath had called a general election under the slogan "Who Governs Britain?" He lost; but Labour was returned with no overall majority, and in October Wilson decided to call another general election to confirm his mandate. Labour won again, this time with only a slim overall majority of three.

The summons was an unusual one. Denis, who for two years had been shadowing the Chancellor of the Exchequer in opposition, was waiting for news from Wilson when the permanent secretary at the Treasury knocked at our Highgate door with the news that he was now Chancellor of the Exchequer — Wilson had forgotten to tell him. "Mrs Healey, I come," said the visitor, "to commiserate not to congratulate." Denis was about to take up his position on the bed of nails where he would suffer for the next five years. We moved to 11 Downing Street in March 1974 unsure how long we should be there — but still with surprising confidence.

The houses in Downing Street had been built in the 1680s by Sir George Downing, a man of undoubted enterprise but dubious reputation. At that time there were not many residences in Westminster suitable for honourable Members of Parliament, for it lay in an evil-smelling slum known as Devil's Acre. Sir George, however, saw that the pleasant street that ran through from Whitehall to St James's Park was an excellent place for some speculative building, lying as it did between the two palaces, Buckingham House and the Palace of Westminster.

Only three of the original houses in Downing's elegant terrace remain. No. 10 was remodelled for Sir Robert Walpole in 1732 by the great architect William Kent, who was at that time overseeing his design for the Treasury building. Walpole, generally accepted as the first modern Prime Minister, had approved Kent's work on his country house, Houghton Hall in Norfolk, and wanted a town dwelling suitable for "a gentleman of quality". Some of Kent's work remains: the Cabinet still meets in the room he designed, looking out on the garden from which a gate leads to St James's Park (in our day that gate was always securely locked). No. 10 was altered again in 1781, and in 1824 Sir John Soane added a dining room to No. 11. The original houses had been rather shoddily built and over the years have needed repairs; they have also become interconnected. The upper rooms of No. 11 extended over the ground floor of No. 12, where in our day the Chief Whip had

his offices. Inside No. 10 a corridor leads to No. 11. I
was told that if the door leading into this passage was
kept shut, it indicated that relations between Chancellor and Prime Minister were frosty: Macmillan is said
to have kept it locked to keep out his Chancellor's
Italian staff. In our day, when Wilson, and later
Callaghan, were at No. 10, the door was always open,
since Denis kept friendly relations with both Prime
Ministers.

From the outset Denis was totally preoccupied with
his work at the Treasury, so I organized the move. When
I asked him what we should take, he said absently,
"The piano and all the books." The piano certainly
came, but "all the books" had to be reduced to a token
library of art, poetry and literature — and even this
presented a problem: for there was scarcely a bookcase
at No. 11. "How did our Tory predecessors manage?" I
asked the officials at the Ministry of Works who were
responsible for furnishing official residences. They
thought Macmillan had kept his books piled on the
floor, and offered me two elegant but useless
eighteenth-century bookcases. After much searching,
we discovered in a basement some large, solid,
library-type bookshelves which by the end of our
five-year tenure were stacked to the ceiling.

No. 10 has a private flat above the official reception
rooms and the ground-floor Cabinet Room. Mary
Wilson and, later, Audrey Callaghan made the flat
cheerful and comfortable, but it was small and by no
means grand; and, although Ted Heath had chosen

elegant wallpaper, there were more convenient kitchens in a Leeds council flat.

No. 11, on the other hand, rambled over three floors. The Chancellor's study and the official dining room were on the ground floor. On the first floor was a suite of rooms — sitting room, bedrooms, dining room and large, old-fashioned kitchen looking out over Downing Street. On the top floor, which in the old days accommodated staff, our children had their bedrooms. When Tony Blair became Prime Minister in 1997, he wisely chose to take No. 11 rather than No. 10 as his official residence, since this warren of rooms offered so much more space for his family. The house was comfortable, but lacked the elegance of Admiralty House; and in after years I found it disappeared completely from my memory, whereas Admiralty House still remains.

My study was on the second floor, jutting out above No. 12, and was a splendid vantage point from which to watch the comings and goings at No. 10. As I wrote of Gladstone and Disraeli, I could watch their successors going through the same door. On one occasion I apparently disturbed a Chancellor from the past — as my secretary, Patricia, would have me believe. I was writing *Lady Unknown*, the life of the philanthropist heiress Angela Burdett-Coutts, and was reading aloud a letter she had written to Gladstone when, at the age of sixty-one, she wanted to marry her young secretary. The world was shocked, and even Queen Victoria was concerned. Angela wanted Gladstone's advice, and wrote asking to see him. He replied frostily that perhaps she should see Mrs Gladstone instead. I was speaking severely to him when Patricia put out her arms: they were covered in goose pimples. "I should have told you," she explained, "I am psychic: Gladstone is now standing behind you." However foolish such stories may seem, it is sometimes easy to believe that powerful characters can leave an impression behind them. Certainly Patricia was always careful to tip her splendid hat to the Millais portrait of Gladstone that hung downstairs in the hall, with a "See you next week, sir!"

Often, as I wrote in the house where they had lived, Gladstone and Disraeli came alive. I remembered how Disraeli had known my "Lady Unknown", had turned her into Adriana in his novel *Endymion*, and had recommended to the Queen that Miss Burdett-Coutts should be made a baroness in her own right. I thought with sympathy of Mrs Disraeli who, driving to the Commons with her husband before an important speech, had trapped her hand in the carriage door and, though in agony, had not murmured in case he should be distracted. I should have done the same. Past and present merged.

I liked to work early in the morning in my study, looking down on a Downing Street empty and unfamiliar. One morning I watched the policemen on guard indulge in a mock gun battle along the silent street. High Noon in Downing Street! One Christmas the policeman taking over duty in the early morning knocked at the door of No. 10 and staggered in with a child's toy arrow stuck in his helmet.

At six o'clock came the bevy of cleaners. These ladies should be remembered in any history of Downing Street; they were a special breed. They took pride in shining "their" offices and "their" official rooms: when the cleaning was taken over by a contract firm it was never quite the same. It is not generally understood that those ministers who lived in official residences during their period of office were not provided with domestic staff. However, it was possible to employ help, at one's own expense, from a carefully vetted body of cleaners. At Admiralty House we had had the competent Vera, who became a friend of the family. She was so worried by our student son's long hair that she offered him a week of her wages if he would have it cut. In our time at No. 11 we were fortunate in having the hard-working Mrs Blake.

Below my study, on the first floor, was the old-fashioned kitchen with its large, scrubbed wooden table and vast cold cupboard that could take a whole side of beef; indeed, once a year it took a side of venison — a gift from the Queen's parks and one of the few perks. A huge, ancient gas stove always smelt of escaping gas, which I regularly reported to the Ministry of Works, hoping they would replace it: they never did. It took Elspeth Howe, wife of Denis's Tory successor, to persuade the Ministry of Works to bring the kitchen up to date.

When Denis became Chancellor, in a fit of masochism he insisted that the occupants of government residences should pay rent for the expensive honour. (Mary Wilson once told me that they were out of pocket when they left No. 10.) Some official residences were less attractive than others. No. 1 Carlton Gardens, usually allotted to the Foreign Secretary, was always thought depressing and uncomfortable. George Brown's wife, Sophie, once complained to me, "I told George I have come down in the world to come here." She had left a very comfortable flat near Marble Arch.

Today Downing Street is securely barricaded, but in our day it was still open to the public and a convenient short cut from Whitehall to the Park. I often invited parties of constituents or schoolchildren to tea at No. 11. The little ones would come in hand-in-hand and walk up the stairs to the big drawing room halfway up, where they would sit on the floor and drink their orange juice, or would dance or perform for us. I know from many letters received years later that they never forgot the experience. This handsome room was scarcely ever used by our predecessors and had become shabby, so I decided one piece of furnishing extravagance should be allowed. Repapered, with the splendid Chinese cabinets in place, it became elegant once more and was used for many occasions, including the Treasury Music Society concerts. It had a little balcony overlooking the garden of No. 10 which I opened up, bringing out a cane table and chairs. It was a boon on summer mornings — though on one occasion, when I was having coffee with my editor, a polite message came up from the No. 10 Cabinet Room below: the Cabinet was apparently disturbed by our chatter.

Other occupants of No. 11 have used the drawing room for charity receptions, and I took great pleasure in helping to provide a lift for the disabled to be built in my Baptist chapel in Coleford by holding two receptions there. Originally intended for London exiles from the Forest of Dean, the first reception was so popular that another was organized and a coachload came from Coleford.

Life at No. 11 Downing Street was quite unlike that at Admiralty House since I was scarcely ever needed in any official role. From my study window I often saw guests arriving at the front door of No. 11 for official meals, arranged by government hospitality in the formal dining room on the ground floor — bankers, visiting finance ministers, politicians, sometimes trade union leaders: almost always male. During all the years that Denis was Chancellor, I think I was invited on three occasions only, and these were on the rare occasions when foreign finance ministers brought their wives. Wives were not usually invited to the great banking occasions in the City, though there was one annual City dinner when "top" wives were granted seats in the gallery above the dining hall. I used to feel that yashmaks were in order.

We were, however, invited to the grandest and most formal City occasion of the year — the Lord Mayor's Banquet. There, in the great hall of the Mansion House, the City fathers lined up to greet or frown upon ministers and their wives as they ran the gauntlet on the long walk to the Lord Mayor and his lady, waiting at the end. "The Chancellor of the Exchequer and Mrs

236

Healey" were announced at the beginning of the walk, and one waited for boos — which, fortunately, never came for us. Once, when Barbara Castle was the Minister for Overseas Trade, she and her husband were announced as "the Minister for Overseas Trade and Mrs Castle". As he shook the Lord Mayor's hand, Ted Castle, with his usual ready wit, said, "Call me madam." This was one of the most splendid occasions in the Chancellor's year and the excuse for finery. The loving cup was passed round in a somewhat alarming ritual that involved curtseying to your neighbour as you passed him the great cup.

There were other annual rituals in which, in our day, the Chancellor's wife was expected to play a role — although only a walk-on part. Budget Days had their own pattern. The massed ranks of photographers always arrived in the early morning and waited, stacked up on the pavement opposite No. 11. Our friendly and cheerful doorman, "Denis the door" as we called him, warned me to do my shopping early — though he did not tell me how early. So at 8a.m., armed with shopping basket — and disguised, I hoped, with a headscarf — I emerged to a massed flashing of lightbulbs. It looked pre-arranged, but it was not. Another ritual was the morning walk in St James's Park, escorted by a posse of photographers. This always produced a succession of contrived pictures. The Tory Chancellor Geoffrey Howe and his wife, Elspeth, were once accompanied by their little dog Budget, and I once brought our baby grandson, Tom, who obligingly punched Denis's nose for the cameras. "Never again,

237

Mum," our daughter Jenny rightly insisted, "we don't want him used." Another Budget Day a canny photographer threw a coin in front of me on the path in St James's Park, hoping that I would pick it up, providing a picture and a headline. But their happiest moment came when, as we crossed into the park, a huge black limousine stopped and out jumped Senator Edward Kennedy, who vaulted over the low fence in true Kennedy style to greet Denis and wish him well. It was a photo-opportunity no American politician could miss.

The walk-on wife's next scene was in the afternoon, when she usually stood behind the Chancellor as he came out of the big black door on his way to present his Budget in the Commons. Traditionally he waved the battered red dispatch box that had once belonged to Gladstone, while she smiled proudly in the background. In his first years as Chancellor, Gordon Brown commendably broke the routine. He was not at this time married, and so brought his Treasury team to stand with him — and continued the practice even after his marriage. He was quite right. They deserved most of the credit, having worked long hours on the Budget.

There was, on one occasion, a near-disaster in the last minutes before we left No. 11. Always a tense time, this was usually the moment for what Denis always called "a burst on my banjo" — a few bars of Mozart on the piano. Then, at the last moment, he always went carefully through his speech, marking it with his red pencil. But this time the penultimate page — the one with all the much-anticipated details of taxes to be raised or lowered — was missing. His private secretary paled with horror. There was silence. I much admired Denis's self-control: no criticism, no rebuke and no panic. Quickly, the missing page was sent for; and no one outside the room was any the wiser.

The day always ended with a long series of television interviews and a broadcast to the nation. Now that the media had their answers they could stop following me to the shops to see what I was buying, as they had done for the past week. They need not have bothered. When Gladstone had become Chancellor he asked his wife if she wished to know everything or nothing. The brave woman said, "Everything." I would have replied, "Nothing." In this complicated modern financial world a little knowledge would certainly be a dangerous thing.

Just occasionally, wives were admitted into the arcane world of finance. Chancellors' spouses were sometimes invited to Washington as the guests of the World Bank for meetings of the International Monetary Fund. We were, of course, not allowed into the meetings. Not that I minded: bankers often choose interesting wives, or vice versa! After the official dinner, when men and women separated — as was the custom — we ladies would proceed to a bedroom, kick off our shoes and hear what interesting work the wives did. One night I was astonished when a large and lovely dark lady with a rose in her hair told me the story of her life. The wife of the finance minister in her own country, she was also the youngest child of the local chief — who had chosen her above her seven brothers to succeed him as head of the family. She was also

239

elected Speaker of their House of Commons — and could silence her husband if necessary! That night we had to be summoned by a plaintive call up the stairs from the host: "When are you ladies coming down?"

We were often invited to walk through to No. 10 to join Harold's receptions or dinner parties, and Mary sometimes invited me to tea in the little flat upstairs. Perhaps the most interesting dinner given by the Wilsons was that for the American astronauts Neil Armstrong, Buzz Aldrin and Michael Collins. How improbable Gladstone and Disraeli would have found that night: men who had walked on the moon, and their wives, coming to dine at 10 Downing Street. I was seated opposite one of the wives. "How did you feel," I asked her, "when you saw your husband step out on to the moon?"

"I had an overwhelming feeling," she said, "that the whole world was supporting me and them."

That night the Wilsons had invited special guests to join us at a reception after dinner. Usually this was the opportunity to introduce more VIPs to distinguished guests, but this time Harold had also invited groups of children: some from a school for the deaf and some severely disabled. One of their teachers told me, "Mrs Healey, I am a tough old bird, but tonight I am near tears. The children never come to an occasion like this."

A father brought his disabled son over to me. "Usually," he said, "I am invited in spite of him: tonight it is because of him. He's very clever and loves history." Bright eyes shining, the boy passed his father a glass of

240

orange juice without spilling a drop and smiled at the astronaut.

"What he has just done," I said, "was almost as difficult as your first steps on the moon."

Harold Wilson has been much criticized, but this guest list was inspired. That night, in that historic setting, a boy who loved history had reached his impossible moon. Mary Wilson recorded the evening in her poem "The Lunarnaut":

"What did the earth look like," I asked him
"As you stood there on the moon?"
"Bright," he said, "fantastically bright,
"Brighter than any moonlit night —
"A shining orb of dazzling light.
"And we could see the countries clear as day
"Though miles of atmosphere between us lay,
"And home and friends and loves were far away."

My next involvement with the Spastics Society was to come in 1978 when Mary Wilson and I were both judges in their literary competition of that year — although by that time Wilson had retired as Prime Minister and Callaghan had taken over. My story of Christy Nolan, one of the prizewinners, is better recounted here. I was deeply moved by the astounding poetry of this twelve-year-old Irish boy: it was both luminous and obscure and I asked that he be given a special prize and be brought over from Ireland.

He came to the headquarters of the Spastics Society to collect his prize, slumped in a wheelchair pushed by his devoted mother Bernadette, unable to speak. To my surprise I discovered that he was almost totally disabled — but his eyes were bright, shining with excitement, as he received his award. Denis invited his mother to bring him to 11 Downing Street and arranged for them to be taken on a tour of No. 10. His wonderful mother had dedicated her life to encouraging her son. He had no power of movement, so it was she who held his head so that, with a peg on his forehead, he could tap out his poetry. It seemed incredible that his shaking head held such bright intelligence and that, though he could utter only groans, through his poetry he could speak with eloquence.

The publicity he received after the prizegiving launched him on a successful career as a novelist and playwright. One of the most moving moments of my life came when, years later, I received a letter from him announcing the opening of his first play in Dublin. Because I had helped him in the beginning, he wrote, he would like me to be present at the first night and "would send my air fare"! I always regret that I was unable to be there; but I read with pleasure his account of the prizegiving in his book *Damburst of Dreams*, in which he describes the early life of Joseph, as he calls himself.

"Title of Article or Poem" read The Spastics Society Literary Contest form — Joseph serenely filled-in all the details. Last minute checking and all poor dreams assisted his entry as it winged its way to London. Nora, his mother, answered weakly as the special, delightful, happy phone call brought the news "Joseph has won a special prize, his entry being judged as a work beyond comparison." Many questions were asked as Nora revealed the lively news, one particular query cropped up again and again, "where does Joseph get his vocabulary?" Nora could certainly not give a very satisfactory reply. Dalliantly, joyfully, Joseph longed to be able to say that he only knew that as he typed thoughts, brilliant, bright, boiling words poured into his mind, sometimes with such ferocity that he felt spoiling confusion creep across his turbulent, creative mind . . .

Then he describes the miracle of the flight to London and continues:

Lunch at 12:30 on Wednesday June 28th at the International Students House in Great Portland Street, London and the reception afterwards for prizes to be given will be at The Spastics Society's headquarters — the judges, Lady Wilson, Mrs Edna Healey, Lord Willis and Michael Randolph who is editor of the *Reader's Digest*, will be there to meet the winners — Joseph could feel his heart thumping as he pondered purposefully on the letter which he received telling him of his schedule for possibly, unbelievably the greatest day in his life.

Mrs Edna Healey looked beautiful as she arrived for the prize-giving ceremony. Joseph Meehan purposefully looked at her, as she it was who judged his entry of prose and poetry and had so happily recommended his being awarded a special prize. Cameras flashed, reporters took hasty fortuitous statements from a poor amused Nora. Joseph's all tremendous, wonderful awe-inspiring moment came when Mrs Healey stepped towards him to present him with his beautiful Ingersoll Quartz Wrist Watch. A tall dark-haired man stepped forward, he was introduced to Joseph as Mr Bill Wright, producer of one of Joseph's favourite quiz shows, *Mastermind*, and on behalf of his team presented their avid viewer with a specially lovely gift. There was still another paralysing surprise bewilderingly in store for Joseph Meehan. Mrs Edna Healey delightfully invited him to visit her at her home — No. 11 Downing Street, the official residence of the Chancellor of the Exchequer. Nora and Joseph hurriedly changed prior to being taken on a tour of lovely London by The Spastics Society and which was to end at Downing Street. Mrs Healey, dressed in a frock of fresh green, opened the door of No. 11 and extended a lovely quiet welcome to Joseph Meehan. Taking him on a personally conducted tour she filled-in all the wonderful accounts associated with the history and previous personages who through the centuries have lived or visited in her architecturally beautiful home. A visit to the home of The Prime Minister of Great Britain at No. 10 Downing Street was hurriedly and secretly arranged by lovely, thoughtful Mrs

244

Healey. Joseph and Nora pleasantly found themselves on a whirlwind tour of No. 10. Sincerely, Joseph tried to thank Mrs Healey for the golden, glorious hour which he had spent with her.

As John Carey wrote in the preface to Christy's next book, *Under the Eye of the Clock*, "it should not be possible, after reading it, ever again to think as we have before about those who suffer what he suffers. That is what makes it not just an outstanding book but a necessary one."

As Christy grew older he took part in experiments to control his spasmodic jerking and was able to make use of modern equipment to enable him to type his work. He appeared on television in his wheelchair, interviewed by Russell Harty, wearing a smart white jacket and, though he was still unable to speak, his bright mind shone through his eyes. In later years he had a bungalow built for himself and wrote to tell me of his happiness.

> The mind is its own place, and in itself
> Can make a heaven of hell, a hell of heaven.
> Milton, *Paradise Lost*

Christy is a marvellous example of the triumph of mind and spirit over body. There have been many occasions when I have introduced distinguished men and women to No. 10 and No. 11 Downing Street, but none who gave me greater pleasure and pride. I describe his later career at the end of this book.

★ ★ ★

The Labour government so narrowly elected in 1974 had none of the eager energy that had characterized the incoming administration ten years earlier. Wilson himself had lost his old zest and was secretly preparing for his resignation. Perhaps he had some precognition of the loss of mental power that would later incapacitate him — although he always claimed that he intended to resign on his sixtieth birthday, when he would have served as Prime Minister longer than any other.

Over the years I watched, as Wilson had done, the effect on ministers of continued stress which they are at pains to conceal. There was almost a death wish, or at least a longing for release, in the Labour ministers who had gone through the war in the coalition government. It was most noticeable in Attlee and Bevin. At the end of his life, Ernest Bevin's wife told me that she wanted her husband to give up, but that his doctor had told him that if he did he would not live long thereafter. He was right. When Bevin gave up, he died. Time and again I have seen the appearance of a certain wildness in the eye of politicians under stress — "the horse's eye", I call it. Time to go, I reflect. But, as I have also seen, there is often a deep-seated unwillingness to let go.

On 11 March 1976 Wilson would be sixty — when he had long since chosen to retire. He had earlier given hints to Roy Jenkins, reminding the historian Roy that he would then be the longest-serving Prime Minister. He told only a chosen few — She, of course, whom he had promised he would leave after his sixtieth birthday.

246

She, who had long wanted release, was surprised that he did not want to stay for the celebration of the Queen's Jubilee the following year, and would have been prepared to accept a delay; but Harold was adamant. Over the Christmas holiday of 1975, the news was filtered through to Jim Callaghan — perhaps deliberately — by Harold Lever, then the most trusted and discreet member of the Cabinet. He warned Jim of Harold's decision and told him to prepare to take over. Jim told no one except Audrey and his closest friend, Merlyn Rees.

Even so, when, in March, Harold himself warned Jim of the impending handover, it still came as a shock. During a dinner party given by the publisher George Weidenfeld to celebrate Wilson's sixtieth birthday, Harold had given Jim a lift to the House of Commons for the vote and told him in the car. They found the Labour benches in uproar — thirty-seven Labour members had abstained from voting because of the cuts in government expenditure for which Denis, as Chancellor, had been partly responsible. Denis had exploded and, as Jim later recorded in his autobiography *Time and Chance*, was engaged in a public row, telling the reprobates "with his combination of Yorkshire bluntness and Irish impetuosity exactly what he thought of them, to which some of them responded in kind". The fracas could not have been more damaging to Denis's chances at this crucial moment. But I very much doubt whether it would have made any difference had Denis known that Wilson was shortly to announce his resignation. As they drove back to the party, Jim was well aware that one of the contenders for the leadership had just blotted his copy-book. He found Harold surprisingly light-hearted, chuckling, "If only they had known." It suited him; Jim was his choice as his successor.

The secret had been well guarded, and when Harold made his announcement to the Cabinet on the following Tuesday, it came as a bombshell. He gave Denis forewarning — in the privacy of the lavatory — then called him with Jim and Ted Short, the deputy leader, into his study to brief them before the Cabinet meeting.

According to the Cabinet papers revealed in January 2005, on the morning of 16 March 1976 Wilson announced that he was to resign and explained the timing to his colleagues. His preferred departure date, he said, had been "party conference 1975", but that summer's pay and inflation problems had caused him to revise his departure date to late December. He said he had told the Queen on 9 December that he would go in mid- or late March. His timing, he stressed, "was not related to any recent events". By this he meant the Watergate revelations in the United States and the banking crash in London. He gave his reasons for his decision: "leader of this Party for thirteen exciting and turbulent years — nearly eight of them in government. My period as Prime Minister has been longer than any of my peace time predecessors in this country." He had led four administrations and been on one or other front bench in the Commons for more than thirty years. He did not want to deny others the chance to succeed him since his Cabinet contained "the most talented team this century since Campbell-Bannerman's 1906 Liberal government". He denied that he was stepping down because of his age, noting that Attlee, Churchill, Macmillan and Douglas-Home had all been a similar age when they *became* Prime Minister. "These reasons represent the total explanation of my decision," he said. He felt his counter-inflation policy was safe whoever succeeded him; but I suspect that, seeing the old financial and political problems recurring in the months ahead and feeling his physical health in danger, he doubted whether he would have the energy to find new solutions.

Harold Wilson has been much criticized, yet though it sometimes seemed that he was more often concerned with manipulating a Cabinet roundabout than with setting his team of horses on a straight political road, nevertheless the first years of his government, especially from 1964 to 1967, were of lasting importance. As his biographer Bernard Donoghue wrote, "he strove to reform the antiquated Whitehall machine ... he created a new minister of economic planning and of technology and appointed a distinguished scientist as education minister". Other social reforms were introduced by ministers he appointed, and under his direction; but the achievement of which he was most proud was the creation of the Open University. It is also often forgotten that he was at heart a kindly man. Jim Callaghan never forgot how, at the time of his resignation as Chancellor, Harold gave him unfailing support and showed great understanding.

At the time Wilson decided to stand down, the party leader and therefore in this instance the Prime Minister was exclusively chosen by the parliamentary Labour Party. The candidates were Jim Callaghan, Roy Jenkins, Tony Benn, Michael Foot and Denis. Roy and Tony withdrew after the first ballot. Denis stayed to fight the second ballot. I thought he too should have withdrawn at that point — but I did not then, or indeed at any time, attempt to influence his political decisions. In the final ballot, on 5 April 1976, Callaghan defeated Foot by 176 to 133. So he became Prime Minister. It was the last time that the Shadow Cabinet alone would be able to make the choice.

Had I had a vote, it would have certainly gone to Jim Callaghan. I had always felt at ease with Jim and Audrey — though it was not until much later that I realized why, and how similar their Baptist backgrounds were to mine.

Jim's father, James Callaghan, a petty officer in the Royal Navy, had applied to join the Royal Yacht, then based at Portsmouth, where Jim spent his early years. How surprised the petty officer would have been to know that years later his son, as Prime Minister, would accompany the Queen on the Royal Yacht for the review of the fleet during the Jubilee celebrations. My own father, had he known that his daughter, as wife of the Secretary of State for Defence, was there too. How he would have loved the music of the bands! Jim lost his much-loved father early, as I did. The four years he spent at Brixham when his father retired and became coastguard there were some of the happiest days of his life, giving him an enduring love of nature and the country and a deep patriotism that lasted throughout his life. There was always something "shipshape and Bristol fashion" about Jim — shoes polished, trousers pressed. His mother had maintained these standards after her husband's death — notwithstanding the difficulties of that period of their lives, when they moved from the coastguard's cottage at Brixham to a succession of uncomfortable lodgings in Portsmouth. Thanks to their mother, a strict and devout Baptist, Jim and his sister were brought up in supportive Baptist communities where the rhythm of life was remarkably similar to my own. Jim was grateful for the support shown to his family by the Baptist community, and he never forgot the importance to his widowed mother of a pension supplied by the Labour government at the time.

The Portsmouth Baptists made sure that the young man away from home was given the protection of the Baptist community in Maidstone, when he moved to Kent to work. Having left school with a limited education, he became a clerk in the Inland Revenue office and rapidly established himself as a trade unionist. Here he acquired experience denied to his more fortunate university trained colleagues. It was at the Baptist chapel in Maidstone that he met Audrey Moulton, whose father was the Sunday School superintendent. Audrey had been brought up in a comfortable home; her father was a successful businessman and they had books, music and culture, and holidays abroad. Audrey should have gone to

251

university but, modest in her ambitions as always, settled for a domestic science course and began teaching. Later she took a course in economics provided by the Co-operative Society, where her tutor was the young Hugh Gaitskell, then a lecturer. At this time she was a sixteen-year-old at grammar school, and Jim remembered very clearly the first words she spoke to him. He never forgot the tall, slim schoolgirl with the lovely smile who told him that one of the Baptist ladies was "expecting you for tea today". She was unlike anyone Jim had ever met, and — as he told me at the end of his life — he loved her from that moment to his dying day. Her love and constant support were of crucial importance to him. Their wedding was traditional, Audrey in white satin and Jim in morning dress.

Jim's political career progressed rapidly. As MP for Cardiff South from 1945, he rose from junior minister in the Ministry of Transport to Education and then the Navy. He would always remember with pride that it was at his insistence during his time at Transport that zebra crossings and cats' eyes were introduced on the roads. He swiftly rose to Cabinet rank. I first met him, when as Foreign Secretary he invited us to Dorneywood, his official house near Chequers. I had admired him as Home Secretary; there was something reassuring about his combination of firmness and understanding. At the Home Office he was responsible for Irish affairs, and his calmness under stress was much admired on all sides. His period as Chancellor of the Exchequer was difficult, and he himself was unhappy with his performance there. The financial world was an unfamiliar one to him; but in opposition he had taken instruction from university professors and had made every effort to understand the theory and practice of economics. When as Chancellor he was forced by circumstances to devalue sterling, he chose to end his tenure of office with an honourable, dignified and characteristic resignation.

So now, when he stood as candidate for the Labour leadership and the premiership, I had no doubt that his experience in the three major offices of state gave him an unrivalled qualification. His practical experience as a trade unionist, too, was an additional recommendation.

He himself was profoundly conscious of the importance of the task ahead. When Merlyn Rees went to see him to congratulate him on his success, he found him sitting head in hands. "I am overwhelmed," he said, "when I consider that I am now responsible for the greatest country in the world."

CHAPTER
TEN

11 DOWNING STREET: THE CALLAGHAN YEARS, 1976–1979

Denis found the next years at the Treasury the most demanding in his career. In his years at Defence he had been in his element in a world he knew well; at the Treasury, he was in unfamiliar country. He had been Shadow Chancellor for only two years before he became Chancellor with a Budget to prepare almost immediately. Until he found his feet, he was unwillingly dependent upon other people's advice. However, perfectionist as always, he had worked for those two years at full throttle to master the unfamiliar briefs.

Fortunately, in the crucial three years ahead he had, in Jim Callaghan, a Prime Minister who had himself suffered the testing trials involved in a Chancellor's life. Jim's understanding support was crucial, for in the following years troubles came thick and fast from a number of different but related sources, economic and political. Denis had long and gruelling sessions with international financiers, with Cabinet colleagues, with trade union leaders and with the Labour Party itself. At the same time there were family concerns which increased the strain.

High office imposes equally high levels of stress. Those who lightly criticize hard-working ministers have no idea of the strain involved, nor the long hours that their jobs entail — hours that would drive many of their critics to march out on strike with banners flying. It was fortunate that Jim Callaghan understood better than anyone the strain of a Chancellor's job and the importance of taking breaks. He often told me that he had found the Treasury more stressful than any other ministry. He knew from experience the helplessness a Chancellor feels when the pound is under pressure from a financial world over which he has no control. So when he became Prime Minister he encouraged his ministers to take a holiday in the long, hot summer of 1976.

Now that the children had grown up we missed our family holidays, though I had said goodbye to the igloo and the camping Healey-ville without regret. This summer Denis and I decided to take a motoring holiday driving to Scotland on our own. In those days of relaxed security, we travelled apparently without any accompanying officials. It was only afterwards that I realized that the police had kept an eye on us throughout the journey. Armed with a list of secondhand bookshops along the route, Denis was able to indulge his book-collecting mania. He tracked one bookshop to a remote cottage in Scotland, peered with excitement through a dirty window to the piles of dusty books, and knocked at the door — then, with

255

characteristic humour, greeted the astonished owner with, "I've come about the tax!" The vision of the unmistakable Chancellor of the Exchequer on his remote doorstep rocked the poor man on his heels. I wish I could recall whether we bought any of his books.

We stayed at a hotel in the lovely village of Ullapool, where a policeman greeted us with a friendly handshake: "I'm always telling them up here that one day the Chancellor's going to catch them out." We had scarcely got into bed when the hotel manager knocked at the door. "I'm sorry," he apologized, "I have had a call from Special Branch to say that they have received a death threat to you. But don't worry, they'll have someone sent down in the morning!" Was it his Scottish sense of humour? I was never sure, but I did not sleep that night.

There was no telephone in the bedroom, so when a little later the telephone downstairs rang again, with a call for Denis, he had to pad down in slippers and pyjamas to speak on the phone in the hall. It was an ever-wakeful official from No. 11 — there was an international financial crisis which needed Denis's immediate attention: sterling was under pressure. So, with the front door still wide open on that hot night, the sensitive financial affairs of the nation were conducted at full throttle in the unmistakable Healey boom.

In spite of these interruptions, we were refreshed by our break in the green calm of Scotland. It was as well that Denis had taken that holiday, because the following months were, as he wrote, "The worst months in my political life." We drove back through a sun-baked Britain to hear the rumbles of the approaching storm, the now notorious financial crisis of 1976, when a run on the pound made it necessary to ask for support from the International Monetary Fund.

In early September sterling came under pressure again, partly because of industrial trouble at British Leyland and a threatened seamen's strike. I had been looking forward to a rare chance to accompany Denis to an IMF conference in Manila. Denis had been particularly preoccupied in the days leading up to our departure, and I had been so busy that I had not followed the news. On the morning we were to set off I had packed, cleared out the fridge and seen our cases put into the car before I realized something was wrong. The Governor of the Bank of England met me at the door of No. 11 — white-faced. "Edna," he whispered, "I am so sorry." I was puzzled. Denis had not spoken of the crisis during the morning. This was a typical example of the ability to compartmentalize which often saved him. The falling pound was locked in one such compartment. His diary reflects the same ability: "lovely day: pound falling."

We drove with Treasury officials to the airport and our cases were put on the plane; the VIP section was shut off so that Denis could talk to the Prime Minister, who was at the Labour Party conference in Blackpool. Now they told me we were to go back to Downing Street; still no one told me why. I had become invisible. Finally I interrupted with, "Will someone tell me what's going on?" And they did. The pound was still falling fast. We returned to London and cancelled the visit — I am ashamed to say that my immediate thought was that I had emptied the fridge and there was nothing in the larder.

It may seem surprising that, although we are very close, Denis had said nothing to me of the developing crisis — but, as he later explained, "What could you do about it? I wanted to save you worry." I did the same for him at the time of my sister's tragedy, which I shall recount in a later chapter; it is the reverse side of "keeping our own space". It was typical of Denis that, though this was the worst moment of his ministerial life, he showed no panic, not even to me. Yet, as he recorded, "For the first and last time in my life, for about twelve hours I was close to demoralisation." He telephoned Jim at Blackpool, suggesting he go up to speak to the Labour conference. At first Jim disagreed, thinking it would suggest panic. He later told me that he still felt Denis should have gone to the IMF conference, leaving him to deal with the crisis. Again typically, faced with some hours of unexpected spare time, Denis took the opportunity to go to the National Gallery to choose paintings to hang in his office. Time must never be wasted; and during times of crisis he often took refuge in music or art.

A little later, Jim telephoned from Blackpool. He had decided Denis should speak after all. He took the next flight to Blackpool and was allowed five minutes to address the conference, where he faced a hostile audience. To mixed boos and cheers, he shouted: "I do not come with a Treasury view, I come from the battlefront." Forcefully he told them that "a siege economy", which some of the speakers demanded, "would be a recipe for a world trade war, and would bring the Tories to power with policies of mass unemployment".

> If you do not want those alternatives, then we have got to stick to the policy we have got. I am going to negotiate with the IMF on the basis of our existing policies . . . I mean things we do not like as well as things we do like. It means sticking to the very painful cuts in public expenditure . . . It means sticking to the pay policy . . . It means seeing that the increase in our output which has now begun goes not into public or private spending, but into exports or investment.

When he sat down the cheers were much louder — and so were the boos. Friends and enemies alike recognized that his speech had been a *tour de force*. I watched the debate on television and was outraged that his critics had so little comprehension of the real world.

The rest of 1976 was spent in a long series of testing negotiations with a team from the IMF who came to London to arrange the package of spending cuts necessary in order to secure the loan. At the same time there were equally gruelling sessions in Cabinet before ministers would accept the cuts, each protecting the interests of his or her department. Finally, it took all Denis's rude energy to persuade the IMF negotiators to accept the Cabinet's limit of £1 billion spending cuts

259

— half what they had demanded. Jim Callaghan often told me with amusement that Denis had threatened the IMF negotiators that we would call an election on the issue: "He didn't ask me," remembered Jim, "but it worked." Denis dealt with the IMF negotiators with vigour, but it was Jim who handled the divided Cabinet with exemplary skill, patiently, allowing each Cabinet member to have his or her full say. Tony Crosland, whose economic expertise Denis respected, had to be persuaded to accept that the IMF loan was unavoidable and finally withdrew his opposition.

The IMF finally gave their loan and, as Denis later wrote,

> the pound grew stronger month by month . . . When I attended the annual meeting of the IMF [in October 1977] even the British correspondents described me as "walking on water". The Labour Party Conference which followed gave me a standing ovation. The leading American financial monthly, *Institutional Investor*, produced a cover story showing me as the first among the six best financiers of the day.

However, the compliment that touched him most came from Jim Callaghan, who inscribed Denis's copy of his own autobiography, *Time and Chance*: "For Denis, who carried a heavier burden for longer than anyone else and did it with incredible resilience, with grateful thanks, 27th March 1987."

The burden, however, had weighed heavily — and the long, gruelling sessions with the negotiating team from the IMF were only one bundle in that burden. As well as dealing with a divided Cabinet, there were interminable meetings with trade union leaders to persuade them to accept a voluntary pay policy which would make the application for a loan more palatable to the IMF. I would watch from my window as Len Murray and other leaders arrived at the door of No. 11 for working dinners which would last until beyond midnight, when Denis would come upstairs "dog tired". On top of all this, there was hostility in the Labour Party itself, from both the right and the left; and because there was no overall majority in the House of Commons, there was the constant fear of losing a vote of confidence. The Lib–Lab pact, too, brought its own difficulties; the Liberal Shadow Chancellor and Denis often disagreed.

And while all this was going on, 1977 had brought other troubles. It often happens that a private grief coincides with a political crisis when press and public, unaware, are without compassion. In 1977, as Denis was wrestling with a particularly difficult Budget, his father Will was dying. Night after night Denis was driven on the busy road from London to Whipps Cross Hospital, working on the Budget with the car blinds drawn for security. Will had never been an easy father or husband, but Win and his children and grandchildren had learned to accept that behind the apparent insensitivity there was a capacity for loving which he found hard to express — revealed only on rare

261

occasions like the Christmas when he had suddenly made an after-dinner speech, speaking of each of us and the grandchildren in turn with surprising affection and understanding. His character was a mixture of Irish and Yorkshire that never quite resolved itself — as I realized when reading his young man's journal after his death. Here were poems, theatre criticisms and collections of the sayings of Churchill with the heading "Wisps of Winston". (He had admired Churchill when he was in disgrace and vowed that if he had a son he would be named after him. So, somewhat to Denis's later embarrassment, Winston was his middle name.) Denis had inherited something of his father's mixed temperament — his impatience, his occasional insensitivity obscuring a deeper sensitivity — but his character was also steeled with his mother's strong will and keen intelligence. It says much for Win's patience and tolerance that her marriage to Will endured. Even now, at the end, he was a difficult patient — testing his wife's love and proving wearing for Denis during a trying political period.

After Will's death, not bothering to eat properly, Win became increasingly frail. In 1983 she fell and broke her leg and she too had to be visited in hospital. Later, while recuperating with us in our London flat, she had a heart attack and nearly died. I called in a London doctor, who was very concerned. When Denis came home, totally exhausted after a gruelling week electioneering, he seemed, to my concern, unable to comprehend the gravity of her condition. Usually in times of stress he was saved by his ability to keep concerns in separate compartments and could deal efficiently with each in turn. This time he had no energy to make the switch.

Later, again during a period of political crisis, Denis's brother Terry, who had always been the life and soul of every party, became terminally ill. In his last months — at a particularly busy time in government — Denis travelled regularly to Swansea to visit him in the nursing home where he ended his days. It is often forgotten that a busy minister does not work in a vacuum. Vital decisions of national importance have to be taken when private problems are tearing the heart.

It is perhaps not surprising, then, that during those years as Chancellor Denis suffered more ill-health than at any other time of his life. In particular, he developed frequent bouts of toothache that always struck when we were about to go on holiday. We knew the signs — the hand clapped to the jaw, the agonized cry — and "Here we go again!" we would groan. As he wrote in *The Time of My Life*,

The mental fatigue took its physical toll. I had constant trouble with my teeth ... I contracted colds or influenza more often than ever before, developed arthritis in a shoulder, deafness in an ear. I had to prepare one of my budgets when I was bruised all over after slipping on the stairs, another when I had an attack of shingles. When I had my routine medical check-up, the doctor and nurse together found it impossible to get any blood out of me, confirming all the popular myths

about chancellors . . . I could not have survived
my five-year ordeal without the love and support
of Edna and the children — and particularly
Edna . . .

There was another shock in 1977: on 19 February a
brain haemorrhage struck down one of the most
brilliant men of our generation when our old friend
Tony Crosland suddenly died. This was a great shock
and distress for Denis. We had known Tony since our
Oxford days — even though I always knew that as far as
he was concerned I was below his line of sight. Later, in
his early years as MP for West Gloucestershire, he was
diminished by heavy drinking and womanizing and a
brief, failed marriage. Our mutual friends Jack and
Frankie Donaldson, who were his hosts in his
constituency, found him a demanding and sometimes
tiresome guest at this time — meals had to be at his
pleasure and his comfort always came first — but his
dazzling charm and stimulating intellect always won
their forgiveness. His friends saw in him the creative
thinker whose books and articles made him the Labour
theoretician of our generation. Back in our Oxford days
I would have guessed that Tony would precede Roy in
the ascent of the political ladder; but his talent was
wasted in the rackety life of his early years as an MP
and so he had to watch with chagrin his acolyte
reaching the Cabinet before him.

Rescued by his second marriage, he no longer
needed to hide his true kind and generous nature and
allowed himself the release of loving. Again and again,

264

he used the words "my family" with affection to describe his step-daughters — and, at the end of his life, even his civil servants. At the last, Susan had the comfort of remembering his ultimate weekend of their thirteenth wedding anniversary at Adderbury — an occasion she recalled in her sensitive biography of her husband. "He walked through the house, came back to the sitting-room for a nightcap by the fire. 'I'd wondered if Dorneywood [his official country residence as Foreign Secretary] might diminish Adderbury,' he said. 'It's the other way round: it's enhanced the sense of privacy at Adderbury. If I pop off tomorrow, you mustn't think Adderbury has been wasted: already we've had so much happiness here.'" When the blow fell, Susan stayed with him in hospital, beside him to the end.

Roy Jenkins was abroad when he heard of the death of the man who had so inspired his student years, and, though they had since drifted apart, was shaken. Giles Radice recounts in *Friends and Rivals* how, on the Saturday, Roy had woken at 6.30 a.m. in Rome having had a vivid dream about Tony, who had said, in an unmistakable, clear, calm voice, "No, I am perfectly all right. I am going to die, but I'm perfectly all right." At about 8 a.m. the BBC rang Roy saying that Tony had died — at almost exactly the moment Roy had awoken from his dream.

After Tony's death, Jim was prepared to move Denis to the Foreign Office — but, as Denis wrote, "Jim was again relieved when I told him I would prefer to stay at the Treasury for the time being; I had broken my back in planting the tree, and I wanted to be there to gather the fruit. So he chose David Owen to replace Tony as Foreign Secretary, warning him, and the Lobby, that he might have to give it up when I was ready to leave the Treasury."

It happened that the day Tony died I was sitting at a dinner next to David Owen, who urgently asked me to persuade Denis to stay at the Treasury. The next day, Jim surprisingly asked him to become Foreign Secretary. Embarrassed, he later hastened to assure me that he had had no idea at the dinner of his impending elevation.

He feared Denis's removal would shake the pound again. If Denis had moved to the Foreign Office he would have become a great Foreign Secretary, the position for which he had been trained; and Tony at the Treasury would have been where he longed to be. As it was, both men were working against the grain. It was only after intensive study and unremitting grind that Tony was just beginning to understand and enjoy the Foreign Office, and the strain had been enormous for a man who insisted on understanding completely every ministry to which he was moved. I believe the stress contributed to his early death. Characteristically, Denis decided to resist the temptation to move and stay and finish his job.

Contrary to some writers' theories, there was no rivalry between Tony and Denis. Each respected the other's expertise, and both wanted and fully expected eventually to swap jobs. The two had much in common. They both had powerful minds; both could be arrogant

266

(though Tony had some vanity, Denis none). Both were domineering — Denis could be sometimes accused of bullying. Tony used a rapier, Denis a hammer. Neither was burning to become Prime Minister. Denis and Tony wanted to *do*; Roy, on the other hand, as he admitted, wanted to *be*. Neither Denis nor Tony would go out of the way to collect acolytes, nor spend time gossiping in the tea room of the House of Commons. However, both valued the friendship of the ordinary men and women in their constituencies, constantly quoting the opinions of Grimsby and Leeds — sometimes to the irritation of their Cabinet colleagues. Tony combined a deep seriousness with an apparent frivolity — as did Denis. Tony sought, in lecturing and writing, to produce a forward-looking structure for democratic socialism; his greatest legacy is his written work. Denis, as he frequently says, sought to prevent another world war, and his record at the Ministry of Defence is a legacy of which he can be proud.

Roy Jenkins's talent, on the other hand, was for understanding and listening to people, and for simple human kindness. He bothered to visit our mutual friend Leo Pliatzky when he was dying in hospital. He was the one minister, according to Mary, who regularly went to see Harold Wilson during his sad last months. Just before his death, Roy wrote a kind note to Tony Benn after Benn had made some critical comments about him.

These differences in character inevitably had their political repercussions. Roy always had the backing of a loyal group of friends and acolytes, whereas Tony had admirers rather than friends, and Denis never bothered to collect followers at all.

Denis found relief from the life of a Chancellor in the limited amount of time he could spend with his wife and family, but in this difficult time our marriage might have come under stress had I not had my own resources. The life of a Cabinet minister's wife can be very lonely: Mary Wilson once said to me as we sat having tea together in the little flat at No. 10, "I sometimes feel that life is passing me by." She found her salvation in her own work. The successful publication of her volumes of poetry gave her great satisfaction.

As Chancellor of the Exchequer, Denis was almost totally immersed in his work. I dreaded the quiet tap at the door and the arrival of a soft-footed messenger with another load of papers that must be seen and absorbed immediately. High finance moves in a wide, unsleeping world: I have on occasion been awakened in the middle of the night by a messenger bringing a red box which shared our bed, or the quiet voice of a secretary using the telephone on my bedside table. Even on holiday red boxes followed us to the cottage. Red boxes, indeed, would pursue him hourly, to the point where I began to lay a place for them at the dining table at No. 11. Reading his diaries, I realize, too, how many of his meals were taken elsewhere, with colleagues or officials or journalists, or eaten as working meals downstairs in the official dining room — to which, of course, I was never invited.

As Chancellor, Denis travelled strictly on business and usually alone. He still paid his monthly visits to the constituency, too, so that I was often on my own at weekends. Even when he was in London, he was usually out in the evenings. At that time Parliament sat until 10p.m. from Monday to Thursday; since at this time Labour had a very narrow majority and often risked defeat, attendance was obligatory and all-night sittings were frequent.

Even when he was present, there was the problem that many wives of powerful, famous men face: the fading into invisibility. I knew exactly what Mary Wilson meant when she told Cherie Blair in 2004: "As we walk to the platform I have a curious feeling. I always have it. I feel like the invisible woman. I feel their eyes sliding across me as if I wasn't there, straight across to him. They want to see him, not me. Sometimes they call to me, things like, 'Take care of him, look after him, we need him.'" Even Shirley Williams once confessed to me that, introduced as Mrs Neustadt, she disappeared, whereas "Shirley Williams" produced immediate delighted recognition. I have stood with other wives in a line-up of ministers waiting to be introduced by Harold Wilson to some visiting dignitary and noted how we were all passed by as though we were not there. According to his biographer, Harold was no anti-feminist — he made Barbara Castle, for example, Minister of Transport — yet in all the years that Denis worked with him I do not think that he exchanged more than a dozen words with me, or indeed was aware of my existence. Fortunately, like

269

many other wives of politicians, I did not take this too seriously and, like them, found the solution in my own work. In my experience the happiest political marriages are those where the non-political wives or husbands pursue their own careers quietly. Nowadays, with an increasingly intrusive and censorious press, wives are only too glad of the "cloak of invisibility".

For the first years of Mary Wilson's marriage she had stayed out of the limelight, bringing up their three children and making Harold a comfortable home; but during the period when Harold was Prime Minister, Mary's own talents were recognized when in 1970 she published her first book of poems. It was perhaps her father who gave her a lifelong love of poetry. A remarkable man, he had studied (like David Livingstone) at the weaver's loom and had made his own way to training college, thereafter becoming a Congregational minister. So Mary was brought up, like Harold, in the traditions and values of the Congregational chapel. When recently I described to her the painting which hung in our Sunday School room, depicting Christ with his arms encircling children of all colours and nations, Mary remembered how her father had told her: "You are the little fair-haired English girl in that picture." That painting remains in my mind as it has in Mary's, a lasting symbol of the brotherhood of man.

Mary's poems share something of the quality of those of John Betjeman, who remained her close friend until his death. She is proud to possess seventy-five letters from him, valuing his criticism and advice. He obviously loved her undemanding calm. "Let's have some Wordsworth, Mary," he would say, and she would read aloud long poems to him as the clock ticked by and he fell asleep.

Her own poems have given great pleasure to many. Georgian in tone, with a simple directness, they are often deeply moving. In "The Old Manse" she describes vividly her return to her old home and her parents:

> Within the study, where the sunlight never falls,
> My father writes his sermon, hooded eyes
> down-bent;
>
> . . .
>
> I see my mother in the kitchen, making bread,
> Setting the pliant dough in shallow pans to rise;
> Her long brown hair is coiled around her head —
> How young her form, how shining blue her eyes!
> The door stands open on the morning sweet,
> And all the hens come clucking to her feet.
>
> . . .
>
> Silent and empty now, the Old Manse stands,
> Weedy and desolate, its garden lies.
> All, all is changed; and yet, it cannot be!
> Now is the dream — Then, the reality!

The success of her first volume led to the publication of a second in October 1979. The four poems commemorating the sudden death in 1974 of her great friend John Webster, the organist at University College, are particularly poignant.

They telephoned to tell me you were dead —
No ageing years for you, no lasting pain,
And I am glad that you have gone ahead
And I remain . . .
Yet, having said this, I am desolate;
How could you go away, my dearest friend?
How could you go, and never say goodbye
Before the end?
Of all the evenings when we sat and talked
Nothing remains, no, not one whispered word;
And when I try to recollect your voice,
No voice is heard.

This grievous loss came at a time of political victory celebrations when, jostled by crowds and with a broken heart, Mary had to go on smiling as journalists told her, "How happy you look, Mrs Wilson!"

Mary's poetry was popular, and the sales of her volumes helped them to buy their little house on St Mary's in the Scilly Isles which, over the years, became their haven, a refuge from the world of politics. This was perhaps Mary's greatest gift to Harold, and one that should never be underestimated. Wandering in his old shorts and sandals along the quay, idly watching the seabirds, he could be himself. Every Prime Minister needs a refuge. It was for this reason that Lord Lee of Fareham in 1917 bequeathed Chequers to the nation as the official country residence of the premier. But though Mary appreciated the comfort of Chequers and used it on official occasions, when Harold was there it was not like their own simple home on the Scilly Isles

272

where they could be themselves. On 24 May 1995 Harold was buried on the island, and each year on the anniversary of his death a service of remembrance is held there. Mary is touched by the messages that year after year are left on his grave, thanking him for all he did during his years as Prime Minister.

Like Mary, so many other highly intelligent wives of ministers in my day had interesting careers. Audrey Callaghan was a most effective county councillor and a wise chairman of the Trustees of the Great Ormond Street Children's Hospital; Jennifer Jenkins, is a lecturer and was a distinguished chairman of the National Trust; Susan Crosland, a brilliant writer and biographer, her life of Tony a moving record of a wonderful partnership; Molly Hattersley, headmistress of a large comprehensive school; Debbie Owen, a highly successful literary agent (with Delia Smith and Jeffrey Archer on her books). Giles Radice's wife, Lisanne, who wrote and lectured on international affairs, like me concentrated increasingly on her own work as the political pressure on Giles increased. Other MPs' wives, like Colleen Rees and Patricia Ashley, acted as highly competent secretaries to their husbands.

There were many such wives on all sides of the House. When John Major was Prime Minister, Norma found great satisfaction in her well-regarded life of the opera singer Joan Sutherland and her splendid *History of Chequers*. Her own success must have brought great consolation in difficult times. I much admired the successful partnership of Geoffrey and Elspeth Howe. When Geoffrey became Chancellor of the Exchequer,

Elspeth, as I had done, compensated for the difficulties of life at No. 11 by taking up her own work, studying for her degree in economics. Her outstanding ability was recognized by her appointment to a number of public bodies, notably as chairman of the Equal Opportunities Commission and a governor of the BBC. She was created a baroness in her own right and, with typical independence, she takes her seat on the cross benches. Highly intelligent, she is also deeply caring. She showed her concern for the homeless by once spending a night in a cardboard box with down-and-outs on a London pavement, accompanied by her little dog Budget. Strong-minded and independent, Elspeth was often — and wrongly — assumed to have written Geoffrey's famous resignation speech. "She made the bullets and he fired them," it was said. In fact, Geoffrey had needed no urging: behind that quiet and unassuming manner lies great strength and determination. Still, not many Westminster wives can claim literally to have rescued their husbands, as Elspeth did. On holiday, when Geoffrey collapsed in the swimming pool, her presence of mind and competence saved his life. Our long friendship with Geoffrey and Elspeth has surmounted political differences and survived many a shower of good-humoured badinage across the Chamber in the House of Commons.

It did not worry me that Denis and I rarely discussed politics. I had my own work to occupy me, and the last thing Denis wanted at the end of a long day was a chat about world affairs — unlike Tony Crosland, who found talking over his problems with Susan a relaxation.

When people asked me what Denis thought of some political issue, I replied, "Do what I do — read his speeches." In any case, many of the issues worrying him were foreign to me, the language — "demand management", "Keynesian economics" — incomprehensible.

When the children were young I had gone alone on visits to the dentist, school concerts and other delights, almost as a single parent. Our children had learned to accept their father's preoccupation. I once heard Cressida, when a little girl, attempt to break through by saying, "Dad, I fell out of a tree today and broke my neck." "Did you, dear? Well done," he absently replied. As the years went by I often had to go alone to family weddings and funerals. If there was a problem, there was rarely a right time to raise it. A sense of proportion was essential; domestic problems had to be seen in the context of world crises.

Now that my birds had left the nest, I was often alone during the years at 11 Downing Street. Jenny was now married to her childhood sweetheart Derek, an award-winning graphic designer — and the kindest and most helpful son-in-law. Jenny is an excellent teacher and school manager and continued to teach while her children, Tom and Kate, were young. Highly intelligent and competent, she is also a most affectionate and considerate daughter. Denis listens to her grass-roots wisdom on the state of education, often delivered with a brisk common sense that he much admires. Tom, having taken his degree in marine biology, turned his skiing skills to good use in becoming the editor of an international snowboarding magazine. Kate took a degree in graphic design and then, almost by accident, found a job on the Labour Party magazine. Determined to be accepted on her own merit, she concealed the fact that she was Denis Healey's grandchild. It is not always easy to be family of the famous.

After Oxford, our son Tim became a writer, broadcaster, record maker, impresario and folk music expert. Lively and witty with a keen mind, he has the same wide-ranging literary knowledge as his father, and can sometimes outquote him and even correct him: no mean feat! He is happily married to the clever and lovely Jo, who after marriage took a good degree at St Hugh's, Oxford, and is a great help to Tim in his work. Fond grandparents that we are, we are devoted to their children: the beautiful and talented Susie, who works in radio and television, and Charlie, who follows Denis's example and is reading philosophy at university.

Our daughter Cressida is most like Denis in strength of character and determination. Like him, too, she has always been something of a lone wolf — travelling abroad on her own when quite young, working in a restaurant in the south of France. After gaining her degree at Leeds University, she made her way to America with friends, and, deciding that San Francisco was her kind of place, settled there, making a living in part-time jobs in order to qualify as a practitioner in alternative medicine. At that time she also became a black belt in aikido. Then, after an intensive seven years' training, she gained her doctorate in clinical psychology. She now provides psychotherapy and supervision, writes on her area of expertise, and is a successful lecturer. Though mostly absent, she returns for holidays and we keep closely in touch; and she is most dearly loved. Denis has often accepted speaking engagements in America so that he could visit her.

This is the close and happy family which has always been so important to Denis; and he is never happier than when we are all together. Jenny always remembers how during a political crisis he found time for the grandchildren, making a special journey to buy a particular toy for Tom, at that time a baby. Denis needs no acolytes; as he often says, he would always rather go home than gossip in the tea-room in Parliament. Some might say this has been his weakness as a politician; but it has also been his great strength.

Throughout 1977 and 1978, while the economic pressures lifted, the political problems increased. Labour's slim majority meant that every narrow vote had the potential to bring down the government. Jim would often greet me with: "Well, I'm still here!" It was a time when sick and even dying MPs were wheeled to Parliament to vote. Now the government survived only by making a pact with the Liberals. Denis, who had shown monumental patience during the economic crisis, now found the Liberal Shadow Chancellor, John Pardoe, a trial and there were frequent clashes. But the most difficult, and most essential, compromises had to be made with the trade unions leaders. Night after night Denis would come home totally drained by long sessions of reasoning and argument.

The opinion polls were moving against Labour, and it was clear that the date of the next election would have to be carefully chosen. On 18 August 1978 Jim and Audrey Callaghan came over from their neighbouring farm to our newly acquired Sussex home at Alfriston for tea, over which we indulged in the usual easy, friendly chat about their farm, the crops and the pigs Audrey was rearing. Then Jim suggested he and Denis took a walk around the garden. Audrey and I watched them strolling along the hill, talking hard, stopping to make a point. We both knew perfectly well what they were discussing, but I do not believe either of us mentioned it. Wives of politicians learn discretion even among close friends. I would not have asked Audrey if Jim had decided yet whether to call an election, and she would not have told me. I had early learned, as wife of the defence minister, the folly and danger of idle talk; I knew that most political decisions mean making hard choices, and that wise judgement depends on knowing the whole picture.

Denis describes their conversation on this occasion in his autobiography:

> [Jim] was minded to go through the winter if we could survive the votes on the Queen's Speech. Both the Labour Party's organisers in the country and all but two of the Labour Whips in Parliament preferred delay. I warned him that the growth and output and living standards would be slower during the winter; but Jim thought that by the spring the longer experience of improving living

standards would count for more with the voters. Neither of us foresaw the industrial troubles which lay ahead, or our defeat on devolution, which was in part their consequence. What weighed most heavily with Jim was the general view of our organisers that we could not expect more than another hung Parliament if we held the election in the autumn. He was sick to death of the continual compromises required for our survival as a minority government; I think he would rather have lost than be condemned to a repetition of the previous three years.

Had they asked my advice, which they did not, I would have said: "Take this autumn." I had seen the stress of these years of minority government — ministers constantly scratching around for votes from Liberals, constantly battling with trade union leaders for wage restraint. And I had seen this kind of weariness before, during the Attlee government after the war, when the will to fight diminished and something akin to a death wish took over.

Jim's decision to put off the election was disastrous. Over the autumn months, the trade union battles over pay and the accumulation of strikes culminated in the "winter of discontent". Callaghan's equable, "Sunny Jim" demeanour seemed to show a lack of understanding of the country's mood. At the Trades Union Congress in the autumn of 1978, he teased the delegates about the date of the forthcoming election, which they had expected and indeed wanted soon. To

279

their mystification, he sang "There was I, waiting at the church . . ." — and they had to infer that the election would not take place that autumn. During the winter we watched each night with sinking hearts the reports of strikes and television images of overflowing dustbins, rats and unburied coffins.

On my visits to Leeds in the spring of 1979 I was aware of considerable and growing unease at grass-roots level, and I went up to the constituency for the general election of 3 May with foreboding. During the election campaign Denis was expected to tour the country, speaking at marginal seats and appearing on television, and this time was unable to get to the constituency until eve of poll. I did my best, but too often the campaign felt like *Hamlet* without the prince. It was enlivened by the colour and excitement contributed by our Asian constituents, who festooned their houses and the battle bus with gaily coloured streamers. Loyal old friends were as hard-working and supportive as always. The McGee family enlivened the battle bus: Eamon's lovely wife, expecting her eighth child, joggled along cheerfully, hoping she could last out until after the election. Douglas, phlegmatic as always during elections, mocked me: "If someone doesn't smile at her, Edna thinks we have lost the election!" It was at times like these, and with friends like these, that I understood why Denis could never desert the Labour Party.

As usual we listened to the results in Leeds Town Hall; and we groaned as the losses mounted. In the cold dawn we went back to our hotel knowing that we had lost. Denis kept his seat; but the Tories had taken the country.

Early the next morning, on the long drive back to London, we listened to dreary music on the car radio, interrupted by drearier reports of falling Labour seats, and I began to prepare in my mind for a hasty move from No. 11. This would be nothing like our exit from Admiralty House; this time, we would have to leave in full view of the press in Downing Street. We had a piano and hundreds of books to be moved, and it was now Friday. Who would move a piano on a Saturday?

All through Friday I packed frantically, watching the comings and goings in Downing Street through the kitchen window. At sunset I called Denis with his camera to catch a shot of Jim Callaghan as he left No. 10 to hand his resignation to the Queen. Obligingly, the sun shone on his still smiling face as he waved goodbye to the photographers. As I wrapped my china in newspaper, I saw Margaret Thatcher arrive, watched her waving to enthusiastic crowds in the street below me and heard the voice that then carried the flat accent of her native county, quoting words usually, but wrongly, attributed to Francis of Assisi: "Where there is discord, may we bring harmony. Where there is error, may we bring truth. Where there is doubt, may we bring faith. Where there is despair, may we bring hope." She looked young, attractive and full of vigour — but she brought me despair.

Denis was totally immersed in winding up his office, but I was determined to get out of No. 11 before the cameras came to welcome our Tory successors. So at dawn on Saturday morning I parked my car at the steps to Horse Guards Parade and, with the help of the policemen at No. 10, lugged my personal belongings out to it, leaving the rest for the removal men. Oddly, I don't remember the removal van — or the exit of the piano. Fortunately, the interior door between No. 11 and No. 10 was closed, so there was no danger of a greeting on the stairs from the new incumbents. Denis's official car had already been removed, as swiftly as it had appeared when he had been appointed Chancellor. Our friendly policemen from No. 10 came to offer help and to say goodbye. "You'll be back," they said reassuringly. But we were not. This was the end of Denis's ministerial career. It was the beginning of eighteen years of Tory government. Labour would not be back until the victory of Tony Blair in 1997.

CHAPTER
ELEVEN

THE WORLD BEYOND WESTMINSTER: A LIFE OF MY OWN

In these often lonely and constantly changing years, I was increasingly glad that my own career was taking off. Throughout my marriage I had tried to keep something of my own alive. This was not so common in the early days, when a woman's career was expected to end with marriage. I recalled being asked in earlier years, "Why do you want to go to Oxford? You'll only get married."

However, I had missed teaching, and from the early days of our married life had found pleasure and satisfaction in giving lectures for the WEA. Given confidence by my speaking tour to America for the English Speaking Union, I became a freelance lecturer for Foyles Lecture Agency, talking to a wide variety of audiences. Later, after the publication of *Lady Unknown* in 1978, my heroine's friendship with Dickens introduced me to the Dickens Fellowship, and I became their president for two successive years in 1979 and 1980. Here I made lasting friendships in a world beyond politics, in particular with the Professor

283

of English at Birkbeck College, Michael Slater, whose encyclopaedic knowledge of Charles Dickens and all his works was a constant source of information and whose encouragement I have always valued.

As president of the Dickens Fellowship I was asked to talk about Dickens to the English departments at universities in Tokyo and Kyoto. Denis was at this time in opposition, and, as a correspondent to the Japanese newspaper *Asashi Shimbun* (the Japanese equivalent of the *Times*), had been invited to its centenary celebrations; I was invited to accompany him. We spent a week in Japan which opened a window for me on to a fascinating country, more foreign and exotic than any other I have ever visited. I was interested to see how powerful the influence of Dickens was here, where his concept of charity was totally foreign. An elderly professor told me with beguiling courtesy that his one ambition in life was to translate my *Lady Unknown* into Japanese. He never has done.

I was also invited to address the Dickensians of Boulogne. They asked me to speak in French! I countered Denis's immediate "You can't do that!" with "Yes, I will" — and I did. The press photograph taken at the lecture showed an audience friendly but bemused.

Over the years I have gained much satisfaction from public speaking, learning to relate to an audience — usually speaking for an hour and mostly without notes. Building on the invaluable advice of my old Forest of Dean schoolmaster, Bobby Noble, who made me reduce my subject to a postcard plan and then put it aside, I learned my own basic rules. I came to realize the importance of eye contact with an audience and picked up various wicked techniques to keep it awake: stop talking and the most profound sleeper will wake with a start. Silence in a speech is important, like space in a painting. Long experience has also taught me never to underestimate an audience — there will be much knowledge and experience under the grey heads before you. The tough, horsy lady may shyly bring you her delicate and sensitive poetry; the rough old man smoking a pipe may correct the translation of Chaucer's medieval English, which you hoped no one would notice was your own.

Throughout my life I have found talking to an audience a refreshing way of finding my own identity, especially if no one asks me during question time, "What does Denis think about so-and-so?" I find it a help to have my critical and sensible sister, Doreen, in the front row; with the most delicate of gestures she can indicate "Enough" or even "Pull your skirt down — you are showing your knickers." She also told me what I often felt, that I had the same relationship with an audience that my mother had when she sang. It has been an important outlet for me, married to a politician who, at the end of the day, has had enough of words. His eyes, understandably, will glaze over after two minutes' conversation: so it was a relief to know that I could hold the attention of an audience for an hour and that I was visible.

However, I realized I needed the discipline of writing. Manipulation of the voice can conceal much emptiness of thought. In Highgate I found a compelling subject in the story of the banker Thomas Coutts and his granddaughter and heiress, the nineteenth-century philanthropist Angela Burdett-Coutts. Our return to the Holly Lodge Estate during the opposition period of 1970–4 had reawakened my interest in their history.

In 1953 we had moved to a larger house on top of the hill in Holly Lodge Gardens, built on the site of the kitchen gardens of Angela's villa, now demolished. It had an extensive view of London from the East End to Kensington and beyond to the Surrey hills — at night a jewel box of distant lights. Little is left of Angela's extensive gardens: only the broken stone basin of a little pool, two elegant eighteenth-century stone urns and a summerhouse remain. Splendid wrought iron gates, with an inscription explaining that her grandfather had placed them there, still led to an old carriageway winding between high rhododendrons. As I later discovered, Hans Andersen had walked there with Angela and admired her rhododendrons — now house-high. From our front porch we could look beyond the ancient gingko tree and watch the sun go down over Hampstead Heath; at the rear we backed on to the overgrown Highgate Cemetery, where so many distinguished corpses rest. Mrs Dickens and her baby daughter lie among the tangled undergrowth. Often, looking out of the back windows, I thought of Christina Rossetti lying there and remember her words:

> Remember me when I am gone away,
> Gone far away into the silent land; . . .

286

Better by far you should forget and smile
Than that you should remember and be sad.

We were not at all disturbed by our silent neighbours, although sometimes peacocks screamed eerily at night from Waterlow Park beyond the cemetery. For the children it was deliciously romantic, an idyllic playground. They climbed over into the wilderness and dared each other to explore the catacombs where, they declared, skeletons could be seen through iron bars. They told us that an old servant used to come regularly to polish her master's coffin.

Now that we were living in her grounds, I was haunted by the history of Coutts's granddaughter. Gradually I unravelled her extraordinary story — her inheritance as a young woman of the immense fortune of her banker grandfather, and her long life occupied in spending it for good causes at home and abroad. Deeply religious, and impelled by an idealism inherited from her father, the radical MP Sir Francis Burdett, she believed that God had given her "great means" for a purpose and devoted her life to practical and inspired philanthropy. She financed explorers like Livingstone and Stanley in Africa, and helped to finance Rajah Brooke — the White Rajah of Borneo. In return he bequeathed Sarawak to her in the first draft of his will. The list of her charitable works is endless. She built not only churches, but also workers' flats. She provided drinking fountains for horses and costermongers' ponies. She financed research into the potato famine that had decimated the Irish rural population, and established a training school for fishermen — horrified that the Irish had starved while surrounded by a sea full of fish, all for lack of boats and training. Once I had a letter from an old Irishman who had been educated in the fishing school she had founded, and who had just placed a bunch of flowers on her tomb in Westminster Abbey.

As a young woman she was in love with the old Duke of Wellington. It was a gentle, autumnal romance, she in her thirties and he in his eighties. Wellington praised her "clear-eyed" vision; he was fond of her, but kindly rejected her offer of marriage since he was "old enough to be her grandfather". At the same time she was for many years the great friend of Charles Dickens, who considered her his "dearest friend" and "the noblest spirit we can ever know".

Her friendship with Dickens — hitherto not fully told — was to guide her in what she called her "reproductive charity". For many years he acted as her unofficial almoner, helping her found a "home for homeless women" — a euphemism for prostitutes — and advising her on the construction of her East End flats and shopping market. He gave much time and thought to her work and in return, she paid for his son Charley's education at Eton and helped him in his later career.

Fearing fortune-hunters, Angela remained single until finally, aged sixty-seven, in a mirror image of her early attachment to Wellington, she married her young American secretary, William Ashmead Bartlett. Charles Dickens would have been interested in this May and

December story had he still been alive. At the end of her life she was created Baroness Burdett-Coutts by Queen Victoria — the first woman to receive the honour in her own right. She is buried in Westminster Abbey near the great west door.

Back in Highgate in the early 1970s, with more time to spare, I began researching her life and became determined to write it. Finally, the late Lady Elwyn-Jones, the wife of the Lord Chancellor, and herself the author of many books under the name of Pearl Binder, persuaded me to stop talking about the miraculous story in my head and take a synopsis to a publisher. As we sat in the Central Lobby at Westminster, she held my hand and made me solemnly promise. I often thank her memory. I managed to convince William Armstrong at Sidgwick & Jackson that here was an extraordinary story and that I had to tell it, and he was brave enough to take me on and give me a small advance. Some years later, thanks to wise advice and editing by Margaret Willes and John Goldsmith, my biography, *Lady Unknown*, published in 1978, became a best-seller. It started me on a writing career which has now given me the greatest pleasure for over twenty-five years. To Margaret I owe a particular debt of gratitude. A skilled editor, she came with her colleague to 11 Downing Street to tell me that my first draft "wouldn't do". "Now be tactful," her colleague had said as he rang the bell. Ignoring his warning, she cheerfully and bluntly told me all that was wrong with it!

I became obsessed with my subject, and the years of research were a constant source of pleasure during long periods that might otherwise have been very lonely. Looking out from our house on the Holly Lodge Estate, I walked in my mind down the avenue of rhododendrons with her as she had done with Wellington and Hans Andersen, or stood on the hill and looked down with Dickens to the twinkling lights of a city he would help her transform. Rajah Brooke would send her seeds from the Far East for her garden. Henry Irving would rehearse here, strutting his Hamlet on her terraces. Here the Duchess of Teck would come to stay with her daughter, Princess May, later to be Queen Mary: Angela would send her splendid furs to keep her warm when travelling. A neighbour once told me that during the war she had seen the old Queen Mary standing outside our house — reflecting. Perhaps she was remembering the time when, as I discovered, a gardener had slapped her hand for pinching straw-berries in the kitchen garden on that site.

As I investigated Angela's life, the pageant of Victorian life unrolled, bringing to life the great men and women of the time. They wrote to her from all over the world. Once I was lent a black tin box of old letters by one of her family, with the words, "I don't know if there is anything of interest here." When I got home with them I could not wait to open my front door but sat in the porch, lifted the lid and found on top a bundle of faded blue letters addressed, "To you at Holly Lodge". The first words were: "I want you to be the first to know that I have just discovered Lake

Shirwa." The letter was signed "David Livingstone". My spine tingled. Straight away I took the letter to my neighbour who worked for the Student Christian Movement, and with whom a young African student was staying. When I showed him the letter he was moved to tears: a legend had come alive. It was a moment of which every researcher dreams. In the same box were letters and photos from the young Princess of Teck, signed "May", and some in French from members of the French royal family.

Angela had also inherited her grandfather's large house on the corner of Stratton Street in Piccadilly. In her drawing room Thomas Moore sang his Irish songs: once, as he played, he watched his audience desert him for the young Charles Dickens, and wept. Scientists such as Charles Babbage and Michael Faraday were her friends. Babbage showed her his "calculating machine", the forerunner of the computer; shy Faraday watched London's fireworks from her top window. Liszt came, and was surprised that tactfully she had removed the piano so that he should not be expected to play. Here came guests from all parts of the world, from all classes: missionaries, explorers, royals and republicans. Both the French King Louis Philippe and Louis Napoleon were at different times her guests. Queen Victoria liked to sit at her window in the Stratton Street mansion and watch the passing show in Piccadilly — her own life running in parallel to the extraordinary career of the woman who became known as "the Queen of the Poor". Yet by the time she died in December 1906 Angela had already been almost completely forgotten. I was glad to have revived her memory. I chose the title *Lady Unknown* because much of her generosity was given anonymously, her letters of donation signed "An Unknown Lady". The book was a success, attracting some favourable reviews; the one I most prized was that by Angus Wilson, who wrote, "Mrs Healey has a nose for a good story".

Denis was delighted — and somewhat astonished. I remember his surprised comment as he read the proofs for the first time: "But this is good!" I wondered whether he would ever have known what I was if I had not written that book; he is always a more attentive reader than listener. From the beginning of my writing career, I have been careful not to show him early drafts which might then be influenced by him. It has always been most important that they should be entirely my work, though I have always been grateful for access to his profound knowledge of art, music and literature, and his advice on the last draft.

In writing about Angela Burdett-Coutts I had thrown some new light on Charles Dickens's "dearest friend", and their friendship had revived my interest in his work. So next I was persuaded by George Weidenfeld to write a new life of Charles Dickens. This great publisher has a gift for sowing the seed of a book in half an hour in the most unsuspecting acquaintance. However, I soon realized the magnitude of the task and, daunted by that and the consciousness that so many great writers had gone over this ground before me, to his surprise gave back the advance. Yet, after reading again on microfilm several hundred of Dickens's letters addressed to Angela as "My dearest friend", many of them at that time still unpublished, I know that my interest in him has remained; perhaps one day I shall have the courage to take on this great project.

Angela's close friendships with so many of the greatest men and women of her day led me into thinking about the nature of genius: what it was that made some go, as Livingstone said, "beyond other men's lines", often at the cost of wife and family? As I discovered, when the divine fire strikes it often burns the grass around. So I chose to write the biographies of the wives of three men of genius who, in the middle of the nineteenth century, for better or worse changed our lives: Jenny, wife of Karl Marx; Emma, wife of Charles Darwin; and Mary, wife of David Livingstone. Of each man it was so often said to me "I didn't know he had a wife" that I was tempted to make that the title of my book. It became, in fact, *Wives of Fame*.

Each husband wrote in praise of his wife. Karl Marx's Jenny died before him, leaving him mourning and desolate: "all is but dust and ashes now my vital and luminous wife is dead". Mary Livingstone, who crossed African deserts with David, was, he said, "my guardian angel and a brave woman". As for Charles Darwin, his wife Emma was his "wise counsellor" and "infinitely superior to me in every moral sense". Yet all three had been forgotten. I was the first to write a biography in English of Jenny Marx, any biography of Mary Livingstone, and a full biography of Emma Darwin, though her daughter, Henrietta, had edited a collection of family letters which gives much of her background. Years later I wrote a fuller life of Emma since it was clear to me that while Darwin's fame had grown, Emma still remained relatively unknown.

Jenny, Karl Marx's wife, has been equally neglected. Beautiful and highly intelligent, she might have married a minor prince. Instead, she was wooed by a neighbour, clever young Karl Marx; but he had to wait seven years before he was allowed to marry the much sought-after Jenny. With extraordinary devotion she followed him from Trier, his birthplace, to Paris and then to Brussels, where in 1848 she witnessed the birth of the Communist Manifesto. She helped support him in his impoverished exile until finally they moved to London in the 1850s and settled in squalor in Soho, where they brought up two daughters and a son who later died. Their mother sent a young serving maid, Lenchen, who lived with them in their poverty. Devoted to them, she shared their misery and on one occasion must have shared Jenny's husband. Marx had sent his wife to beg support from her Dutch uncle Anton Philips, the founder of the electrical firm. (When I stood outside the house in Soho where they had lived, I was amused to see, on a nearby hoarding, an advertisement for Philips Electrical Company.) In her absence an illegitimate son was conceived. Engels, a successful businessman in Manchester, without whose financial and literary encouragement *Das Kapital* would probably never have been finished, was persuaded to pretend paternity of the child, who was given away for adoption. It was some years before the child's true paternity was acknowledged and he was discovered living in London. With all his faults as a husband, Marx was devoted to Jenny, and this had been presumably a rare lapse; in any event, finally Jenny forgave him, and her daughter, Eleanor, described how in the last year of Jenny's life they were like lovers once again. At her death, Marx was stricken. She is buried with her husband in Highgate Cemetery, over the wall from Holly Lodge Gardens. Yet in the history of Marxism Jenny scarcely has a face.

I have always believed in the importance of seeing the childhood background of my subjects, and I followed each of the three women to their homes. One holiday, I visited Marx's birthplace in Trier with Denis and imagined the young Karl walking through the vineyards with Jenny and her clever father, chanting Shakespeare and talking of Greek drama. On this visit to Trier we had been astonished to see hanging on the walls of the Marx Museum a letter from the British Labour Party refusing to contribute to the repair of the museum, signed "Denis Healey, Secretary of the International Department of the Labour Party". Were they expecting him?

In 1984 I had the chance to visit Moscow with Denis and Neil and Glenys Kinnock as guests of the Russian government on an official delegation. I took the opportunity to ask about Jenny Marx — and our hosts were surprised at my interest. She had the disadvantage in their eyes of aristocratic connections, being a descendant of a Duke of Argyll. I wanted to see what records they had of Jenny in their archives and, though I was told at our embassy that I should not get permission, our Russian hosts obligingly laid on a morning's visit to the archives and an interpreter to help me. It was an interesting glimpse into another side of Russian life but not, I am afraid, particularly useful. There was little about Jenny. For details of her life I had to trawl through many volumes of the Marx–Engels correspondence.

Emma Darwin, the most attractive of the three wives, well deserved the fuller life which I was later to give her. When I was writing *Wives of Fame*, I went to the Shropshire village of Maer, where she spent her childhood, and to nearby Shrewsbury, Charles Darwin's home town, to see the countryside in which he and his cousin Emma had grown up. (Darwin's paternal grandfather was the great scientist and poet Erasmus Darwin; his mother was the daughter of Josiah Wedgwood. Emma's father was Josiah, a son of the great potter. So Charles and Emma, both grandchildren of the elder Josiah, were first cousins.) I decided to travel from Shrewsbury to Maer on the top of a bus, a substitute for the ponies that used to carry the cousins between their homes. I alighted near Maer and asked a policeman, sitting in his car at the side of the road, how to get to Maer Hall. The policeman looked at me and said, "Don't I know you?" (I had recently been on television.) When I told him who I was, in alarm he lifted his car radio and telephoned his headquarters: "Guess who I've got here — Denis Healey's wife!" he said. "Has she no security?" came the reply. "None," he said. Back came the order: "Stay with her until she gets back on the train." I was obviously out of my senses! So for that part of my research I had a police escort who drove me to all the places I wished to visit. When working, I completely forget the present and am out of the real world. I had no idea how odd it must have seemed for a leading politician's wife to be wandering alone in the fields.

Emma was a brilliant musician, a good linguist, better educated than Charles and widely travelled. At first he had not dared to woo her; but after he returned from his famous tour of the world on the *Beagle* he was emboldened to propose to her, and was amazed that she accepted him. His moving tribute to her, written to his children at the end of his life, shows the depth of his love and her importance to him.

> You all know well your Mother and what a good Mother she has ever been to all of you. She has been my greatest blessing and I can declare that in my whole life I have never heard her utter one word which I had rather been unsaid. She has never failed in the kindest sympathy towards me, and has borne with the utmost patience my frequent complaints from ill health and discomfort. I do not believe she has ever missed an opportunity of doing a kind action to anyone near her. I marvel at my good fortune that she, so infinitely my superior in every single moral quality, consented to be my wife. She has been my wise adviser and cheerful comforter throughout life, which without her would have been during a very long period a miserable one from ill health. She

has earned the love and admiration of every soul near her.

Yet, when I recently wrote a fuller life of this remarkable woman, I was still often asked "Did Darwin have a wife?"

Mary Livingstone, my third subject, was to lead me to another new life — as a writer and presenter of television documentaries.

After I had given a lecture at the Livingstone Museum in Scotland, describing the importance to David of his forgotten wife, Mary, the religious affairs director of Scottish Television, the Reverend Nelson Gray, asked me to write and present a television documentary on her life. Emboldened by ignorance, I agreed, and drafted a wordy synopsis. "And where do you think all those words are going?" asked the director, Jim McCann. "TV is about pictures."

So, with the help of John Goldsmith, the counsellor and friend who had edited *Lady Unknown*, a new script was written; and before I knew what had happened I was setting off with a film crew on a month's trip to Africa, following in Mary's footsteps from her missionary parents' home in Kuruman to the Kalahari Desert with her husband, David Livingstone. Looking back, I am amazed to realize that I left Denis for four weeks when he was totally preoccupied with his campaign for the deputy leadership of the Labour Party.

298

As a novice presenter I had much to learn. After my first attempt, the director and crew stood in embarrassed silence. I was standing by the spring at the Kuruman mission station in South Africa where Mary was born, declaiming as though from a platform to a Literary Society. Wisely, John Gould, the young sound man, suggested: "Play it back to her and she'll hear what she is doing." He was right; I did. "Television is one to one," said Jim McCann, the director; "tell it to your mother at home." So, with advice from him and his cameraman, I became more at ease. We rarely needed lights, but Hector, the electrician, carried a great white screen and became "Hector the Reflector". My unhappiest moments were spent standing at the slippery edge of the Victoria Falls while Jim — a long way off — shouted through his walkie-talkie, "Forward, move forward!" and the foaming spray urged me to my death. Aptly named in Africa Mosewatunga, "the smoke that thunders", the falls were breathtaking, especially when at four o'clock each evening they were arched by a sparkling rainbow. To photograph this the assistant cameraman was held over the edge. I shut my eyes.

Jim, a sensitive director, insisted that I should go alone for my first sight of the little mission house built with their own hands by Mary's parents, the missionaries Mary and Robert Moffat. Jim had set the scene in the Moffats' study; the shadow of a bearded man flickered on the walls in the firelight, while a soft Scots voice read from his translation of the Bible. Jim had found it unutterably moving and knew that I would too. I was glad to be alone and taken back more than a hundred years.

The Revd Nelson Gray, the "Wee Rev", was a constant source of encouragement and amusement, even when we got into difficulties. At the beginning of our adventure he drove John Gould and me from Johannesburg to Kuruman in a hired car following the van bearing Jim, the crew and the equipment. On a long, dark, silent road through a forest, we lost the van and ran out of petrol, then severely rationed. Nelson commanded: "Edna, as a white woman you should get out and stop the next car." I did not follow his reasoning but obeyed and waited, trembling, fearing snakes more than people, until a van stopped. Silently the enormous driver hitched our car to his vehicle and pulled us to Kuruman, where Jim and the crew were waiting apprehensively. To have lost the wife of a famous politician in the dark heart of Africa would have been some achievement.

The young Scottish weaver David Livingstone had come to Kuruman as a missionary. Having married Mary, he took her to help him build a new mission station at the edge of the Kalahari Desert. We followed them there, hiring an ox wagon in which I sat, thinking myself Mary as, with young children and pregnant again, she prepared to set out with him to cross the unknown desert in search of a fabled great river, the Zambezi. Somewhere in the limitless waste ahead she must find shelter to have her baby. Soon afterwards they had to find a place to bury the infant. We filmed at the site of their first home, slashing away the thorn bushes to find the baby's grave. A pile of rubble is all that remains of the house they built with their own hands. A brass plaque marks the site: on it, the inscription, "David Livingstone lived here". Not a mention of Mary! No word of the wife who helped build the house and brought up the children in this desert, who shooed away wild beasts from the door when David was sitting comfortably, who struggled up through the thorn trees on hot afternoons to the school she ran for African women where she talked to them in their own language, which she spoke fluently. I was angry, and this time my piece to camera came straight from the heart.

With the help of Jim and the crew I became more comfortable as a presenter. "Sit on that log and write two short sentences and learn them," Jim ordered, "while I go and look for elephants." "Shut your mouth when you have finished speaking," advised the cameraman, "then I know you have stopped." I gradually improved, though I know there were times when Jim wished Scottish TV had sent what he called "a proper actress" who would be happy to do her bit to camera, unclip the microphone, go away and be quiet — not a writer and researcher who wanted to take an interpreter and talk to the village women in their huts. However, thanks to Jim and the crew, *Mrs Livingstone, I Presume* won an award from the Radio Industries Club of Scotland as the Best Single Factual Programme in 1981, and also a silver medal in New York.

Encouraged by the success of *Mrs Livingstone*, STV asked me to do a similar film on the Scottish missionary Mary Slessor, who had worked devotedly for Nigeria's people for many years in the early nineteenth century. This meant another month's filming, this time in Nigeria — an even more demanding experience than before. The resulting *One More River* also won awards and, I hope, recognition of a most remarkable woman. Nigeria in 1983 still bore the marks of the Biafra civil war, the country disorganized and even dangerous. However, I had remembered my Sunday School prize for attendance, given at the Coleford Baptist Chapel, *Mary Slessor, the White Queen of the Okoyong*, and was thrilled at the thought of following her to the land where she had died.

A tough little red-haired Dundee Scot, Mary Slessor had bravely fought against cruelty, particularly towards women. Among the Okoyong at that time, twins were considered the product of union with the devil and were killed at birth. She rescued many of them: the descendant of one still lives. She taught a gospel of loving kindness with fierce determination, confronting drunken and angry chiefs, travelling with her family of little adopted children, paddling up rivers and on one occasion whacking with a saucepan a hippo that attacked her boat. Teacher, doctor, nurse and later administrator, she left a legacy that is still remembered. Our visit fortunately coincided with the anniversary of her arrival in Nigeria, so we could film hundreds of women singing and dancing, wearing T-shirts decorated with her picture, twins in her arms, and thronging through the streets of Calabar to the remembrance service in the church.

Ted Williams, the director of this film, coped with a steady nerve with all the difficulties that beset us. From the beginning there had been dangers. At Lagos I had been sent ahead alone to the hotel in a taxi while the crew struggled with officials to get the equipment out of the airport. My taxi was stopped on a lonely road by thugs dressed as soldiers who bullied the driver, demanding to know what I had brought from England. I sat quietly, hoping to escape notice, and we were finally released. The terrified driver must have bribed them. Next day, the plane to Calabar had run out of fuel and we had to wait for hours. I sat on my case, surrounded by our equipment, reminding myself of Denis's advice: "When in difficulty, sit quiet and let it wash over you." Finally, a Nigerian bishop who had been sent to greet us came to our aid and sent us scurrying across the tarmac to the plane — someone had found fuel.

Our hotel at Calabar was equipped with radio, television and a refrigerator — but they rarely worked, since electricity came only in fits and starts. Lights, however, came on for long enough to show the enormous cockroaches. I had been warned that here, standing on their hind legs, they were big enough to drink from a pint mug. The next morning, as we drove to the first shoot, we saw a dead body lying by the roadside. When we returned that night it was still there, but covered by a sheet — and there it stayed for the next two days. No one dared remove it in case they were implicated in the death. This was the background for the rest of our stay.

In spite of the dangers and difficulties, the warmth of the welcome we received from Nigerian church members revived my spirits. The descendants of Mary's adopted son joined us for some of our tour, and sang and prayed with us before her grave in the little cemetery at Calabar. I prize the gift they gave me: carved sticks used as tooth-brushes in an embroidered bag. I felt honoured to interview Dr Francis Ibiam, the distinguished Nigerian who, taught by Mary, had gone to Aberdeen University to train as a doctor and returned to practise in his home country. When he came to have lunch with me in Calabar, the surprised hotel waiters knelt in reverence.

One day we paddled a canoe up a shallow river to an island where Mary had built a school and church. The villagers were waiting and greeted me with much ululating as our canoe approached the shore. "They're going to carry you ashore, Edna," the cameraman warned with much relish. And so they did — as they had done to Ma Slessor. Four enormous Nigerians bore me aloft on to the island to welcoming shouts of "Ma Slessor, Ma Slessor!" To them I was "Ma" returned from the grave. They sang hymns she had taught their people decades earlier and, to my amazement, I heard one old familiar tune sung in moving African harmony. As I looked at the crowd of singers, among them a lady wearing a Portuguese tall hat and a man dressed — in the sweltering heat — in full evening dress with top hat, I felt how barbaric to them must have seemed the costumes of the Western world. But they wore them to pay us a compliment in memory of their beloved "Ma Slessor".

One of the oddest occasions was a village ceremony at which the chief, wearing a woollen crown and in full ceremonial costume, received us and blessed us with a libation of Gordon's gin poured on the ground. An interpreter introduced the team one by one. I was "Edna Healey, the presenter and writer — and, incidentally, also the wife of Denis Healey". Immediately he heard this, the traditional tribal chief vanished. "I remember hearing him speak when I was at the LSE in London!" he said, astonished, in excellent English. Then he blessed us with new enthusiasm.

The most moving moment in making the film came when we were following Mary to her last home, deep in the African forest. The director had come earlier to ask the chief's permission to film in his village. He was dying: his son, now a lawyer in America, had come home for the expected funeral. However, the old chief promised he would stay alive "until Mrs Healey comes to make her film". I interviewed him and he told me the story of how, as a little boy, he had gone to fetch the doctor when Mary Slessor was dying. He remembered her well, and sang for us in his quavering voice a hymn she had taught him. To hear the old words and tune I remembered from my Baptist childhood sung in the dark African hut touched me deeply.

That day I stood in the forest on the site on which Mary had built her house. She had made the cement for the floor, laid it with her own hands and then, looking up, had ordered the Lord: "Now Feyther, you set it."

Standing there in the silence of the forest I remembered her last letters, written here in the Great War which had brought her such sadness. She had not heard from friends for a long time. In her loneliness she had remembered her home in Scotland and how her mother had sent her to church with a clean handkerchief and a peppermint to suck during the sermon; and how she had welcomed gifts from Scotland, especially the scented soap. "Missionaries are not made of iron," she wrote. Remembering her words, "We are travelling not towards death but to the East and the sunrise," I wrote what I hoped were moving words and prepared myself to speak for her when we returned the next day.

To our horror, as we rounded the bend in the path we saw that the chief had ordered the forest undergrowth to be scythed: my silent wood was now covered with bright flags from tree to tree and a bevy of grass-skirted women were waiting there with whistles and drums to dance for us. The poignancy of Mary's last moments had vanished. With all the tact the director could muster, he persuaded the welcome party to let us remove the flags after a token amount of filming and tried to recall the earlier mood. But the magic had gone.

Filming in Nigeria had its horrors. Food was scarce, communication with home difficult. I had managed with difficulty to get a message to Denis through an

English engineer from an oil company: "It's the survival of the fattest." War in Nigeria had destroyed buildings and palm plantations. Life in the interior was still primitive, still disfigured by much cruelty. Yet though I wanted to kiss the English soil on our return, when it looked as though the crew would have to return because some film was fogged I immediately asked to go with them. In spite of our difficulties I had learned to love Africa and our African friends. Fortunately, it turned out not to be necessary.

Our film, shown on Scottish TV as *One More River*, won an award as the Best Religious Film of the Year. Though she died in 1915, Mary Slessor has never been forgotten in Calabar. At the airport in Lagos an African porter had told me: "She lives in Calabar." Coming as we had during her anniversary celebration, we had shown how true this was. I hoped our film would revive memory of a remarkable woman.

I had enjoyed my foray into the documentary film world and only wished I had started when I was younger. However, I returned to my writing encouraged and renewed.

CHAPTER
TWELVE

THE CRUCIAL YEARS,
1979–1983

The years from 1979 to 1983 were crucial in the history of the Labour Party and, indeed, of the country; for us, they were years of great change, not only in our political life but also in our family affairs. It was a time of beginnings and endings, of deaths and entrances, of personal tragedies and, for me, the growth of my new career. It will be convenient to describe these parallel lives separately, but it should always be remembered that behind the public life of politicians there is a private life, and that when, as often happens, the demands conflict, the stress can be intolerable. We were fortunate that our happy and stable family life was a support for Denis in these testing years.

Those readers who find the arcane world of party politics a desolate landscape may wish to take a quick gallop through this chapter. For them, I give here a brief summary of what happened: for those brave souls who can bear the tedium, and for myself, I must also try to explain in more detail through the remainder of the chapter why and how these events unfolded as they did.

After Margaret Thatcher's victory in May 1979 Jim Callaghan remained leader of the Labour Party in opposition until November 1980. Then, in the contest for the party leadership, Michael Foot defeated Denis — who had been expected to win, and thus to become Prime Minister if Labour won the next election. In 1981 Denis defeated Tony Benn in the contest for the deputy leadership: had Denis lost, there would have been a massive exodus from the centre and right of the Labour Party into the new Social Democratic Party and a parallel move to an unelectable extreme left. As it was, in the years following 1981, the fightback began to return the Labour Party to ground on which the "sane left", as Barbara Castle called it, could work together with the centre and right of the party.

Meanwhile, from 1981 to 1983 a party so riven by bitter faction-fighting and policy disagreement forfeited support in the country — just as Margaret Thatcher's success in the Falklands War bolstered support for the Tories. Labour lost the general election of 1983, and more than another decade of Conservative government until the Labour revival, under the combined leadership of Neil Kinnock and Roy Hattersley, paved the way for victory under Blair in 1997.

Since other political parties have suffered similar, apparently terminal, breakdowns and recoveries, and since Labour's fate in these years was of such importance in our own lives as well as in the history of the party, I must look back and record these events in more detail.

★　★　★

After the 1979 election Jim Callaghan was persuaded to stay on for eighteen months as leader of the Labour Party — expecting and wishing Denis to succeed him, but, as he said, wanting to "take the shine off the ball" for him. In fact, as Denis wrote, "it took not only the shine but the leather too". Even after defeat, Jim was still popular in the country, and the cheers and affectionate good wishes from the general public were balm to his bruised spirit. He was not in a hurry to go, and it was not until 15 October 1980 that he announced his resignation. Meanwhile the extreme left gained ground.

The party conference in Brighton in October 1979 was rancorous with bitter feuds and vicious recriminations. One trade union leader welcomed me cheerfully with: "There'll be blood on the carpet this week, Edna!" Nevertheless, Denis greeted Tony Benn, the rising star of the left, with the usual cheerful bonhomie that always overlay their mutual wariness, and obliged the press with a photograph: Denis and Tony shooting each other — with their cameras! But there was not much good humour around at that conference. The militant left were on the march. They had been steadily gaining ground in local constituencies, drawing with them many of the more moderate and idealistic left, so that now they largely controlled the election of the constituency members of the National Executive which arranged and chaired the annual conference and planned the future programme of the Labour Party. As a result, the NEC at this conference of 1979 was dominated by the left wing of the party; and it was here that two resolutions were passed which were to be of vital importance to the future of the party and which were to alter the course of our own lives.

The first of these was a resolution to give local parties the power to deselect their MPs between general elections — a power which some on the left wing of the party would use later to persuade or even to bully their members not to support Denis in the leadership election. He himself had firmly established the right to independence in his own constituency, quoting the reply of Frederick the Great's general to his king's demands: "Please tell His Majesty, that after the battle my head is at his disposal, but during the battle I propose to use it in His service." Mandatory reselection, as it was called, by a minority of the constituency was, he considered, not democracy. Labour MPs represented 11.5 million voters, whereas Labour Party constituency members at that time numbered fewer than 300,000. Now, a minority of dedicated Labour members could deselect a Member of Parliament who had been elected by the constituency as a whole.

The second decision of the 1979 Brighton Conference, equally important in the leadership election, was to set up a commission in the new year to decide on a new electoral college, which would in future elect the leader and the deputy leader of the Labour Party — hitherto elected by the votes of Labour MPs alone. This commission recommended a new constitution, with an electoral college composed of

311

trade unions, constituency members, the socialist societies and Labour Members of Parliament.

Together, these proposals meant that Labour MPs would no longer have sole choice of a future Labour Prime Minister and that their local parties could deselect them should they vote the "wrong" way or refuse to disclose their vote. The two resolutions would not be ratified until the following Labour Party conference, in October 1980. It was therefore in the interests of Denis's opponents to encourage Jim Callaghan to delay his departure as leader of the Labour Party until after the next party conference, so that his successor could be chosen by the new rules. Similarly, it was important for Denis that the election should take place under the old rules.

In the new year of 1980 Jim decided to call a conference to discuss the defeat of 1979 and to plan the future. This was probably a mistake; the mood was bitter, and what Denis's biographer, Edward Pearce, describes as "the new brutishness" was "very much on show".

Denis, speaking in the afternoon, took the podium to cries of "Out, out, out!" Beginning his speech, "Comrade Chairman, friends and those who shouted 'Out, out'," he robustly lambasted "those who would keep the Tories in power" unless "every dot and comma of their own particular ideology is accepted . . . in the next election manifesto". Labour would not win again "if we go on ideological ego trips or accept the clapped-out dogmas which are now being trailed by the Toytown Trotskyists of the Militant Tendency". By sheer force of personality and power of argument, Denis finally dominated the conference; at the end there were more cheers than boos, and even opponents were impressed. As Susan Crosland recalled in her life of Tony, "It was a *tour de force*." But there were "Toytown Trotskyists" and others who would never forgive Denis.

For many on the right and centre the Labour Party seemed lost in a nightmare of destructive hate, but others of the extreme left saw a rising dawn when the ideologically pure would march to the beat of the Red Flag to a dream world where the gallant constituency members would rule the Party. At one blast of the trumpet they believed the towers of capitalism would collapse. Michael Foot and Barbara Castle and "the sane left" listened to the wild cheers of a motley band with increasing impatience and hostility. They knew from experience the stern reality of power.

Many right-wing Labour members had become increasingly disenchanted and were looking for an excuse to break altogether with the Labour Party. The bitter Wembley conference was the last straw for those, like Shirley Williams, who saw the inevitable destruction of the Labour Party as they knew it. David Owen listened to speeches like that of Terry Fields "with his gorge rising". He was appalled not only by the rancour but also by the prospect of a new constitution that would increase the power of the militant left. It was at the Wembley conference that David Owen, Bill Rodgers and Shirley Williams decided that the time had come to make a break. Roy Jenkins, watching from his new post

313

at Brussels, agreed. He was already considering the formation of a new party.

For many of those who were determined to remain, Denis Healey seemed the obvious successor to Jim Callaghan. He was popular in the country. In opinion polls he was rated highly — even above Margaret Thatcher. He had an excellent international reputation. His early experience in the army and in the Labour Party's International Department had given him unrivalled knowledge of the world, and his expertise in foreign affairs was acknowledged on all sides of the House. Direct and unpompous, he was nationally recognizable — his image boosted by Mike Yarwood's television imitation, complete with shaggy eyebrows and distinctive voice — and he was usually greeted in the streets with a smile, even after his Budgets. Though his career at the Treasury had started uncertainly, at the end he had been acclaimed by the members of the IMF as the best Chancellor among them. It was not only his devoted wife who saw him as the obvious choice for Prime Minister.

During the campaign that began in October 1980 he had an excellent, experienced team, "the lynchpin" as Denis wrote, the Flint MP, Barry Jones, now in the Lords. Observant, sensitive and totally loyal to Denis, he could not have done more to promote his cause. I particularly welcomed his kindness and concern for me during this trying period.

On 1 October 1980, at the Blackpool conference, Giles Radice pledged his support and became Denis's campaign manager. The son of a businessman, Giles was educated at Winchester, a public school which produced a number of Labour politicians, including Hugh Gaitskell and Dick Crossman. Unlike Chris Mayhew, Giles never felt encumbered by his middle-class background; he had an easy relationship with his constituency and with the unions which his fellow Wykehamists would never quite achieve. After Oxford he became head of research at the General and Municipal Workers' Union and was one of their sponsored MPs, sitting for Chester-le-Street in 1973 and later for Durham North. So he balanced his middle-class background and education with a deep understanding of working-class politics. His benign face, under a shock of prematurely white hair, gave him the look of a Wizard of Oz or a biblical patriarch. He was direct, honourable and much respected; it was his misfortune to come to political maturity during Labour's years in the wilderness: he belonged to that generation of talented politicians who, in the long wasteland of opposition, would never reach the political heights they deserved.

His marriage to his clever and vital wife, Lisanne, and his happy family life gave him the stability which supported him through the trying years ahead. Lisanne, a talented writer and lecturer, is a much-loved and important partner in his political life. At Bournemouth in 1985 he reflected, "It is always lovely for me to have her calming presence at a conference," and he dedicated his *Diaries* "To Lisanne, without whose support my political life would not have been possible."

315

Giles had been a member of the Fabian Society when Shirley Williams was its chairman, and had been her parliamentary private secretary in 1978 when she was Minister of Education. At the time of the leadership election Giles, like Denis, spent many hours trying to persuade her not to leave the Labour Party. Had Denis won, I believe she would have stayed.

Eric Varley, another key member of Denis's team, was one of the most promising politicians of his generation. Elected MP for Chesterfield in 1964, four years later he had become Wilson's PPS, sharing his centre-left views with many of the Bevanites, and was well on his way up the ladder at forty-seven when Labour lost the 1979 election. After Labour's defeat he joined the fight against Militant and gained a place on the NEC. He once described himself as "an extreme centrist". Quiet, upright and competent, he was a great source of strength in the leadership campaign. Had Denis succeeded, he would undoubtedly have won high office.

One of the most active of Denis's supporters was Roy Hattersley. An acclaimed writer, whose skilful pen was used to great effect during the campaign, he was a fellow Yorkshireman and had much in common with Denis — a north-country realism and directness, a dry humour and a deep-rooted loyalty to the Labour Party. He had been involved in Labour politics since his Sheffield boyhood, influenced by his mother Enid, the city's formidable mayor. At Hull University he was chairman of the University Labour Club, and his seven years' experience as a young Sheffield City councillor after that gave him a lasting understanding that politics is the art of the possible. At the age of thirty-two he became MP for Birmingham Sparkbrook, and rapidly rose to ministerial rank in the Wilson government. Later, as Denis's Minister for Defence Administration, and in opposition in 1972 as Shadow Minister of Defence, he showed the outstanding ability that might well have led him to the leadership of the Labour Party. He was forty-three and heading for the top when Labour lost the 1979 election. Had Denis become leader he would certainly have been promoted; they had worked well together when Denis was Minister of Defence.

In addition to these political heavyweights, Denis had invaluable financial advice from his old Treasury team, led by Joel Barnett, MP for Heywood and Royton, who had been Treasury Chief Secretary when Denis was Chancellor, and Edmund Dell, who, as Secretary of State for Trade, had played a vital part in the IMF negotiations. We had known Edmund's brother Sidney in the Labour Club in our Oxford days. Very able but unassuming, he was a great loss to the Labour Party when he left Parliament in 1978 and subsequently joined the SDP.

Denis had come top in the Shadow Cabinet poll and was expected by some to be elected unopposed in Callaghan's place. In the event, there were four candidates. Michael Foot, the darling of the left, was widely admired in the party. Peter Shore, an academic former head of research at Transport House, was popular with anti-Common Market members. At times surprisingly eloquent, he could produce bursts of Churchillian oratory in defence of our island, that "precious stone set in a silver sea". Those on the left who opposed the Common Market could forgive him his otherwise right-wing views; but he was a shadow in the public mind. The fourth candidate was John Silkin, a wealthy solicitor married to the film actress Rosamund John; he too had made little impact on either the party or the general public. He was not expected to be serious competition for Denis.

Foot was the only serious rival — and he had been reluctant to stand. His wife, Jill, was said to have persuaded him that to stand aside would be letting the party down. I hardly knew her — we had only once been guests at their dinner table — but I had liked her and admired her as a film-maker and had been waiting impatiently for her history of the suffragettes which, alas, was never to appear. Michael always spoke with a deep love of her beauty and intelligence, and she had considerable influence on him.

Already sixty-seven, and appearing more frail than he was, Foot seemed an improbable leader, though regarded with great affection by the Labour Party and with some respect across the floor of the chamber. It was suggested by those on the left who opposed Denis that Michael might be an effective leader in opposition and could retire in favour of Neil Kinnock or Tony Benn later on. His roots are deep in the same soil as my own, west of England Nonconformity. Radical yet liberal in the widest sense of the word, he combines a deep understanding of history with a prophet's vision

318

of the future. He was one of the great parliamentary orators, speaking with passion, yet often with humour too, as when he rose to attack the Tories: "Look at them, these unlikely novices for a new Trappist order, these bashful tiptoeing ghosts, these pale effigies of what were once sentient human beings, these unlarynxed wraiths, these ectoplasmic apparitions, these sphinxlike sentinels at our debates — why are they here?" Often he spoke with a rapier wit that deflated opposition; but he possessed a fundamental gentleness that endeared him to the Labour Party and even to his opponents.

But, like Alec Douglas-Home, he was diminished by television. No one seeing him shambling across Hampstead Heath with his stick and his little dog could imagine him, like Wilson, leading a "white-hot technological revolution", and it was easy to mock the figure in the "duffel coat" among the warriors at the Cenotaph. Jill tried her best to improve his image, but complained that in two minutes Michael could turn a jacket from Harrods into a jumble-sale bargain. Those who watched him, lost among his papers, chairing a committee, often despaired.

In the first round of the two-stage election by the PLP, Denis led with 112 votes to Michael's 83. Silkin and Shore were eliminated with 38 and 32 votes respectively. Denis made no comment to me, but I knew he was disappointed; he knew Michael could pick up enough left-wing votes to defeat him on the second ballot. Memory plays tricks. Barry Jones assures me that at this point I rang him in great distress and foreboding for a twenty-minute conversation. I do not remember this at all. In my memory I was calm and stoical. Knowing how Denis would hate leading the party in opposition, with all the bitterness and argument it would entail, I remember half-dreading his victory.

So, on the grey afternoon of 10 November 1980, the scene was set for the event that was to change the history of the party and our own lives. I waited in the House of Commons Families' Room for the declaration of the result, which would be announced to the parliamentary Labour Party in the Grand Committee Room in the House of Commons. Denis, meanwhile, waited with Barry Jones in the little office next to Foot's on the Shadow Cabinet corridor; the result would be brought to them at 5.55 — five minutes before it was announced to the parliamentary party. Denis remembers the tense moments, hearing the footsteps along the corridor as the messenger, Phyllis Burt from the whips' office, stopped first at Michael's door, knowing well what this meant, and bracing himself as he opened the envelope she brought. Then he walked along to the Grand Committee Room, where, as he remembered in his autobiography,

The moment the result was announced I rose to congratulate Michael, and announced that I would be proud to serve under him as Deputy Leader if the Party wished, as I knew he would have served under me if I had won. There was a great storm of cheering and banging of desks. I glanced at Tony

320

Benn. His face was ashen. So I knew I had done at least one thing right.

Barry, kind and considerate as always, came to the Families' Room to bring me the result. Harriet, Denis's loyal secretary, came in in tears — and, to my surprise and pleasure, Michael Foot's wife, Jill, joined us, greeting me with a hug and "I'm so sorry". For myself, knowing what lay ahead, disappointment was mingled with relief, and I suspect that Jill's pleasure was not unmixed.

Our good friend Frank Giles, then the editor of the *Sunday Times*, had heard from his reporters that "Edna was distressed and thoroughly unhappy . . . Denis was completely stoical." Pearce quotes Ian Aitken, political editor of the *Guardian* and old-time Bevanite, as enthusing: "It's marvellous . . . I'm delighted . . ." but then adding ". . . though it will be a disaster for the Party."

While most of the press followed the rather shaken Michael Foot out of Westminster Hall, one cameraman followed us and caught the sight of our backs disappearing through the door of our flat. As we ate our quiet supper, Denis, still showing no emotion, said steadily, "Well, back to the drawing board." Neither then nor at any time did he show bitterness or resentment.

Why did Denis Healey become "the best Prime Minister we never had"? He was generally acknowledged to be supremely equipped for the job, and he had friends and admirers in England and all over the world.

321

But he was a doughty warrior who battled sometimes too roughly: even his friends could be sharply stung by a well-directed arrow that left its irritant poison; even his wife sometimes did not escape. I sometimes felt as though I were accompanied by a great dog, leaping joyously at friend and foe alike, saying, "He's only playing, he doesn't mean to hurt." As his staunch supporter Roy Hattersley wrote, "He bites your legs." It went against the grain with him to canvass support from colleagues, and though he was deeply grateful to those who worked so hard for him, I doubt whether he often thought to tell them so.

Also — oddly, perhaps, for one who is so sure of himself — he is always a reluctant self-promoter. On the contrary, he would often deliberately downgrade himself, pretend to be old and shambling, pull a mad face, or, to my constant annoyance, choose to use coarse or brutal language — inexplicable in one so sensitive to the beauty of poetry. His temper, too, usually under tight control, could sometimes flare with an explosion of strong language — as had recently happened in the chamber of the Commons, losing him some supporters. And he had also made many enemies on the left who were determined to prevent his becoming leader.

Looking back on the history of this period, I cannot help wondering whether I should have taken more part in the Healey campaign, and feeling some guilt that I had been content to be merely a quiet support. But I am assured that I could not have made much difference. The truth was that he had not a burning desire to be Prime Minister, and that I could not have given him. Yet had he been elected he would have given all his formidable talent and energy to the job and would have done it well. My own greatest regret is not that he never became Prime Minister, but that he never became Foreign Secretary, a job for which he was supremely equipped and for which he had long hoped.

The election of Michael Foot was a complete disaster for the Labour Party, as even one left-winger, Eric Heffer, recognized when he said to me later, "What fools we were not to vote for Denis!" Many others told Barry the same story.

This was a time when I lost patience with the Labour Party. I thought their decision was just plain daft, and for the first time, like many of my friends, seriously considered following those who were about to break away. I was persuaded to remain by Denis's arguments. I remembered how, long ago, when he was International Secretary at Labour Party headquarters, he had watched with despair the disintegration of the Italian Socialist Party, the PSLI, into *piselli* — little peas. Now he prophesied that the same would happen to the SDP; and he was right.

On the night of his defeat as party leader Denis had immediately been elected deputy leader. He summed up the position in which he now found himself:

As Deputy Leader, I was now ex-officio a member of the National Executive and of the Liaison Committee with the TUC, as well as of the

Shadow Cabinet. I was also Shadow Foreign Secretary. In fact, from the Leadership election in October 1980 to the General Election in June 1983 I was as busy as I had been at the Treasury — but with far less to show for it.

Denis was not a patient member of the NEC. Not the best of listeners at the best of times and with an almost pathological hatred of wasting time, he would while away the tedious hours cutting articles from newspapers, slashing away with what we called his "snickerskee", a small razor blade. My sympathies were with the committee: I suffered this performance at every breakfast. He collected clippings — usually from the *Financial Times* — for his files, and would apparently be deaf to all around him until challenged, when he would reel back, as on a tape recorder, all that had been said in the last half-hour. This trick had its uses. When on one occasion in the NEC Benn was extolling the virtues of the "alternative strategy" of his guru, Wynn Godley, Denis, apparently unheeding, was snipping out a newspaper cutting; looking up, he asked if Tony could mention one reputable economist who supported him, and then solemnly read out the cutting in hand — a letter from Godley explaining the difficulties of the "alternative strategy".

A more agreeable activity, in addition to his regular visits to the constituency, was the travels round the country he made as deputy leader. At this time polls showed him as one of the most highly regarded of politicians; this public popularity was comforting in the trying and exhausting years as deputy leader. His bushy eyebrows made him instantly recognizable, and his genuine love of people — especially of children — made him easily accessible. Walking in his wake, I invariably caught the wash of pleased recognition — our children called it "the look" — and again and again the comment, "Well, that's made my day!" He never minded acting the fool, whether with Dame Edna Everage or other comedians of the day, and Mike Yarwood's brilliant mimicry — he caught the singular quality of Denis's voice (our daughter Jenny called it the "fluff on the needle"), with its undercurrent of Yorkshire — actually increased his popularity. To those of his critics who found his enjoyment of foolery childish and lacking in seriousness, he would retort: "Except ye be as little children ye shall not enter the kingdom of heaven." And when erudition or high seriousness was demanded, he could always — as he says — "wipe the smile off their faces".

As Shadow Foreign Secretary he kept up his foreign contacts with visits abroad, fulfilling some engagements he had made as Chancellor, and sometimes I was able to go with him. He loved to chat to passers-by or fellow travellers, find out where they came from and use his wide knowledge of the world to relate to them. He would easily slip into another language to talk with knowledge of their homelands: an Italian waiter would be regaled with a joke in his regional dialect, Neapolitan, Tuscan or Venetian. His Italian, acquired during the war, was fluent, his French and German almost equally good; but he also had learned something

325

of the language of every country he had visited. He always joked that he could say in every language, "In the name of the Labour Party I wish you a successful congress" and "I love you, beautiful lady" — but that he had to take care not to confuse them! This linguistic skill was immensely useful, though it made Roy Jenkins call him, with some irritation, "Mr Knowall". "He was annoying," Roy once said, "even when he knew more than I. His assurance when he knew less was intolerable."

From the outset, the role of deputy leader was exhausting; but the months from April to October 1981 were, as Denis wrote, "the busiest and least agreeable of my life". For, encouraged by his growing support, Tony Benn now decided to challenge Denis for the deputy leadership of the Labour Party. He chose to announce his decision at the bizarre time of 3.40a.m., appropriately on April Fool's Day. Denis heard the news in Hamburg, where he was speaking on the Common Market in his capacity as Shadow Foreign Secretary. The next day, in Bonn, he was officially asked for the second time to accept nomination as Secretary-General of NATO; again he refused. "It was not a lonely impulse of delight which kept me in politics," he later wrote, quoting his favourite poet, Yeats. "It was my dogged determination to do my duty." Aware that Tony, in spite of the caricatures of his round-eyed madness, was no April Fool, and conscious that in the contest for the leadership he had not fought as hard as he might have, this time he did: "and it was all for the sake of a job which I found disagreeable and which in itself was not worth having" — in other words, for the sake of his ineradicable loyalty to the party. Above all, to have taken an easy escape route at this point would have been betraying old friends in his Leeds constituency, like Douglas Gabb and the loyal engineer Jack Gallivan who at the difficult Brighton conference of 1979 had been given the Labour Party Award for Long Service.

In this campaign Denis used all his formidable skills, his powerful intellect and personality, and the Irish fighting spirit. There were radio or television interviews almost every day, three or four meetings with trade unions and constituency parties every week — all in addition to his continuing constituency work as a Leeds MP, meetings of the Shadow Cabinet and travels as Shadow Foreign Secretary.

This time around, Denis had an extra and invaluable assistant. Richard Heller was a friend of our son Tim, a frustrated civil servant who, longing to strike a blow at Mrs Thatcher's government, offered Denis his services as research assistant. They met, Richard recalled in his unpublished memoirs, "in a dismal waiting room in Westminster Hall, then the man said, 'The pay is rotten, the conditions are terrible and the prospects are negligible,' and I said, 'You don't have to talk me into it.' I was hired."

Heller liked to describe his job as "American style 'chief of staff' or, in the elegant French, 'chef de cabinet' ". In fact, as he wrote, Denis was "a senior politician running a major campaign, managing with one secretary — the indefatigable Harriet Shackman — and one dogsbody".

I did whatever had to be done each day, with no opportunity to delegate. One morning, after an all-night voting session, I discovered that Denis had been locked into his office after snatching a nap on the couch. He said, "Richard, I have the most awful job to ask you to do." Finding himself locked in, he had been forced to answer a call of nature in a water bottle. He asked me to dispose of this. I can now claim to be the only person who has ever taken the piss out of Denis Healey.

During the leadership campaign Denis's supporters had complained to Richard that "Denis had placed too much reliance on MPs recognizing that he was the best leader". This time, Richard saw to it that "everybody who wanted something from Denis got something, and with the electoral college that meant not only MPs but any local ward party or trade union branch and even individual Labour party members. Everyone got a letter ... an article ... a signed photograph ... replies to questions."

Benn, as Richard wrote, had already cornered the vote in the constituencies. "His supporters were well-organised to take over branches and committees — often simply by boring ordinary party members into going home before the vital votes were taken. Sometimes they used veiled threats or outright hostility and I can well recall the characteristic low hissing in local party meetings of any speaker who supported Denis." In addition, "Benn had about 60 or 70 people working non-stop on his campaign, all well dug into the Labour party. Denis had me and Harriet."

However, inexperienced politically though Richard was, no *chef de cabinet* could have worked more tirelessly, more loyally or with such good humour. With Barry Jones, he kept in touch with MPs and with the former excellent team of the Healey campaign committee in the Shadow Cabinet — Eric Varley, Roy Hattersley and Giles Radice — and learned from their experience. He also valued the support given to Denis by old friends like Merlyn Rees. Merlyn held the neighbouring seat in Leeds, and Richard found him invaluable "for his honesty and the respect he commanded across the party", and for advice on problems in the Leeds area. Also, as one of Jim Callaghan's closest friends, he was Richard's "best channel for approaching Jim", whom surprisingly Richard found "forbidding". As he wrote, "Giles never turned down any of the chores in the campaign. He edited a pamphlet based on Denis's best recent speeches and articles, called *Socialism with a Human Face*, which offered a reference point for 'Healeyism'. For such a giant mind, Denis himself had always been oddly reluctant to define himself ideologically. Even more than Roy Hattersley, Giles turned the Healey campaign into a battle of ideas, and in doing so persuaded us all that it was a moral necessity to win."

Richard shrewdly notes that "one of the unintended consequences of the Deputy Leadership contest was to give Denis, for the first time in his career, a solid base of support in the Trade Union movement". One of the people, according to Richard, who can take credit for that was

> John Golding MP from the Post Office Engineering Union, who had organised the lonely resistance to the left on the NEC. An ex-whip and an ex-Employment junior minister, John . . . had many personal friends on the Left of the union movement, particularly those with a shared interest in fishing, horseracing and greyhounds . . . David Warburton — a combative down-to-earth speaker and writer, always ready to mix it with the Bennites — was indispensable.

During this campaign I saw more of David and other trade unionists than at any other time. They came to stay with us, and I learned to admire their directness and pragmatism.

There were also three women who played an important part in the campaign. We had known all them since they were young girls: Gwyneth Dunwoody MP, one of the most powerful women in the Commons, was the daughter of Morgan Phillips, under whom Denis had worked at Transport House; Shirley Summerskill was the efficient doctor daughter of our old friend and Highgate neighbour Dr Edith Summerskill; and Betty Boothroyd, later a distinguished Speaker of the House of Commons, had been a bonny young Yorkshire lass whom Denis had selected as winner of a young speakers' contest in Leeds in 1952.

It was now obvious that Tony Benn, for all his idealism, was attracting the most destructive forces of extremism — groups outside the Labour Party who were gradually taking over local constituency parties. They came in coachloads to shout Denis down at public meetings. I watched the scene on television with growing fury as the young hordes shouted, "Healey out, out, out!" and with anguish as Denis, red-faced and furious in an improbable red jersey, tried in vain to shout down the screaming mob, which even Michael Foot had difficulty in quieting. There were anarcho-syndicalists, waving a black flag on a ten-foot bamboo pole; Socialist Workers and young Communists, chanting, brandishing clenched fists — all having come determined to make it impossible for Denis to be heard. And then I remembered, ruefully, that I too, at their age, as a student at Oxford, had gone on an unemployment rally and had chanted happily, "Down with Citrine and Bevin!" knowing little about either. But I do not recall in our cheerful chants the viciousness of this campaign.

These were scenes, condemned by Michael and most of the left wing, which brought the Labour Party into the greatest disrepute, but which Tony failed to discourage. Foot, in his memoirs, describes how one rally was "wrecked by a sectarian mob, screaming applause for Benn and execration on Healey". It was the sight of this that turned Foot and so many of the moderate left against Benn, and demonstrated the real

331

danger to the Labour Party brought by Benn's followers.

Here it is necessary to try to understand the magic and the menace of Tony Benn's appeal, as one of the Labour Party's genuinely charismatic figures at the height of his influence. I have always been taken by his charm and idealism — but then, I have never had to work with him. I had felt there was some truth in Tony Crosland's famous remark, "There is nothing much wrong with Jimmy [his nickname; another Tony would be confusing, he said] except that he is a bit cracked." Tony had been Benn's tutor at Oxford, was his neighbour in London and knew him well. Benn's devoted followers obviously thought, then and now, that "it's through the cracks that the light comes in" and certainly it can be argued that many world shakers have often been thought "a bit cracked".

In his favour, Tony Benn had a happy marriage and family life; I always admired his talented American wife, Caroline, who was a successful lecturer and writer with a particular interest in education. Their son, Hilary, became an MP for Leeds, a Blairite and a competent minister. Caroline bravely endured a painful cancer until, tragically, it killed her. I last met her at a Labour Party conference walking with difficulty, arm in arm with Tony who supported her with the greatest tenderness. After her death he wrote a moving tribute to a partner who had loyally supported him all their married life.

He came from a privileged background: both his grandfathers were MPs. Born and bred in a great house on the site of the Millbank Tower and educated at Westminster School and Oxford, at twenty-five he became MP for Bristol — and in 1959 Gaitskell brought him into the Shadow Cabinet. In the 1959 election he produced and presented the party television broadcasts, developing the skill as an orator and broadcaster which he would keep all his political life. His Commons career was threatened when, on the death of his elder brother, he inherited his father's title and became Anthony Wedgwood Benn, 2nd Viscount Stansgate; so he campaigned for the right to disavow his peerage and remain MP for Bristol. Henceforward he affected a singular mid-class accent, took his tea in large tin mugs and liked to be known as plain Tony Benn.

In the Labour government of 1964 Wilson made him a Cabinet minister — first as Postmaster General, then as minister for new technology, in charge of the Concorde project. His delight in the new technology was increased by the knowledge that it provided many jobs in his Bristol constituency. But he was always happier in opposition, and after the unexpected Labour defeat of 1970 all his energy was directed to encouraging the party to move leftward. He was, observers recall, "exciting, inspirational, sometimes dangerous". At first the "sane left" saw in him Bevan resurrected; but they were uneasy with the revolutionary elements he encouraged, and gradually dissociated themselves from him. Meanwhile, an assortment of revolutionary groups, Trotskyites and Communists and others with outlandish names — the "Militant

Tendency" and "Rank and File Coordinating Committee" — brought their banners to his support. Their aim, to infiltrate constituency parties and take over the Labour Party, conveniently chimed with Benn's "power to the people" campaigns.

In 1979, at that bitter first party conference after the election defeat, Benn was in his element, helping to carry motions for the mandatory annual reselection of Labour MPs and to give the NEC the final say over the party manifesto. At Blackpool the following year, Benn was at the height of his powers. His apocalyptic speech was wildly cheered: the next Labour government must "within a matter of days" bring in an act to extend public ownership, and within weeks Britain must withdraw from the Common Market. If the Lords objected, there must be an instant creation of a thousand peers if necessary. Shirley Williams observed wryly: "Even God took five days to make the world." But though he was wildly cheered, many of the "sane left" were infuriated by his attacks on a Labour Cabinet of which he had been a member and from which he had not resigned.

On Sunday 28 September 1981, I sat on the platform at the party conference awaiting the count of the vote for the deputy leadership. I must have been in this unusually elevated position because Denis was, at this time, an ex officio member of the NEC. I seem to remember that I sat next to Neil Kinnock and that I said with intense conviction, "If you abstain now, you will become leader of the Labour Party." I also

334

remember Neil's cheerful abuse of Denis to his other neighbour.

Throughout the lengthy voting procedure I sat watching Denis on the front row, knowing by the way he was opening and shutting his despatch case and rattling his keys how on edge he was — though he otherwise showed no nerves.

The result was bound to be close. Tony would get a majority of the 30 per cent that the constituencies were given, Denis expected to get the majority of the 30 per cent allotted to the parliamentary party. But the trade unions cast their 40 per cent in a single block for each union, and no one knew how this would go, since each union chose a different method of deciding. Some consulted all their individual members, others "sounded" opinion, some delegations voted as their national executive committee instructed — and some, as Denis recalled, "ignored consultations and instructions alike". On the first ballot Denis won 45.37 per cent of the college, Benn 36.3 per cent and a third candidate, John Silkin, 17 per cent. When Silkin withdrew for the second ballot, the delegation from the union that had sponsored him decided, on the floor of the conference, as Denis wrote, "how and by what majority is unknown, to vote for Benn. So I scraped in to victory by a hair of my eyebrow — 50.426% against 49.574% for Benn".

Intensely relieved, I jumped up and, probably to his embarrassment, rushed forward to give Denis a great hug. I had always felt that this vote would be a crucial landmark, not only in our personal lives but in the history of the Labour Party. And so it was: as Giles Radice wrote in his diary that evening, "By beating Benn, however narrowly, Denis has saved the Labour Party."

From this point onwards a fierce battle against Militant was fought by those on the centre and right wing of the party and, as deputy leader, Denis was deeply involved. Realizing, as he told Giles, that he had not been sufficiently aware of the growing power of Militant in the constituencies during the campaign for the leadership, he now took this threat seriously, and spent time and energy in the fight to restore the balance of the party.

The deputy leadership campaign, which had marked the highest point of Benn's popularity, was at the same time the beginning of the decline of his influence over the following years. Had Denis lost, there would certainly have been a haemorrhage of right-wingers from the party, and the SDP might indeed have "broken the mould". As it was, his victory on 28 September 1981 marked the beginning of some of the most tiring and tiresome years of his political life.

There had been great initial enthusiasm when, on 26 March 1981, Shirley Williams, Bill Rodgers and David Owen, along with Roy Jenkins (now returned from his Commission presidency in Brussels), had set up the Social Democratic Party. Launched at David Owen's home in Limehouse with the "Limehouse Declaration", it attracted considerable support immediately, and for a time Roy Jenkins saw himself as a future prime minister of a new party that would bring in a new era of non-confrontational middle-of-the-road politics. Shirley had lost her seat in the 1979 defeat and Roy still needed to get back into Parliament; but they were leaders of an army already formed and waiting, even with funds to support it.

Like many others, I was tempted to set off after them in this new dawn; but I was persuaded by Denis's arguments, based on his long experience of European politics, that this was a party without roots and would fail. He was to be proved right. But at first the prospects looked bright. The polls of December 1981 showed that 51 per cent of the electorate were in favour of a Liberal–SDP alliance. Some of our brightest and best friends were leading the way. I had known Roy and Jennifer for forty-five years; we had been neighbours and colleagues in government. I liked and admired David, who had been a clever young minister under Denis at Defence. I was also very fond of his bright and lovely wife, Debbie. I had not known Bill Rodgers so well, but Shirley I had long loved and admired. George and Grace Thomson and their daughter had been our friends when they lived in the flat above us in Admiralty House. Their departure was a real wrench, and though our political ways separated they still have remained good friends.

The triumphal progress of the SDP was halted in 1982 by Margaret Thatcher's resounding victory in the Falklands and the subsequent revival of the Tory party. When the Argentinians invaded the Falklands I heard the news on my hotel radio in New York, where I had

337

gone to give a literary lecture: it was an uncanny experience, switching on the radio and hearing Denis's voice recorded from the debate in Parliament. He had been on his way to a conference in Greece and had immediately flown back to London. I listened in surprise to Michael Foot's belligerent speech — General Galtieri seemed to have become fused in his mind with Adolf Hitler.

In the general election of 1983 Roy Jenkins was returned for Hillhead Glasgow, but Bill Rodgers lost his seat in Stockton, and eventually the party that had been formed to end dissension itself split. Roy and Shirley led the majority of the SDP into a merger with the Liberals under the name of Liberal Democrats; David Owen remained obstinately with the rump of the SDP until they finally obtained fewer votes than the Monster Raving Loony Party! In due course all four went to the Lords: Roy, Shirley and Bill as leaders of the Liberal Democrat Party, and David representing his diminished band there.

Labour's humiliating defeat in the 1983 election was not surprising. Against the television image of Margaret Thatcher, headscarved and triumphant, driving a tank like a modern Boudicca, the elderly man hobbling with his stick and little dog over Hampstead Heath had no chance. Denis had given Michael Foot his loyal support, but it was an impossible partnership: their views on defence and much else were totally divergent. The manifesto was a mass of contradictions and appealed to no one.

I did my usual election stint in Leeds and saw it coming. I knew the signs all too well: old supporters could not meet my eyes, and I could not blame them. This seemed the nadir of our political fortunes, when old friends asked: "Can you put your hand on your heart and say that Labour will return to power?" I lied when I said I could.

As deputy leader, Denis had to be in London and all over the country — especially in marginal seats. As always, Douglas Gabb and the constituency party members were loyal and heroic during a difficult and depressing campaign. Now that Denis had his office in the smart Labour Club at Seacroft, campaigning was at least more comfortable. The days of slugs on the walls were over. There was less dangerous canvassing at night for me, too — but the usual round of clubs, with their smoke-filled rooms and the thump and screech of bands, left me with blinding headaches. Denis could not get to Leeds until eve of poll, and was totally exhausted after a dispiriting and badly organized tour of the country. He concealed his weariness under his usual boisterous good humour: but we had no doubt of the outcome. Although his seat was safe, nationally the Labour Party had reached its nadir. Yet in fact the fightback had already begun.

Michael immediately resigned and Neil Kinnock became leader, with Hattersley as his deputy, bringing a crackling energy and common sense that would help transform the Labour Party. Denis, after consulting his friends, quickly decided not to enter the contest. It was the end of any expectation of becoming leader, and he

339

accepted it with his customary good humour, immediately offering the new leadership his services. Throughout all his political career, I have never known him moan in disappointment — at most there would be a "Well — back to the drawing board". Nor would he ever have dreamed of "taking his bat home". He continued to use and lend it. He cheerfully accepted Kinnock's invitation to stay on shadowing Foreign Affairs and, without rancour, played second fiddle on visits to a world he understood better than anyone.

CHAPTER
THIRTEEN

FAMILY LIFE: ENDINGS AND BEGINNINGS, 1979–1983

Our sudden and unexpected ejection from 11 Downing Street in May 1979 meant reorganizing our domestic life. We did not return to live at Holly Lodge Gardens. Our eleven years in Westminster, first at Admiralty House and then at 11 Downing Street, had convinced us that we were country people at heart, so we had bought a house in Alfriston, near the East Sussex coast, exchanging the cottage in the first place for a small flat in Chelsea. While we looked for a London base we were grateful for the hospitality of Diane and Harold Lever, who accommodated Denis in their splendid home in Eaton Square while Parliament was sitting.

Leaving Highgate was a painful break. Here I had been inspired to start my writing career; here the family had been so happy. When we took down the mirror from the wall of Cressida's room, we found her moving message, "My heart is here". For many years I could not bear to go past our old house, whereas I pass Admiralty House and No. 11 without a pang. But in Alfriston, where our main home has been since 1979, we daily revel in our incomparable views of the river winding to the sea and the "blue goodness of the Weald".

Some newspapers immediately confused our house with that of Jim Callaghan, at a nearby farm, and for many years we could not persuade the press that we did not possess a farm. They even took a photograph of the house with the caption "The Healeys' house which Mrs Healey says is not a farm". Eventually I decided I must introduce some sheep so that "the scripture may be fulfilled".

We had taken our tiny Chelsea flat in a hurry after leaving Downing Street, and after a while we moved on to a small house in West Square near the Elephant and Castle, where we enjoyed the use of a charming communal garden with four ancient mulberry trees. Blown down in the great gale of 1987, they were carefully re-rooted by the council and now they flourish again. Our immediate neighbours there were Merlyn and Colleen Rees and Jim and Audrey Callaghan.

Merlyn and Colleen were long wound into the pattern of our lives. Merlyn was a much respected neighbouring MP for Leeds; Colleen, whom he had married in 1949 — one of the nicest wives in Westminster — was his secretary throughout his parliamentary career. She was competent, intelligent and caring, and a great help to Merlyn. Merlyn's father had walked to London from south Wales in search of work, and Merlyn's roots lie deep in the Welsh mining tradition. Politically motivated from his grammar school days, he became chairman of the Labour Society and President of the Students' Union at Goldsmiths'

College, where he trained as a teacher. Like Denis and other Labour leaders of his generation, he was tested in war as an operations officer in the RAF. A squadron leader, he served in Italy and France and was offered a permanent commission which he refused. His sights were still set on a political career and he took a postwar degree at the LSE, later teaching economics and history.

After Gaitskell's death he won his East Leeds seat in a by-election in 1963, and in the Labour government of 1964 quickly made his mark under Denis in the Ministry of Defence — first in the Army Department and then as an under secretary of state for the RAF. Again, like Denis, he was well equipped by his military service for the job. His quiet competence had impressed Callaghan when he was Chancellor of the Exchequer, and over the following years they became not only close colleagues but close friends.

Much respected throughout the party, Merlyn was elected on to the Shadow Cabinet, and when Labour, under Callaghan, regained power in 1974, he was made a Privy Counsellor and appointed to the difficult and dangerous job of Secretary of State for Northern Ireland, where his outstanding achievement was to end internment without trial. This was a trying period for Merlyn and his family alike: under threat from the IRA, they had to be constantly guarded by Special Branch officers; on one occasion their sons were threatened with kidnapping and were embarrassed to be escorted home from school.

When in 1976 Wilson retired and Callaghan became Prime Minister, Merlyn became Home Secretary and Callaghan's personal adviser. After the defeat of 1979 he shadowed Home Affairs, Energy, and Industry and Employment until, like Denis, he left the Commons in 1992 to become a peer. Even after he was struck by Parkinson's disease he was able to continue to play a part in the Lords, thanks to the steady support of Colleen. Both have given devoted and unstinting service to the Labour Party, in Leeds and at Westminster alike.

Outside Westminster politics there was a different world in which I was increasingly involved. During this period Denis and I were like passengers in two trains running on parallel tracks. We waved from time to time, even stopped at stations for brief encounters, but mostly we were each absorbed in our own work. Yet paradoxically it was also a time of deepening mutual love and understanding.

It has often been said that our marriage was one of the happiest in the Palace of Westminster. That it was so was partly because we each kept our own space. I had my own interests and my own problems, and I tried not to add to Denis's public responsibilities with my private worries. Similarly, Denis never burdened me with his ministerial problems. Some marriages succeed by sharing difficulties: for us, a trouble shared is a trouble doubled.

There were bereavements and tragedies in my life in these crucial years.

In 1979 my quiet, retiring elder brother Bert died. "Look after Mum," our dying father had asked him — and he had kept his promise, never marrying but living with her and Doreen at the family home, then moving with them to a well-designed, comfortable little house that my sister had built. Totally unsentimental, Doreen does not look with regret at the empty place where our house was, nor remember the tin bath with affection.

After his retirement as a skilled dental mechanic my brother had enjoyed his golf and quiet evenings with friends in the "back room" at the Angel Hotel. I see him digging the good red earth in the garden and, foot on spade, watching his pet robin pulling at worms. "Dig your own potatoes, Tim, that'll make you feel better," he advised our son through a "black dog" patch. Reserved and shy, he left few possessions but his last years were happy. His friends from the Angel carried him at his funeral, shoulder-high, arms linked in the old way. I remember him with such affection: how, shoulders straight and head held high, he taught me to waltz in the Broadwell Memorial Hall.

Throughout my whole life, my sister Doreen (Dode) has always been my support and comfort. When, in our childhood, I gobbled all my Saturday sweets, she, the careful one, always gave me half of hers. As we grew up and I took the high road, she made the home road a welcoming one for me and a comfortable refuge. Always self-deprecating, she was a skilful needlewoman and a first-rate cook, and has more common sense and wisdom in her little finger than many intellectuals have in all their swollen heads. It was she who initiated the move from the old house, planned and furnished the lovely new home, kept house for my brother Bert and took care of my mother to the ends of their lives; now she lives alone.

Like many single women of her generation, she is the backbone of the Baptist chapel and her local community, raising funds and visiting the sick. Kindly, unpretentious, loving without sentimentality, she also has a fund of pithy and memorable wise sayings. "Never judge a man till you have walked a mile in his shoes." "Spend it," she would urge — though she is herself extremely careful; "there's no pocket in a shroud." A surrogate mother to all her loving nephews and nieces, she has always been the heart of the family. She made the last years of my mother's life comfortable and happy.

In the next year, 1980, my much-loved elder sister, Ivy, died. Hers is a sad story which I want to tell more fully because it is the kind of dark shadow that hides behind many homes. It is also an example of how, married to a public figure under great stress, a wife may not wish to share a pain which would only increase the husband's burden and which he could not help to ease.

During the years when my world was expanding and my home life increasingly comfortable, Ivy was suffering the disintegration of her personality, the breakdown of her marriage and confinement in a mental hospital. Her husband emigrated with their five children to Australia and she finished her life quietly in an old people's home.

346

It is a tragic story, painful to relate. Always "the little mother" to her younger siblings, when our mother was busy it was she who looked after us. At Christmas she made the cake and mincemeat and filled our Christmas stockings. Later, when she left college and was earning a salary as a teacher in Walsall, she made clothes for me and bought my first dance dress. Intelligent, sensitive and caring, she gave me good counsel when I set out for Oxford. She was a competent pianist and sang well with a sweet, light voice. I remember her in the school's annual Shakespeare play, as Feste in *Twelfth Night*, standing at the side of the stage, slim and elegant in her jester's costume, her light green eyes filled with tears as she sang "Come away, come away, death, and in sad cypress let me be laid". It had not seemed odd that she was physically sick before the performance — she was always unusually nervous, hiding in thunderstorms and fearful of strangers. Although she and my mother loved each other, there were frequent rows, for my mother was always impatient and often tactless. I dreaded these flare-ups, often over trivialities, and, especially after my father's death, would act as peacemaker.

For all her sensitivity and nervousness, the outcome need not have been tragic had she married a gentle and sensitive husband. But Gilbert, a clever science teacher, had a fierce energy: he liked climbing mountains, played the violin like a demon and enjoyed bruising arguments about the Spanish Civil War. Only because of his driving persistence was she persuaded to marry him. During the war she had twin babies and was pregnant with a third when Gilbert was called up to the

347

air force and posted to India. During air raids on Birmingham, terrified, alone and heavily pregnant, she had to carry the twins in the blackout to the air-raid shelters in the garden. I stayed with her one holiday and carried the twins during a raid, not knowing which way up they were, and realized how stressed she was.

After the war, Ivy's restless husband moved her and the children from the neat, manageable little home in Walsall to a succession of lonely, rambling houses in the Home Counties. Like our mother, Ivy liked an orderly house; we joked that she would dust the lumps of coal in the coalshed. Gilbert was like a hurricane blowing through her life. The fifth child died at birth, and by the time the sixth was born Ivy was a nervous wreck.

Gradually, her affection for her husband ebbed and her demeanour changed. Once, on a visit, I saw with alarm her usually gentle face contorted with hate. She seemed indeed "possessed by a devil". Finally she shut herself away in a room in a wing of the big house with a store of food. At this point, Gilbert finally realized that she was in a perilous state of mind — though he still could not understand why she was so stricken. He sent her to me for a holiday. We were at Langbourne Avenue, Highgate, at the time, with three young children. I thought that, loving her as I did, I could cure her. But, though with me she was always kind and apparently sensible, she was obsessed by irrational fears, imagining Germans in the neighbours' cellars. I sought help. At that time, the Labour minister Dr Edith Summerskill lived nearby on the edge of Hampstead Heath, and her husband Dr Samuel, a distinguished psychiatrist, kindly agreed to see Ivy. His opinion was that she needed professional help, and that my own marriage and family would be wrecked in vain if she stayed with us. She returned home and Gilbert took her to their doctor, at last accepting that she was mentally ill. After a vain attempt to cure herself, by living away in a caravan on the south coast, Ivy was taken into a mental hospital, where she remained for many years. Diagnosed as schizophrenic, she was given various forms of treatment, including electric therapy, but she became withdrawn and — so the hospital doctors said — unwilling to see any of us. My mother wrote to her every week, but the hospital was far off and gradually we lost touch.

Then one day a new doctor at the hospital wrote to my mother suggesting that a visit from her own family might help Ivy. Immediately my younger sister, Doreen, drove my mother, now in her eighties, on the long journey to the hospital. They found her almost unrecognizable: apathetic, unwilling to talk and uncared-for in appearance. Heartbroken, my sister telephoned me. I drove down from London the next day.

I did not at first recognize the shabby old woman in a faded dress and wrinkled stockings, her hair hanging in a long plait; but gradually I found my sister, still there. She spoke with difficulty, was not conscious of the passage of time, but two things she did remember: mental pain that in her words was "worse than childbirth" — but also, she said, times when she felt protected by a great love. I drove home blinded by tears, stricken to the heart by guilt that I had let her slip out of my life. There were good reasons — she had her own family, I had mine — but I cannot, in retrospect, hide behind them.

When I reached home, I found Denis deeply immersed in a political crisis. Absently he asked, "Had a good day?" I did not tell him anything until much later. He could not have helped, and my distress would only have made things worse for him.

From now on I visited Ivy regularly, and once a month Doreen drove my mother the two hundred miles to the hospital. Gradually we brought back her self-esteem and self-awareness. My sister took charge of her clothes, cut her hair and on each visit took her for picnics and drives round the countryside. She loved the fields of yellow rape and little by little responded to the stimulus. After some time she was stable enough to be moved to an old people's home, where I visited her regularly with an easier conscience. She had regained her old dignity. She had her own private room next to a sitting room that looked out on to green fields. Every day she sat there quietly, reading a little. Her children wrote to her from Australia and, when they came to England, visited her. She always carried their letters and photographs in her handbag. The demon that had possessed her was now held at bay — though sometimes, when she spoke of some of the staff, the haunted look reappeared. In later years she developed cancer; as her body weakened, her real character resurfaced and, though she was always quiescent, she greeted me with the old kindness.

Then one day I was having lunch with Denis when I suddenly felt I must go to her. It was not my time for visiting her, but the silent call came urgently. Her chair in the sitting room was vacant. She was in bed and near death. I held her hand and gave her the love of all her children and our family, mentioning each of us by name. Did I imagine she pressed my hand, or were they the involuntary movements preceding death? I believe she knew I was there and was glad I was with her at the end.

There were few at her funeral in the little church at the crematorium, but one old schoolfriend, who had loved her as a girl, unexpectedly arrived. Looking out to the lovely gardens bright with flowers among the cypresses, I thought of the slender girl on the stage in her jester's costume, singing so sweetly, "Come away, come away, death, and in sad cypress let me be laid."

I have told Ivy's story out of the sequence of time so that her children and grandchildren may remember her as she was. When, after the funeral, we unpacked the small suitcase containing her belongings, we wept to think this was all that remained of her life. But my own daughter Cressida, now a doctor of psychology, has in recent years reunited Ivy's daughters and grandchildren with our family. Looking around the table at our last gathering, I thought how proud of them all Ivy would have been. Gillian became an excellent psychiatric social worker. Her twin has had tragedies in his own life. Ivy would have been proud of his lovely daughters. Jane, who hated Australia, made her way back to England, marrying an Italian she met on the boat. She had two lovely girls with him and, after his death, made a successful career as a secretary and forged a happy second partnership; she has proved a wonderful mother. The love Ivy had always given them as children, they now have passed on to their own. That is her legacy to them.

A year later, in 1981, my mother died at the age of ninety-eight. Bedridden at the end, she was clear in mind almost to the last. In her last years she had mellowed, no longer the "fierce little bantam" her friends once called her. She loved to sit in the cosy sun room, watching the birds in the garden, receiving her friends and dispensing her mellow wisdom, telling young visitors to "pull your socks up" or "run a comb through your hair, you look as though you've been dragged through a hedge backwards". Mary, the daughter of her old friends Mr and Mrs Cullis, now dead, came each night to help get her into bed, and she always thanked her with: "You've been such a good girl, Mary, I shall tell your mother and father when I see them." Such was her confidence in a future life, she was certain of meeting her dead friends beyond the grave.

When the end approached, she was driven in the ambulance through the autumn woods to Dilke Hospital. Propped upright in her best coat and hat, she could still admire, as she always had, the burnished gold of the beech trees. From her hospital bed she kept the nurses up to scratch, watching the interests of the other patients in the ward. "That lady in the end bed," she would tell them, "needs your attention." Once she suddenly said, "I can see the sea from your sitting room" — she was thinking of me and our house in Sussex.

I was so glad I managed to get there before she died. I held her soft white hand as I had done as a child. Her eyes were closed, but I am sure she knew I was there.

My sister and I drove behind her hearse through the woods to the crematorium at Gloucester. Never had the beech trees blazed more triumphantly, and my sister and I had the strongest desire to sing aloud "Hallelujah!" If ever trumpets sounded at the other side, they did then.

Now there were empty chairs at the family feasts. Denis's mother, who had come to live with us after his father died, later moved to a nearby nursing home. She remained intellectually eager right to the age of ninety-nine, contentedly working her way through the works of Tolstoy and Turgenev — and explaining the Russian characters with great confidence to her younger sister Dolly, until little Aunty Dolly, who had been our faithful surrogate parent when we had travelled the world, now in a comfortable old people's home, herself quietly slipped away.

CHAPTER
FOURTEEN

PARTY POLITICS, 1983–1992

In the early 1980s Denis, as deputy leader, was finding his party work more stressful than ever. The struggle to hold the party together required unremitting effort, and there were times when it seemed in terminal decline. The country watched on television the Labour Party tearing itself apart in scenes of bitter hatred, while the SDP was gaining ground in the polls and reaping the advantage of Mrs Thatcher's growing unpopularity.

He could at this time have bowed out of politics and accepted some more rewarding offers; but he chose to stay to help in the fight back to sanity. He refused nominations to become an international civil servant in charge of either NATO or the IMF. In 1983 Arnold Weinstock asked him to become chairman of his company, GEC. To his astonishment, Denis immediately refused. "Edna," Arnold told me, "he didn't even hesitate for a moment." Any one of these jobs would have given him a more comfortable life, infinitely better paid. But loyalty has been always one of Denis's most outstanding qualities, and he chose to soldier on in the Labour Party. Many years later, during the TV programme *This Is Your Life*, Neil Kinnock praised his loyalty: "If you cut through Denis Healey like a stick of rock you would find 'Labour Party' written there."

In 1983 there was some relief in letting the young Kinnock and Hattersley take over as leader and deputy leader. Denis was now sixty-six, and even his phenomenal energy had been sapped by five testing years as Chancellor and four years of stress and frustration as deputy leader of a party torn by dissension. For Denis, the tedium to be endured in committees was as wearing as the stress borne in government. Perhaps only his wife realized how draining the last nine years had been. So he welcomed the "dream team" of Neil and Roy with genuine pleasure.

Roy Hattersley and Denis had much in common. They were both pragmatists, aware that idealism without power was not enough in politics. They had worked well together at the Ministry of Defence, where Denis had chosen Roy as his navy minister, and had forged a partnership of mutual trust and respect. Roy had given invaluable support to Denis during the leadership and deputy leadership contests in 1980 and 1981, and Denis, in turn, had supported Roy in his unsuccessful bid for the leadership in 1983. I had always admired Roy's ready pen, wielded to great effect in both books and articles; I liked his self-mocking humour and his practical common sense. Driven, as he himself wrote, "by the obligation to succeed", he suffered, like so many others, from the tragedy of Labour's long period of opposition, which prevented him from reaching the highest position he merited.

355

Just as Roy was moulded by his early experience in Yorkshire's practical politics, so Neil Kinnock was rooted in the mining community of south Wales. His father worked for twenty-six years as a miner; his mother, a district nurse, was a socialist and a committed chapel-goer, and had a lasting influence on him. Joining the Ebbw Vale Labour Party at fifteen, he continued to be involved in politics throughout his three years at Cardiff University where his talent for oratory came into its own when he won first place in a Welsh University Eisteddfod competition. After graduating, he became a WEA tutor organizer and in 1967 he married Glenys — an equally committed Labour activist and fervent campaigner against apartheid: she chose silver for her wedding ring rather than wear one of South African gold. It was a good, lively partnership, and their combined charm, energy and intelligence were to help to transform Labour Party politics.

I had first become aware of Neil in November 1969, when Denis returned from a visit to Bedwellty speaking highly of the candidate who was to take the place of the retiring MP, Harold Finch. Arriving for Harold's farewell dinner, he had been met at the station by the new candidate, whom he described in *The Time of My Life* as "a red-haired young Welsh lecturer with a pretty wife who was pregnant. He made a rousing speech over the cold ham and salad in the Miners' Institute, with excellent and unfamiliar jokes which I wrote down in my diary along with his name." In the election of 18 June 1970, Kinnock won the seat with a huge majority over the Conservative candidate, Paul Marland (who,

356

incidentally, later became the MP for my Forest of Dean). Neil was to hold Bedwellty until he retired from Parliament in 1994. Denis later heard him speak at a party conference at Llandudno and wrote of his "incandescent oratory with an irresistible moral thrust".

I next noticed Neil at that difficult Labour Party conference in the autumn of 1979, when his passionate speech on education brought the delegates to their feet in a standing ovation. The next morning at the conference hotel, as I passed Robin Day's breakfast table, I stopped to tell him that "yesterday you heard the speech of the next Labour leader". Robin looked doubtful.

When in 1983 Neil easily won the contest for the leadership I was pleased, believing that his charisma, energy and determination, in partnership with Roy Hattersley's solid strength, could generate renewal in the damaged party. Shaken to the core by the party's catastrophic defeat in that year's election, he would never forget how he felt on 9 June 1983. "Never again," he vowed, "will we experience that." For the next nine years he led a fierce battle to rid the party of the extremists who were making the Labour Party unelectable. With great courage he confronted head-on the militants who were infiltrating local parties. He could not have succeeded had he not had the active support not only of the right wing of the party but also of many on the left who realized that the party had been in danger of being destroyed by extremism. Led by Kinnock's courageous attack on militants who had taken over the Liverpool party and supported by formidable fighters like Betty Boothroyd, Gwyneth Dunwoody and others, the party gradually saw militants and extremists ejected or defeated; and, as Denis had predicted, moderates won places on the National Executive, restoring the balance.

My next chance to get to know Neil and Glenys better came in 1984, when he was invited to Moscow on an official visit and took Denis as Shadow Foreign Secretary. Denis had been to Russia many times since our visit with Bevan and Gaitskell in 1959, had met Gorbachev, and had for years kept in touch with Soviet affairs through Russian friends at their embassy and at world conferences. For Neil, the visit was part of a sharp learning curve on foreign affairs in which Denis's long experience was immensely useful. Glenys and I were included in the invitation — not to attend the official talks, but to follow our own programme, which included visits to schools. This was familiar ground for both of us; like me, Glenys had been a teacher after graduating, and had continued to teach part-time after her marriage.

Glenys, who later would make an impressive career as a Member of the European Parliament, is an attractive woman who has always taken pride in presenting an elegant appearance. Glenys, as someone wrote, "could always look a million dollars in clothes from Marks & Spencer or C&A". She and others like her — Jennie Lee in earlier years, and Barbara Castle, who was always immaculately groomed — helped to change the image of Labour women, and prove that clever women did not have to be scruffy. In the working world in which they and I grew up, looking your best was an important part of being your best.

In the early days at party conferences I used to watch the leaders' wives on the platform comfortably knitting — until speakers complained that it distracted them. Glenys not only listened with an informed intelligence, but was herself an excellent speaker on many subjects, especially education. Deeply committed from an early age to the anti-apartheid movement, she often spoke in her own right at fringe meetings. For many years she chaired One World Action, providing aid to underdeveloped countries. Watching her at party conferences, as she sang anti-apartheid songs with Neil, I was impressed by her genuine dedication.

On my previous visit to Russia in 1959, I had been much impressed by the teaching of English and by the eager faces of the young — the girls in their starched pinafores and neat white bows on shining hair, the boys sporting red kerchiefs. By 1984, that generation had grown up into the well-spoken, intelligent young officials we had met in London and the capitals of the world. The new generation of Soviet women we met (who were better dressed than their counterparts had been in 1959: the ubiquitous angora hats of those days had disappeared) were now holding responsible positions in science, medicine and the arts. In London, at a Women of the Year luncheon, I had met the first Russian woman astronaut, Valentina Tereshkova, through her friend Lady Lothian and had admired her greatly.

However, it was not only the neat Russian uniforms and the good teaching of English that were unchanged since 1959; some of the old attitudes remained too. When Glenys and I were taken round Lenin's old offices, our guide, in a hushed voice, showed us the holy relics: "and this is the satchel of our beloved Krupskaya" — Lenin's wife. She was one of the few wives of Russian leaders to receive this treatment. With rare exceptions, as when Mrs Khrushchev accompanied her husband to America and as when, later still, Raisa Gorbachev took a public place alongside her husband, Soviet wives were kept in the background. I did not know their leaders *had* wives until I saw on television their widows in black, leaning over to kiss the marble faces in the coffins.

Glenys had been all her adult life an enthusiastic supporter of CND, and I accompanied her on a visit to the headquarters of the Soviet Peace Movement, where we were surprised by the members' fierce attack on Mary Kaldor and E. P. Thompson, the British leaders of the Movement for European Nuclear Disarmament, because they dared to seek converts to unilateral disarmament and the dissolution of alliances among the Communist countries, and had already made contact with sympathizers in eastern Europe.

Our Russian hosts, rightly proud of their superb ballet, took us to see the great Plisetskaya in *The Spectre of the Rose*. Although now she was unable to dance as she had done when we had seen her in 1959, she still moved with incomparable grace.

360

Once again, too, we were taken on the night train to Leningrad; once again, large ladies in starched white aprons sat on guard in the corridors. The ever-lively Neil and Glenys chatted late into the night with journalists in their smoke-filled compartment. The ageing Healeys, on the other hand, slept in their narrow beds while the train rocked and rumbled through the Russian night.

In Leningrad we paid a ceremonial visit to the harrowing museum commemorating the 640,000 who died during the siege in the Second World War. The story of the heroic endurance of those who survived has never been forgotten. We walked the snowy path with Glenys and Neil to lay a wreath on the memorial — Neil, to our hosts' surprise, bareheaded in an icy wind. Leningrad was a reminder, if one were needed, of the horrors of war. In their different ways, in their different generations, Denis and Neil both dedicated much of their political lives to its prevention.

Since our last visit the Russians had lovingly restored their beautiful city — traditional values were no longer dismissed as decadent, and the past was once again accorded due respect. The great palace of Catherine the Great, Tsarskoe Seloe, destroyed by the Germans, now shone, elegant and exquisite in the winter sun. Later, when writing the life of Emma Darwin, I saw some of the plates decorated with English country houses that had been made for the Empress by her grandfather Josiah Wedgwood. A Scottish architect, Cameron, had designed with classic grace one lovely room.

361

PART OF THE PATTERN

Our Russian visit ended with an unforgettable walk along a snowy railway platform. Denis began singing "Lara's Theme" from the film *Dr Zhivago* and, to the astonishment of our accompanying hosts, the four of us danced together along the platform to our seats on the train as the flakes fell on and around us. A decade later, Neil Kinnock recalled the occasion in the "Golden Book" presented by our family and friends on our Golden Wedding:

> We went to the station to catch the night train (to Leningrad), the Red Star, it was snowing heavily, as we walked along the ice covered platform, Glenys took Denis's arm and Edna took mine. As a small army of journalists and cameramen followed us on the long walk through flickering snowfall, Denis and Glenys (there's a poem here somewhere) began to hum *Lara's Theme*, as the march continued their voices rose, Edna and I joined in, followed by all the rest of the group. Glenys and Denis began to waltz, it wasn't the most elegant of dancing but at least they kept their feet until we reached our carriage. The people with us laughed helplessly. The railway staff and police showed stunned amazement. The whole episode gives us a magical memory of the Healeys, whose great gift for fun is amongst their best qualities. It is one of the things that makes them loved. I confess to a fleeting thought that Glenys might have been captivated by her dashing dancing partner. Fortunately, she saw him as the train

came to a halt in the grey Leningrad dawn. Edna looked wonderful. But the waltz king was not a pretty sight.

It had been a particular delight of this Russian trip that it gave me a chance to know Neil and Glenys better — a bright partnership of charm and intelligence. Glenys had always been politically motivated, "taking on" as she told Eileen Johns, "the things that interest me . . . which millions of women like me are concerned about . . . health, education . . . I don't speak on behalf of the Labour Party but as an individual who is political and as a wife and a mother." Had Neil become Prime Minister, Glenys would have made an impressive partner at No. 10. As it was, the defeats of Labour in 1987 and 1992 impelled her to make a career of her own as MEP for South East Wales. As Neil told his biographer,

We were driving down to see Rachel [their daughter] after she had started at university . . . we were by ourselves . . . chatting about the European elections and who would stand to replace the retiring MEP. There was a pause and then Glenys said "I'm going to do it", and I nearly drove off the road . . . [it] was just dawning on us that she could act as if her first obligation was to herself, for the first time in her life.

I knew exactly how she felt. Like her, my new life started when our children had grown up. In addition to her work in the European Parliament, Glenys has published a collection of interviews with remarkable women, *By Faith and Daring*; she is still president of One World Action and she is joint president of the ACP Parliamentary Assembly.

Throughout the years I had watched Neil's progress with particular interest, admiring his strength of purpose, his idealism grounded in common sense. He had gradually moved towards the centre of British politics — to the disappointment of some of his comrades on the extreme left — and was now, in the mid-1980s, capable of uniting the Labour Party. Certainly, by the time the next general election came around, Neil and Roy Hattersley had led a remarkable revival in public respect for the party. But at the same time I noticed a widespread hesitation in accepting Neil as a potential Prime Minister because he is Welsh. I once heard, to my amazement, young men discussing this in a railway carriage.

"He'll never be Prime Minister," one said, "he's Welsh."

"What about Lloyd George?" I interrupted.

"Not a red-haired Welshman," the other continued, ". . . and not a bald red-haired Welshman!" And they roared with laughter.

This prejudice was rooted deep — perhaps centuries deep. To the Anglo-Saxons, "Welsh" literally meant "foreigner" — and "Taffy was a Welshman, Taffy was a thief" has echoed through the years.

In the last days of the 1987 election campaign, when the parties were neck and neck, some sections of the press used every opportunity to trip up the Labour Party; even I was used as a target. On the morning of the eve of poll, I was dressing in the hotel bedroom, watching Anne Diamond interview Denis on foreign affairs on television. Suddenly she whipped out a copy of the *Sun*, with the headline "Healey's Wife Had Private Operation" — a reference to a hip replacement I had had in a private hospital three years earlier. I had never made a secret of it. At the time I was told that there was a three-year wait for the operation on the NHS. I was in great pain, was no help to Denis and had a book to finish writing. Livid, I shouted at the TV: "I am not a chattel! Why don't you ask me? I make my own decisions! I paid for my operation." In the studio, Denis was equally furious and almost clouted the producer.

That night the Leeds MPs held a great rally in the town hall for Kinnock and Hattersley. The two arrived at the back of the hall and made a ceremonial progress through the cheering audience to the sound of trumpets. Seeing me at the front of the hall, Neil suddenly left the procession, came over to me and, giving me a great hug, whispered, "Sod 'em, Edna!" before returning to the procession to the platform. He then inserted into his speech an unscripted passage, in effect challenging his audience to "look in the mirror and ask what would you have done", and attacking the "politics of envy". Then he called me on to the platform with the other MPs' wives, to rousing cheers.

This was typical of Neil's generosity, courage and loyalty. Other leaders might have ignored the attack, which was intended to embarrass him; but, as so often in his career, he chose to meet the challenge head-on. It was a gesture for which I have always been most grateful.

The next day, as we toured the polling booths as usual, we had more support. One of the policemen in charge said of the interviewer, "Why didn't you hit her, Denis?" We had many letters backing me; only one that was hostile. Most said, "If I had the money I would do the same."

Remembering the state of despair in 1983, I considered it amazing that in just four years the Labour Party had come so far. But as I had gone round the constituency in the last days before the election I had felt that, in spite of the wild enthusiasm at the rallies, the public were not yet convinced. Two particular obstacles were Neil's opposition to nuclear defence, and the popularity of the Tory policy allowing council tenants the right to buy their homes; in a constituency full of council housing estates the policy had been popular, and it was difficult to persuade the new home-owners that the Labour Party now agreed to the policy. Neil, himself brought up in a council house, understood how much this had meant to ordinary people.

The Kinnock–Hattersley team had been effective. The party organization had been taken by the scruff of its neck, and in the campaign of 1987 film directors Hugh Hudson and Colin Welland commissioned one of the most admired party political TV broadcasts ever made. Directed by Hugh Hudson of *Chariots of Fire* fame, it showed Neil and Glenys walking wind-blown on cliff-tops above the sea, like young gods coming down to save the world. Neil and Roy had led a renewed Labour Party, had made it electable. But not yet.

Defeat in 1987 was a blow; but although Labour did not win that election, it was clearly now in a position where it could expect to win again. And, as Peter Kellner wrote, "Kinnock was credited with beginning the process of Labour's recovery, rather than blamed for leading only a small advance." The team seemed well on its way to victory next time.

After the disappointment of 1987 Denis finally resigned from the Shadow Cabinet. Neil Kinnock remained leader, easily defeating a challenge from Tony Benn. However, when in November 1990 Margaret Thatcher was replaced by John Major, ironically it was the quiet man who spoke from a soapbox on street corners who defeated the charismatic Kinnock in the election of 1992. That year, Labour had been full of enthusiasm across the country, and confident of victory; but wider support was strangled by an unprecedentedly hostile press which attacked Neil personally with great venom.

The final pre-election rally at Sheffield should have heralded victory. The applause from a vast crowd was the wildest yet — and it was not only for Neil, for this was Roy Hattersley's home town. Neil has described the euphoria of that occasion as he and Glenys walked through the hall. Turning as they reached the platform, facing a delirious crowd, he was carried away, and his triple cry of "Well, all right!" went over the top. Hubris brought its penalty. Major's low-key approach brought a surge in Tory support in the country; Labour lost the election. Neil resigned and, in July 1992, John Smith, who had been Neil's Shadow Chancellor, took over as leader. In 1994 Neil retired from Parliament to become a European Commissioner and accepted a peerage.

Gerald Kaufman, who never praises lightly, wrote: "I voted against Neil Kinnock in the 1983 leadership election ... [This] was one of the most serious mistakes I have made in nearly a quarter of a century as an MP. Kinnock turned out to be the most decisive, the strongest, the toughest and, in my judgement, the greatest leader the Labour Party has ever had." I could add from personal experience: and the most loyal.

CHAPTER
FIFTEEN

TOWN AND COUNTRY, 1992–2005

After the disappointment of the 1987 election Denis had decided it was time to leave the Commons. The Labour Party had not won this time, but it was on the way back. He could now retire as MP for the Leeds constituency he had represented for forty years. His replacement in 1992 was to be George Mudie, whose efficiency as a young man I had noted in the trade union headquarters during the 1970 election. Later he was to rise to become a competent whip in the parliamentary Labour Party.

In 1987 Denis was seventy; he had served for five years in war and more than forty years in the Labour Party, many of them in excessively stressful work. In 1992 he accepted a peerage with the title of Baron Healey of Riddlesden — his Yorkshire village home. He was introduced into the House of Lords at the same time as his old sparring partner and friend, the Tory former Chancellor Geoffrey Howe. Elspeth Howe and I watched the ceremony with our families, looking down from the gallery at all the mock-medieval dazzle of brass chandeliers on gilt and stained glass. The House of Commons Chamber had been puritan plain in contrast.

Down below, the aspiring Baron Healey made a splendid entrance in a robe of scarlet and ermine between two supporting barons, Lord Longford and Lord Cledwyn, his sponsors. He was preceded by Black Rod, followed by the Garter King of Arms in a tabard of red, blue and gold, carrying in his right hand his silver gilt sceptre of office and in his left the new peer's "letters patent of creation" on a vellum scroll. They progressed with much bowing: there were bows at the Bar of the House, at the table where the clerks sit, and again at the Woolsack, the seat of the Lord Chancellor: a rich red cushion stuffed with wool, in tribute to the importance of the medieval wool trade. The Lord Chancellor, in white wig, black tricorn hat, black gown and breeches, stockings and buckled shoes, greeted the new peer, who knelt with difficulty and offered his letters patent, which were read aloud at the table: Her Majesty commanded him "to be personally present at our aforesaid parliament . . . to treat and give your counsel". His Lordship then read aloud the Oath of Allegiance and signed the Test Roll. Eventually, the three peers made their way to the back benches — where, in a final flourish of ritual absurdity, they rose up and sat down three times, each time doffing their three-cornered hats. Finally, on the way out, the new peer shook the hand of the Lord Chancellor and the assembled peers made their traditional sudden startling shout of welcome.

Much of this baroque oddity was removed when the Lords reformed itself in 1999: now there is not so much bowing, the tricorn hats are no longer used, elderly peers no longer have to kneel, and the ridiculous bobbing up and down is no more. However, something must be said in praise of spectacle and pageant; it brings history to life and marks an important occasion. If it did not exist we should probably invent it.

I enjoy my visits to the House of Lords. Wives have privileged seats in a special enclosure at the entrance to the Chamber, where one feels part of the procedure. The House of Lords is unlike the Commons: it is another and more civilized country. Their lordships and ladyships do not shout across the Chamber; there is no Speaker to call "Order, Order!" The Lord Chancellor or his deputies preside, but the members keep order and regulate the length of their speeches themselves. Only rarely do they have to rebuke a member of the House for "rough speaking", and even then it is in a decorous phrase: when debate becomes heated a member may move that "the standing order on asperity of speech may be read". They vote, not with the Commons' abrupt "aye" or "no" but with the quieter "content" or "not content". Other members of the House are referred to not by name but by rank: the Archbishop of the Church of England is "the Most Reverend Prelate the Archbishop . . ."; a bishop is "the Right Reverend Prelate, the Bishop of . . .". Dukes, marquesses, earls, countesses, viscounts, barons, baronesses are all referred to as "noble"; admirals, field

371

marshals or marshals of the Royal Air Force are "noble and gallant"; lawyers are "noble and learned".

Their lordships allow themselves a gentler humour. When Alice Bacon, a former fellow Labour MP of Denis's in Yorkshire, was introduced she was greeted at the Woolsack by the Lord Chancellor, Lord Hailsham — the former Quintin Hogg. As he shook Alice's hand, he whispered to her: "Hog greets Bacon."

The composition of the Lords has now changed: the number of hereditary peers is limited, making it a more politically balanced chamber. Life peers are still created by the Queen on the advice of the Prime Minister, but the political parties choose from among the hereditary peers those they wish to remain. The House of Lords holds much varied wisdom. Bishops, lawyers, academics, members of the armed forces, doctors and scientists, trade unionists and now the people's peers together make a unique chamber of experience. It is regrettable that their informed debates are not generally reported. This is an age reluctant to grow old: it needs to learn from the voice of experience.

The Lords' power is limited — they can delay the passage of a bill that has passed the three stages in the House of Commons, but ultimately they cannot defeat it. They can return it to the Commons three times for further consideration; if the Commons continues to pass it, in theory, the Queen could be asked to create more peers to get it through the Lords; this was Tony Benn's favourite apocalyptic answer to their lordships' intransigence. The threat is usually enough.

It is more comfortable to be a wife in the Lords than in the Commons. Nothing is more pleasant than to sit waiting in the armchair by the fire in the hall at the Speaker's entrance to the House of Lords, greeting old friends from all sides of the House, the arguments of former years forgotten. Here I can meet Conservative friends like Lord and Lady Howe; other friends from my Oxford days; improbable lords like Hattersley and Kinnock; Lord Barry Jones, fondly remembered from the days of the Labour leadership contest; the eversprightly Lord Barnett, trim and fit from his daily exercise in the Lords' gym. I can welcome with pleasure the deserters to the Liberal Democrats: the still much-loved Lady Williams, warm and affectionate as always; Lord Owen, still young and handsome, his wife Debbie as lovely as ever. It is good still to see those to whom time has not been kind: Lord Merlyn Rees, once so upright and steady, now, like me, walks with sticks; even the formidable Lady Falkender has dwindled into a wheelchair, accompanied by the still trim and lively Lady Wilson.

While policies were considered calmly in the House of Lords, party strife progressed noisily in the "Other Place". We liked and admired John Smith and his bright wife, Elizabeth, who was persuaded by Denis to succeed him as the very successful president of Birkbeck College. They came to stay with us in Sussex for discussions with Denis, and impressed me with their early morning energy, so that we were surprised as well as profoundly shocked by John's fatal heart attack on

PART OF THE PATTERN

12 May 1994. He was replaced by the vigorous young MP for Sedgefield, Tony Blair, for whom Denis had spoken in the by-election at Beaconsfield in 1982, and who brought new hope to a party that by now had been in opposition for fifteen years. The victory that was to follow in 1997 was the culmination of years of hard slogging in which Denis and his colleagues had played an important part.

I did not know Tony personally at that time, but met him and his brilliant wife, Cherie, occasionally in the years that followed, after he became Prime Minister. I have always been impressed by his energy and drive, and remained convinced of his honourable intentions in respect of the Iraq war, even when I disagreed with his policy. Decisions on how or whether to act in situations like this are cruelly difficult to take, especially for a man still young in experience.

I became startlingly aware of Tony Blair's youth on one occasion some years ago when he and Cherie invited us to dine at Chequers. It was a small party, and the other guests arrived before our hosts. Their youngest child Leo had been born not long since, and Cherie and Tony were still upstairs, having just returned from an official visit abroad. We waited in the somewhat cheerless great hall. I remembered Chequers from Attlee's time, when it was all dark varnish and reminded me of an Oxford college. I saw it again when Ted Heath had rightly, but against expert advice, stripped away the varnish and made the great hall light and cheerful. Now we waited till a tousled young man with a baby tucked under his arm came down from the

374

landing above and I realized that he was the age of my own son. Cherie had just been feeding the baby. We chatted, and I told him I had first come to Chequers when Attlee was Prime Minister. "You knew Attlee!" he exclaimed, astonished, as though I had said I knew Gladstone. Then I remembered that when Denis went into Parliament Tony was not even born; and by that time Denis had fought in the war and, as a Labour Party official, gained a wide knowledge of the world. Denis's pessimistic forecasts at the beginning of the Iraq war were based on a lifetime's experience and proved depressingly accurate.

We occasionally visited the Blairs after Tony became Prime Minister. Wisely, they had decided to live in 11 Downing Street, which — as I well remembered — was a rambling building with many rooms, whereas the flat above No. 10 was small and inconvenient and more suitable for the new Chancellor, Gordon Brown, who in 1997 was unmarried.

During the Blairs' time in Downing Street we were often invited for the anniversaries of our ageing generation. On his ninetieth birthday, a somewhat shaky Michael Foot held forth with his old fluency in the garden. On another ninetieth, Jack Jones forgot old quarrels and Blair made a charming speech; Jack's son told me that his father had at first wondered whether he should accept the invitation, but decided to be friendly. Jim Callaghan at ninety spoke of how, in his time as Chancellor in No. 11 and as Prime Minister in No. 10, his family had enjoyed playing "hunt the red boxes" through the hallowed halls.

★ ★ ★

In 1995 Denis and I had our own special occasion: we celebrated our Golden Wedding. Our daughter Jenny insisted that we have a family party at her home, rejecting the idea of a celebration in the House of Lords. Our families were joined by old friends from the Langbourne Avenue days: Fred and Margaret Bell; their son Paul, the little boy who sobbed at the piano at Mrs MacAdoo's, now a distinguished structural engineer, who with his wife and family have remained lifelong friends; Margaret Boyd, now widow of Sir Francis, knighted just before his death for his years of service to journalism at the *Guardian*. Friends came, too, from my writing world: John Goldsmith, who had been my first editor and had taught me how to write a television script, and Anthea, his wife. Suddenly a young man in black leather arrived on a motorbike bearing a huge bunch of flowers. It was one of my grandson Tom's friends, Rob, who had spent many Christmases with us and had, in recent years, inherited the diaries of Kenneth Williams. I had introduced him to my agent, and now he is delighted to be recompensed when they are performed. Jenny had helped Rob's mother clear Kenneth's flat after he died, and was saddened by its desolation and air of loneliness.

Jenny fed us magnificently and then presented us with a surprise. We unwrapped a huge parcel and found a glorious bound volume, edited by her and most professionally produced by her husband, Derek, entitled simply "Edna and Denis". It was our "Golden

376

Book" — a record of our lives illustrated by old photographs and with contributions from family, old friends and political colleagues. We were deeply touched.

There were comments from our children, some of which I have quoted, friends from Langbourne Avenue — Paul Bell's memory of Denis in a pair of blue shorts singing "Two lovely black eyes": "The Healeys were great campers, setting trends like track suits and unconventional tents, a generation before anyone else. Not many campers had a wobbly tooth, swung you around by an arm or leg while singing 'Down in the Sewer'."

Sir Patrick Nairne, Denis's private secretary at the Ministry of Defence, remembered:

When Edna left the lunch on a hot plate for the Secretary of State and Permanent Secretary Sir James Dunnett, it all went well until they reached the pudding over which Sir James and Denis poured some sauce from the hot plate until Denis stopped . . . "hang on, I think this is mushroom soup we're pouring". More seriously, I had great admiration for Denis's courage and coolness; the Labour government's major defence review was not popular with the three services and . . . as decisions were taken the Secretary of State had to explain . . . why . . . When he talked to a large gathering of Army officers I can vividly recall sensing the cold wave of hostility towards the Secretary of State but Denis is at his best as a speaker on such occasions. Within ten minutes I could sense the audience warming to his calm, reasonable address.

Douglas Gabb, Denis's constituency agent, wrote to Jenny:

Speaking as an agent, I never had any worries with your father and mother as the team we were fighting for. The Tories never had a chance. The absolutely sincere love and devotion they displayed for one another, the care and concern they publicly expressed for all their children convinced the general public that what was printed in the literature we produced for the elections was genuine.

Others came from Dr June Goodfield, our neighbour in Sussex:

Denis boisterously bursting into the sun room at Tile Barn where my old white-haired mother would be knitting, looking out over the incomparable view. "Hello Queen Eleanor" accompanied by a smacking kiss delivered with such . . . warmth . . . it made her eyes and cheeks glow with pleasure . . . she adored him. He is wonderful with old people.

Jack Donaldson, to whose HQ Denis was attached as staff captain in Naples during the war, described him as "the first officer . . . in the British Army who was clearly more intelligent than I was . . . They are my oldest and best friends . . . I'm so happy they have managed to get to a Golden Wedding, the fifty years together are God's greatest gift to man."

And from Roy Jenkins came a kind and characteristic comment:

> We both qualify as two remarkably uxorious politicians exceeded so far in connubial longevity by Gladstone, Lloyd George . . . Baldwin, Alec Home and Harold Wilson and practically no one else . . . Denis has always known a great deal and has known it with depth and subtlety as well as with certainty . . . I frankly admit that on at least three-quarters of subjects he knows more than I do and is brilliant at making up information on the other quarter. I vastly admire the indestructible strength of his personality, his wit and his resilient courage, which I think owes a great deal to the emotional stability which stems from the strength of his relationship with Edna. On their 50th anniversary I salute one of the most remarkable couples in England.

The presentation of the "Golden Book" was followed by Denis reciting in my honour the poem written by Tennyson to his wife, which he can never read without blubbing:

There on the top of the down,
The wild heather round me and over me June's
  high blue,
When I look'd at the bracken so bright and the
  heather so brown,
I thought to myself I would offer this book to
  you,
This, and my love together,
To you that are seventy-seven,
With a faith as clear as the heights of the June-
  blue heaven,
And a fancy as summer-new
As the green of the bracken amid the gloom of
  the heather.

A few lines and he broke down. I said, "Give it to me," and tried to read it, and similarly collapsed. In the end our son Tim took up the book and finished the poem — to the amusement of all. It was the happiest, if most tearful, of times and no grand party in the House of Lords could have compared with it. Nor can any book I have written ever compare with our "Golden Book". By the time this one is published we shall have had our Diamond Wedding.

In 1997 there was another celebration — this one given by the Labour Party to celebrate Denis's eightieth birthday at a hotel in Brighton. Tony Blair was there, along with members of the Cabinet. Speeches praising the "old warrior" were made; Tony Blair recalled that he had looked up to Denis when he was a young man as one of the icons of the Labour movement. Barbara

Castle, honest and aggressive as always, refused to flatter and reminded the audience of Denis Healey's shortcomings, which somewhat took the shine off the occasion.

There was another and more heart-warming celebration on Denis's eightieth birthday itself in the august surroundings of the House of Lords. Party differences diminish as we grow older. Old opponents spoke kindly, and Ted Heath surprised all present with the warmth and humour of his speech.

For all the grandeur of the House of Lords, both Denis and I have since childhood felt the beauty of the countryside to be an important element in our happiness, and have always been grateful to the National Trust as the guardians of our heritage. Throughout his boyhood on the edge of Ilkley Moor, Denis had, as he wrote, "explored every beck and crag on the moors above us — as a boy built dams with stone and tussocks of grass and, as a young man, explored the upper Dales on foot and on bicycle, staying in Youth Hostels". When I came to Keighley he took the greatest delight in showing me the land he loved so deeply, and we spent the happiest of courting days here. So when, in 1991, as Denis was about to leave the House of Commons, he was asked by Roy Jenkins's wife Jennifer, at that time the distinguished chairman of the National Trust, to preside over the Trust's fundraising appeal for the Yorkshire Moors and Dales, he jumped at the chance.

The appeal was launched on a September day. We should have made a spectacular descent by helicopter to a splendid marquee beside a river on the wild moor at Yockenthwaite. Unfortunately, heavy rain and dense mist hid the magnificent scenery and made our arrival not only dramatic but somewhat dangerous. However, the beautifully decorated marquee that rose out of the mist was a magical vision, lit by chandeliers. Denis lifted the spirits of the waiting photographers by posing in borrowed wellingtons in the swollen, icy river.

This tract of land in Upper Wharfedale had been given to the Trust by Graham Watson, "a hale young man of eighty-two with a handsome clean-shaven ruddy face", as Denis remembered. "His passion was riding his motorbike at eighty miles an hour. He was part owner of Lister's Mills and his father had given John Christie the velvet for his new opera house at Glyndebourne in the thirties." Now he was delighted to present this stretch of land in gratitude for the pleasure the Dales had always given him.

In the "Book of Memories" produced as thanks to Denis after the appeal was over, Graham remembered the occasion:

A joyful occasion? Low clouds, drizzle and wet grass, surely not a day for celebration? But why not? Come and meet a noble lord who is to start the Moors & Dales Appeal then . . . was there ever such a lunch in such a place and me between Denis and Edna! Comes the sun and blue sky and the magic of the river wharf above Yockenthwaite.

382

A joyful occasion? Yes, but *we* know that any occasion with Denis at hand is going to be joyful.

The appeal, which closed in May 1998, was a triumphant success on many counts. It raised over a million pounds and produced a handsome book, *Denis Healey's Yorkshire Dales*, with an introduction by Denis and stunning photographs of the Dales by Denis, John Morrison, Geoff Lund, Norman Duerdon and Colin Raw. For Denis, it was a chance to get away from the inbred life of Westminster, to remind himself about life literally at the grass roots, and to forge friendships with the dedicated people who make our National Trust the envy of the world.

Many of these friends recalled their memories of Denis during these seven years in the beautiful memorial album. Praise came from all sides — from farmers and Trust officials and land agents like Dorothy Fairburn and Judy Richmond; but also, most important of all, from his guide, counsellor and friend throughout all that time, the late Adrian Alderson, the Trust's Yorkshire director, who wrote in the album:

Seven years and one million pounds later, your chauffeur bids you farewell. Driving rain and warm farm kitchens, impossible time-tables and woods full of bluebells, I too, will hang up my muddy boots. Thank you for your friendship, the affection for all you met, your gentle pride in the moors and dales of Yorkshire, just thank you for all that. Adrian.

383

Sadly, now his boots are hung up for ever; but we are proud to remember him with gratitude. The adjective "gentle" is not one often used about the boisterous Healey, but it shows Adrian's sensitive understanding of the man who was at his best on his Yorkshire home ground. The National Trust survives because of dedicated and inspired people like Adrian.

These years meant a great deal to Denis, and also to the people he met. There was Walter Umpleby, the old Yorkshire farmer whom we visited in his ancient, unchanged farmhouse. He wrote in the album, in a careful hand,

When Dorothy Fairburn first informed me that you and Edna would like to visit . . . I was thrilled to bits but also had a strong feeling of inferiority. However, within a few minutes of your arrival, you was singing Gracie Fields, "Walter, Walter lead me to the Altar", which probably intentionally broke the ice. I thought it was going to be Walter Walter lead me to your meadows and I will have a look at your flowers. Then when Dorothy volunteered to help you on with the borrowed over-trousers which were far too small, you threatened to have her arrested for sexual harassment, that really put us at ease. The walk up the meadow was most enjoyable and looking over the wall at the cows with their young calves when the sun came out made a lovely end to your visit.

We paid many similar illuminating visits to tenant farmers on lonely farms. Chris Akrigg and his wife and family became great friends. Once, as we took a cup of tea with them in their hill farm at Cray above Buckden, Chris explained how and his wife had "sewn tough strips of cloth over the nether regions of more than a hundred ewes as a primitive form of birth control". As Denis later wrote, "Meeting farmers like this, and the patient craftsmen who led teams of unemployed lads from the Yorkshire towns and cities in rebuilding the dry stone walls and collapsing barns, gave me a new insight into the Dales as the homeland of living communities with their roots deep in the past, and reaffirmed my faith in the strength and value of life at the ground level."

If the years brought new understanding of the countryside to Denis, the chance to meet the former Chancellor of the Exchequer and to find him so approachable was a revelation and a joy to the people he met on their home ground, as they recalled in the "Book of Memories". His friends, farmers Bob and Jenny Dicker, commented that

> meetings with Denis were guaranteed to leave their mark, sometimes a pregnant message, other times a debate about serious or topical issues and invariably something to laugh about ... One highlight of the visit by Denis and Edna was asking to meet members of an employment training team and the encouragement the team felt as a result. Personally the fact that Denis is not

precious about himself or what he does, only committed, is a source of inspiration.

Dorothy Fairburn remembered

> Denis with mac and umbrella in torrential rain, ... building dry stone walls, at the press call for New House Farm as he stood in wet hay meadows with Walter, his immense patience with the press, especially photographers ... balancing on a rock in the centre of the river Wharfe, humming and singing his own musical accompaniment to all our journeys ... constant re-takes with Ruth Maddox on a windy hillside above Cray for BBC Songs of Praise. His *genuine* interest in people be they NT staff, farmers or just the man on the street — Edna's tremendous support and last but not least, dancing the can-can with him at "Music by Moonlight" at Fountains Abbey. Without you the NT would never have made three outstanding acquisitions in the Dales, Heber, Darnbrook and New House Farm.

Judy Richmond recalled

> a President who cared deeply about the moors and dales as not only wonderful countryside but also as home to those who live there. Someone with a genuine interest in the individuals he met and who, with Lady Healey, has the ability to make them all feel special and inspire in them affection

and friendship. A born entertainer, especially of children; an ever-ready camera, unfailing good humour and the ability to make ordinary days special.

I was happy to share many of Denis's visits to Yorkshire and was reminded of happy courting days on Ilkley Moor — long walks along the peat-brown river to Bolton Abbey, or spring days out to the bluebells in the Grass Woods at Appletreewick; cycling for miles along stony roads over the moors to Skipton, where the butcher's shop produced unforgettable pork pies for our picnics. I remembered the visit to Denis's old Bradford Grammar School summer camp at Grassington, where I was invited to launch their new canoe. It gave me almost as much pleasure as the occasion in later years when, as the wife of the Minister of Defence, I launched a submarine.

On a visit to the Trust hostel for trainees next to the Buck at Buckden, we were amused and touched to find it was converted from the barn where in 1945 we had spent our honeymoon. There ought to be a plaque!

When I was asked to contribute to the BBC's programme *Down Your Way*, I chose as my location the Brontë village of Haworth, across the valley from Denis's home in Riddlesden, where many of the girls I had taught at Keighley Grammar School had lived. One of my old pupils, Eunice Roper, had become curator of the Brontë Museum and attributed her love of the Brontës to my teaching. Her tribute to me sent me home with a glow round the heart.

I shared Denis's love of the Dales; his was enriched by long memories of his youth, as my love of the Forest of Dean is deepened by all the associations of my childhood. For both of us, Emily Brontë's poem remains the quintessence of all we love of this wild landscape.

Often rebuked, yet always back returning
To those first feelings that were born with me,
And leaving busy chase of wealth and learning
For idle dreams of things which cannot be . . .
I'll walk where my own nature would be leading;
It vexes me to choose another guide;
Where the grey flocks in ferny glens are feeding,
Where the wild wind blows on the mountain side.
What have those lonely mountains worth revealing?
More glory and more grief than I can tell.
The earth that wakes one human heart to feeling
Can centre both the worlds of heaven and hell.

We are glad that Denis was able to give back to the National Trust some of the deep joy that the countryside had given us and that their work has helped to protect.

We always enjoy visits to National Trust properties wherever we are. We delight in the Clergy House at Alfriston, which was the first to be owned and restored by the National Trust. I was pleased to take our old friend Dame Jennifer Jenkins there and watched with admiration her understanding, appreciative talks with

388

the curator, who was delighted to meet someone who had been such a distinguished chairman of the Trust.

Visits to the National Trust gardens at Sheffield Park in East Sussex have given us the chance to thank Archie Skinner — formerly head gardener there and now our neighbour — for the pleasure his inspired plantings years ago have given us and generations of visitors. We showed him a magical photograph Denis had taken across the lake to a single scarlet tree reflected in the clear water, while in the foreground two swans lifted, white wings outspread. "I planted that tree just there," he told us; "sent a boy over there to get it placed just right." Years later, it gave us a shock of delight. It is sometimes forgotten by the admiring visitors that gardens like this do not just happen by chance.

During Denis's forty years in parliament my life was punctuated — and sometimes punctured — by eleven general elections. During his years as Minister of Defence and Chancellor of the Exchequer, politics decided where and how we lived and to a certain extent even which friendships we could foster. The core of our married lives was, and always would be, the family; and the best and most lasting of our friendships were those we had known at home and as a family. But there were other friends across the world with whom, though we met rarely, we became close. Now we rarely travel abroad and much regret that we no longer meet the company who for many years gathered at an annual seminar organized by our Greek friends Minos and Pia Zombanakis with the central aim of bringing together informed and influential people from all parts of the world — Russia, America, the Middle East, Western Europe and England — to help in understanding the complexities of the modern world of finance. Minos's roots were in his native Crete, and although he is now very prosperous he still values his wealth in acres of olive trees. Tall, handsome, black-haired, he chaired the international seminars with consummate skill, fluent in each language, selecting and assessing each participant with a sharp intelligence. But when he relaxed in the evening and danced, arms wide-stretched, to Cretan music, he was once more a boy from the village dancing among the vineyards.

His beautiful wife Pia was similarly rooted in Greece. I see her now as I saw her first thirty years ago, white in the bright light, slim as a dart on the scented slopes of the Acropolis, pointing upwards and passionately declaiming from the classics like some Greek goddess. The years have dealt kindly with them; Pia is always exquisitely dressed and intensely interested in whatever subject she takes up — raising funds for Russian children, studying Greek Orthodox art or ancient monasteries.

The other wives who attended the seminars over the years were equally interesting and, although geographically distant, became close friends. Among them were an artist who had sailed the Atlantic alone with her husband; the clever mayor of a French town; an American professor; a Russian engineer; and the bright wives of Saudi ministers and the charming American wife of an Arab oil expert. Each of us brought our own work and discussed our various pursuits over a light lunch in the shade while the men sweated over world affairs in hot rooms. Each year we greeted each other as though we had only been a week apart. One year we mourned the sudden death of the wittiest of our number — the wife of a Dutch diplomat — and sadly remembered how, tiny and vital, she would throw herself into the depth of the sea wearing her waterwings and bravely swim. We remembered with pleasure how the year before we had encouraged her to buy the extravagant, stunning emerald ring she coveted. We hoped she had enjoyed it.

Over the years, kind, efficient and elegant Beatrice Vlassopoulos had organized both the conferences and our pleasures — tours through the villages of Greece, visits to churches and galleries, expeditions to simple meals in village tavernas. Denis and I usually took our annual holiday afterwards. Looking back, I remember that these annual weeks were my ideal of what a holiday should be, combining work, pleasure, sightseeing in beautiful places and rekindled friendships with congenial friends. Each year I said, "I am so lucky."

While the pace of life slowed for Denis, for me it was still quickening. After 1987, while he sat among his books on literature, art or photography, I wrestled with the history of banking.

My first book, *Lady Unknown*, on the grand-daughter of Thomas Coutts, had been welcomed by the chairman and directors of the bank Thomas had founded, Coutts & Co., who had allowed me to do research in their archives. So, when the three-hundredth anniversary of the foundation of the bank approached, they invited me to write their history for their celebration in 1993. I agreed, but warned them that I wanted to write a human rather than a banking history, since I knew nothing about banking. The chairman, Sir David Money Coutts — a descendant of Angela's sister, who had married a Reverend Money — gave me every encouragement and allowed me full access to the bank's archives.

So it was that Denis and I reversed roles: while he sat engrossed in literature, my subject at Oxford, I was deeply involved in the world of banking; he read Wordsworth while I struggled with the collapse of the South Sea Bubble. Over a period of years studying the bank's extensive archives, I learned of three centuries not only of banking but of life and the effect money has on it.

At first I worked with the helpful and friendly guidance of the archivist Veronica Stokes, and under her eagle eye. Her successor, Barbara Peters, made work a pleasure and kept me firmly under control — for I could willingly have spent a lifetime studying that cornucopia of gold that was the bank's archives — frequently reminding me that my deadline was fixed. In the beautiful new Coutts building in the Strand a tree and a forest of plants grew in the banking hall and enormous goldfish splashed in a pool. In those days the clerks still wore frock coats and I signed the visitors' book with a quill pen when I lunched with the chairman. It was a pleasant place to work. Angela had established some civilized traditions: a library for the use of the clerks, and a restaurant where they could have a decent mid-day meal. The latter, unfortunately, has since been closed, but I enjoyed it at the time.

Working in the archives I had so powerful a sense of the past that I could understand the rumours among the staff of an unhappy ghostly visitor. Apparently, employees had reported strange shadowy figures and sudden chilly airs. So discreet is the bank that no murmur of ghostly visitations reached my ears when I was working there. However, in 1993 the press learned that the directors of the bank had called in a "ghost-buster" who was supposedly experienced in exorcizing unwanted spiritual visitors. He determined that the presence was a headless gentleman, wearing Elizabethan dress and a ruff, prompting one cynical journalist to question why he would be wearing a ruff if he did not have a head. He decided that this was an ancestor of the Duke of Norfolk who had been unfairly accused of treason and beheaded at a site nearby. The story caused much amusement in the national and international press and gave rise to some frivolous cartoons. The then Duke of Norfolk was not convinced, but nevertheless a service was conducted to quieten the spirit of his headless ancestor and for a while there were no more apparitions.

A second ghost was reported to me when I was writing the life of Angela Burdett-Coutts. The writer Alan Dent had claimed in an article that he had seen her walking along the Strand making her way into Coutts Bank. He came up to Highgate to tell me of this experience. Since he had obviously lunched very well, the spirits surrounding him were more likely to have come from a bottle than the previous century, but he assured me that he had indeed seen her. I suggested that she would have been unlikely to have been walking along the Strand, but would have arrived in her carriage with her great dogs galloping beside her. Besides, Coutts's splendid new bank did not exist in her day.

Living in Westminster as I did for eleven years, I have often had so strong a sense of its history that I can understand how people can seem to be summoned from the past. Ghosts have followed me as I wrote and researched my biographies, though I am sorry to say I have never actually encountered them; they have always been seen through other eyes. On the whole I remain sceptical, though strongly aware that, as Hamlet said to Horatio, "there are more things in heaven and earth . . . than are dreamt of in your philosophy".

In the days when we lived at Admiralty House I would often look across Whitehall at the Banqueting House and, as I picked out the window from which King Charles I had stepped out to die, the red buses would fade and I would remember, as though I had been there, the crowds thronging the street and hear the voice of the boy who said, that, as the head fell, "Such a groan went up as I have never heard before and hope never to hear again." Can such violent emotion fade completely from human memory?

As I have recounted in earlier chapters, a ghost was seen in my bed at Admiralty House, and Gladstone had appeared behind me in my study at 11 Downing Street.

394

When I was writing the life of Emma Darwin, I was told of the ghost in the old home of her grandfather, Josiah Wedgwood, now part of a hotel. There I was dissuaded from going down to the cellars because, said the receptionist, "it's haunted down there". I knew the ghost could only have been that of Emma's uncle, Tom Wedgwood, said to be the father of photography, who had worked on his experiments down there and had contracted violent headaches in the darkness. Later, led to opium addiction by the poet Samuel Taylor Coleridge, he died unhappily and young. They told me also of a second Wedgwood ghost, that of a young child, who was said to watch from the stairs through the banister. This, I decided, was Josiah's daughter, who had died young. His friend Dr Erasmus Darwin had subjected her to his early experiments in treatment by electricity — though to my knowledge no one ever blamed him for her death.

The book that emerged for Coutts' anniversary in 1993 was, I hope, a readable story of human life behind and beyond the cash desks, in which gamblers like the lovely Duchess of Devonshire and the spendthrift George IV are taken to task by the old Scots banker Thomas Coutts. Once again, I did not allow Denis the sight of it until the last draft, when he gave me useful advice. It was more important with this book than with the others that it should be written from my angle, to dispel any assumption that Denis had actually written it. When I went to America to lecture, a judge sitting next to me at a dinner said: "Why are you worried? I expect Denis writes your speeches." At the end, nothing pleased me more than his approval and favourable reviews from bankers.

My history of Coutts & Co., bankers to royalty since King George III, led to an invitation to write the history of Buckingham Palace in conjunction with the directors of the Royal Collection. This again took many years of research in many archives — including those at Windsor Castle, where the curator gave me every help, as did the directors of the Royal Collection. They went through my draft with a fine-tooth comb, saving me from many an error, and making me check my sources again and again. "How does Lady Healey know that?" the question would come. Just occasionally, I could tell my editor in triumph, "Because she was there!" It was entirely due to the directors' painstaking scrutiny that one reviewer could say, "There are surprisingly few errors."

The Queen Mother kindly agreed to see me. At Clarence House we sat alone in a room filled with the scent of roses and sweet peas. It was difficult to reconcile the frail little lady among the flowers with the redoubtable Queen who had, during the war, taken pistol practice in the grounds of Buckingham Palace and who, I was told, would have fiercely defended herself had she been in danger from German paratroopers, as Queen Juliana had been in Holland.

It is easy to forget how very real the danger was for Queen Elizabeth at this time, yet she stoically refused to leave the palace. She remembered how Queen Juliana had fled, escaping with only her handbag. King Haakon of Norway came to Britain, too, and took refuge down below in the palace's bombproof room. The Queen Mother remembered his long figure stretched out on the floor and how he snored. She told me of their wartime experiences and of the day Buckingham Palace was bombed. She laughed as she remembered how reluctant she and the King always were to go down to the shelter when the red warning came, and how as a result she was at the window taking an eyelash out of the King's eye when the bomb fell in the courtyard immediately outside.

I managed to piece together the story of a more humble victim of another air raid on the palace, a policeman killed on duty in the courtyard. One evening, during a short, sharp air raid by 123 bombers of Luftflotte no. 3 based in northern France, a bomber dropped a basket of one-kilo phosphorous incendiary bombs on the area around the North Lodge, where PC 629A Steve Robertson was on duty. Shunning the safety afforded by the steel shelter nearby, and ignoring the orders not to tackle incendiaries unless they were threatening the palace itself, because some contained high explosives which could kill, Steve began to snuff out the blazing devices. His attention totally absorbed in this dangerous undertaking, he failed to hear — or chose to ignore — the sound of another bomber heading his way. A stick of six bombs was aimed at the palace: the first fell on the parade ground of Wellington Barracks, another on the lawns of Queen's Gardens and three on the forecourt of the palace; the last one scored a direct hit on the North Lodge, completely demolishing it. Steve was buried beneath a pile of

397

masonry. I was able to record his history, to the pleasure of his family and police colleagues.

My surprising discovery among the royalty of the past was how impressed I was by old Queen Mary. I had earlier encountered her in researching the life of Angela Burdett-Coutts, as the young and shy Princess May, a frequent visitor at Holly Lodge where she and her mother, the lovable but penniless Duchess of Teck, often took refuge when in financial straits. As Queen she had always been represented to me as formidable and unbending: it was said that talking to her was like "addressing Westminster Abbey". Her habit of acquiring furniture for Buckingham Palace from the houses she visited was legendary, and many apocryphal stories survive. However, I discovered in her a highly intelligent curator *manqué* who organized and transformed Buckingham Palace, who carefully briefed herself for all the formal visits with the King at home and abroad, who had an unexpected friendship with a woman trade union leader, and took a genuine interest in working women. In some ways she was a prisoner in the royal enclosure.

Nowadays we are no longer involved in the annual Westminster rituals, but we still enjoy attending the Queen's garden parties at Buckingham Palace. When Denis was a minister we were always invited to take tea in the Queen's Tent, but since then we usually sit under the trees, admiring the lake, or walk along the famous long flower border among a wonderful mix of people from all over the country and indeed the world. Old friends greet Denis with enthusiasm, and unknown admirers say to him, "You are an icon", or "Thank you for what you have done for our country."

In 2005, we were once again honoured by the invitation to take tea with Her Majesty in the Queen's Tent. Since it was so soon after the cruel bombing of London, security was exceptionally tight, though not visible, and guests were instructed to "bring two forms of identification, one photographic". Waiting for the Queen's arrival, we drank iced coffee and chatted comfortably with old friends like Mary Wilson and former opponents like Margaret Thatcher and Kenneth Baker and his bright wife. Kenneth is remembered by my teacher daughter Jenny for the "Baker Days" he introduced as education minister, and by me for the pleasant radio programme Denis and I did with him and his wife when our shared pleasure in poetry bridged the political gulf. Denis and Lady Thatcher exchanged friendly compliments, Denis extravagantly kissing her hand, she — elegant and indomitable as always — reminding Denis that she was younger than he. Ted Heath's recent death was not mentioned.

I enjoyed seeing Roy Mason and his attractive wife, Madge, again. As a former defence minister he had for many years endured the tightest police protection since his courageous fight against the IRA had made him a target, so that their lives had been unbearably circumscribed. Madge, with her quiet common sense and courage, had always given him unwavering support.

The arrival of the Queen and the royal party was greeted by applause from the crowds outside the enclosure, this year with a particularly warm cheer for the Prince of Wales and Camilla, Duchess of Cornwall. Once again I watched the royal expertise on these occasions as they progressed across the lawn through the lanes of guests from all over the country and indeed the world, to the royal tent, greeting and remembering. These occasions undoubtedly have given a great deal of pleasure to thousands and it is an opportunity to pay tribute to those from all walks of life who have served their communities.

A central figure, outside politics, a focus for celebration or mourning, seems undoubtedly to be needed. In Britain in my lifetime we have been fortunate that our monarchs and their consorts have served the nation with life-long dedication in peace and in war. An elected president who represents a political party is bound to be divisive and his period of office is limited. In this changing, mechanical age a sense of history and continuity seems to me to be vitally important and there is a place for ceremony and tradition. Changes there will be with the changing times, but a democratic monarchy would be difficult to replace. After all, the social democracies of Norway, Sweden, Denmark and Holland have retained their monarchs.

CHAPTER
SIXTEEN

FRIENDS AND FAREWELLS

Denis does not often speak in the House of Lords, but still makes his views known through television and radio, and in frequent lectures all over the country. Now, however, he prefers to talk about art, literature or photography.

One of his most effective television programmes was *Pictures in the Mind* with Bel Mooney, broadcast in 2003, when he described and illustrated his love of great art. Another — in which I took part — was recorded in the garden at our Sussex home with the Poet Laureate, Andrew Motion. In it, Denis walked with Andrew among our autumn trees reciting:

> That time of year thou mayst in me behold,
> When yellow leaves, or none, or few, do hang
> Upon those boughs which shake against the cold,
> Bare ruined choirs where late the sweet birds sang.

It was a moving moment.

Now too, he can enjoy his treasure chest of books, paintings and gramophone records; has time to sit in the sun, looking out to the incomparable rolling downland above the Cuckmere river. At last he can fully indulge his lifelong passion for art, music and literature. When, before our marriage, I went to his home in Keighley, the first thing he showed me was his prized art books. I sympathized with my colleague, the art mistress, who told him then: "I don't come to see books, I come to see *you*." His mother told me that as a little boy of ten he would spend his pocket money on picture postcards of great paintings from a shop near his school. All through our married life he would bring home in triumph beautiful volumes on art history, saying, "I'm saving these as capital for my old age." Now he has time to enjoy them.

He also has time to continue his writing. His autobiography, *The Time of My Life*, published in 1989, is generally acknowledged to be one of the best political autobiographies of the age and achieved immense sales. It was followed in 1992 by *My Secret Planet*, an anthology of his favourite prose and poetry which illustrates the depth and breadth of his knowledge of literature and deserves a prominent place in every sixth-form library, *Healey's Eye*, *When Shrimps Learn to Whistle*, *Denis Healey's Yorkshire Dales* and *Healey's World*. *Healey's People* is in preparation. Our own library of more than sixteen thousand volumes threatens to push us out of the house; but there is scarcely a book here that he has not read, and he knows where each is placed.

Equally extensive and varied is his vast collection of gramophone records, ranging from the Last Quartets of Beethoven to Fats Waller's "Your Feet's Too Big" —

played in reference to my size eight shoes. We often sit sentimentally smiling while records of French or Italian songs send us back to romantic holidays abroad.

Photography remains a passion. Never one for modern devices, he has so far resisted the digital camera which, as I tell him, would cut down the need for our racks of photograph albums. He is never without a camera bulging his pockets; and here at home in Sussex there are incomparable landscapes to be captured. From our house and garden we look north to Ashdown Forest, blue in the distance, and down to the Cuckmere river winding through the chalky Downs to the steel-blue sea. In all lights, in all weathers, his photographs have caught its matchless beauty. Daily, as we walk around, he says, "God, I love this place!" I was amused to find that in the "Golden Book" presented to us on our fiftieth wedding anniversary our family record this repeated exclamation in their childhood at Highgate. An enduring love of home is and always has been central in our lives. The wide Sussex skies and distant Downs remind us both of Denis's home on Ilkley Moor, so different from my childhood memories of the Forest of Dean, where the spring brings a sea of bluebells unrivalled even in Sussex or Yorkshire.

The garden is my passion and at Alfriston, as I did at Highgate, I find myself once again recreating my childhood Forest — daffodils and snowdrops take me back to the Forest of Dean, secret wild gardens in the woods at the Buckstone; banks of primroses and the first wild violets, the scent of wild garlic, and I am back in the lanes of Cherry Orchard and the Staunton woods. I am planting a copse of foxgloves to remind me of Sunday evening walks through the woods after chapel with our father and mother. "Snompers", my father called them, and would say: "I'm as happy as a bee in a snomper." For me, too, the deep remembered love of the country remains the central theme in the pattern of my life.

Here in Sussex I discovered an unexpected link with my old home in the Forest — a reminder to me of how, throughout my life, one shake of the kaleidoscope produces a new pattern. When Denis was Chancellor of the Exchequer, the late Lord Gage invited us to lunch at Firle Place, his magnificent country house not far from Alfriston. As he took us through the great rooms he pointed to a portrait of an eighteenth-century lady sitting reading a letter before a distant house in a landscape. It was, he said, an ancestor at High Meadow House, Cherry Orchard. Immediately, I remembered my Cherry Orchard in the Forest of Dean — the grassy plain, the spectacular view of the distant Welsh hills, the ruins of outhouses where I had picked blackberries, the broken fountain we called Dog Kennel, the strange cave on the hill opposite haunted by the grey lady. It was at Cherry Orchard that on my fourteenth birthday I waved goodbye to my father as he walked to work. I did not know then that there had been a magnificent seventeenth-century house on this site, but I had dreamed of such and sworn that one day I would build a house there.

In 1817 the Crown had bought High Meadow House and estate and is said to have offered them to the Duke of Wellington on behalf of a grateful nation. But the view, said the Duke, reminded him too poignantly of Portugal; so he settled for Stratfield Saye instead. He must have inspected the house; he certainly came down to the Forest with Mr Arbuthnot, the minister responsible for Crown Woods and his great friend, with the entrancing Mrs Arbuthnot. With pride they showed him the great oak plantations that were to come to maturity in the Forest in future generations. When the Gages bought Firle Place in Sussex they could not afford two such mansions and, it was said, did not want their descendants to be seduced by the lovely landscape of the Forest; so they completely demolished High Meadow House, reducing it to a pile of rubble — with gunpowder, so it was reported. (A crossing-sweeper who kept a diary described all that remained in the 1870s.) However, the huge, elegant wrought iron gates from the entrance were brought down the Wye by boat and hauled overland to Firle. Now, as I stand before them at Firle Place, I am back among the foxgloves in Staunton Woods, walking with my father and mother on a summer evening.

In Sussex I have also found again something I valued so much in my childhood in the Forest, and again in Highgate: the easy friendship of a local community. Life at the roots here is vigorous. I am president of a flourishing Historical Society in Alfriston. Trying to understand the past helps with the present, and a community grows from the group. Cheryl Lutring, a founder member of the society, has a particular historical interest that continues actively in the present: she is concerned to revive an old breed of riding horse with a special gait — now forgotten in Britain, although its descendant breed, the American Saddlebred, is cherished in the United States. In addition to giving many displays around the country, she annually presents a demonstration of the imported team at her home in Alfriston for local residents. We sit on the grass and watch elegant ladies ride and drive graceful, high-stepping Saddlebreds in the smooth rhythm of their English ancestors. Once we watched Cheryl's glorious chestnut mare Rare Visions take her last bow: now retired from the display team she pioneered, she was the first of her kind in Britain — a rare vision indeed — and so gentle that children loved to pat her shiny coat. I remembered how so many of my characters from the past rode for days across country; Cheryl's horses enabled me to understand how. Now that horses have almost disappeared out of our daily lives, it is good to remember what a vital part of our history, progress and even our vocabulary they were. Cheryl reminded us of this in a talk to our Alfriston Historical Society entitled "History on the Hoof".

At home there is music as there was in my childhood, when talented musicians performed for their own and friends' pleasure. On one unforgettable June evening our friends Graham and Serena Hughes collected a small orchestra of professional friends to play Mozart in their cottage. The doors were open in the warm summer air, while below couples strolled among the cows along the river towards the church.

The pianist was inspired. As she played and conducted, the reflection from her watch dazzled on the ceiling like a Mozart cherub and we were engulfed in music outside time.

Once a year, friends lend their restored ancient barn for a charity concert performed by brilliant professional musicians from the London Philharmonic Orchestra. Over the years they have come to call themselves the Ludlay Players after the home of our host, Denis's fellow peer Lord Lloyd. Once again there is spontaneous growth, creating and renewing life. So, while I watch with despair the decline in quality of programmes on television, I notice with hope the growing number of small groups who meet at home to sing, as we did in my childhood, to read poetry and to study books. I have had the greatest pleasure in hearing such a group in the village here discussing my own *Emma Darwin*. This communication with readers makes up for the loneliness of writing.

In our political life friendships were made across the world and renewed only once or twice a year; friends and colleagues were met at crowded meetings or on official occasions. No one dropped in for a cup of tea at Admiralty House or 11 Downing Street. Now the years are thinning the ranks; and as time passes, it is only when friends die that I realize how little I really knew many of our political colleagues and companions. I have known best those friends with whom I have spent time in their homes and among their families.

We enjoyed our frequent meetings with Frank and Elizabeth Longford, at their home or our own. Once a year we joined them to celebrate Elizabeth's birthday — the same day, though not the same year, as Denis's. This August day was always fine and the party was always held on the lawns in their lovely grounds with an annually growing family of brilliant children, grandchildren and great-grandchildren — who with such genes cannot help but be brilliant too — and their friends. The proceedings were always led by their daughter Antonia Fraser, the distinguished historian, accompanied by her playwright husband, Harold Pinter. There were annual speeches by Denis, Frank, Sir Nicholas Henderson and Nigel Nicolson. But the best was always by Elizabeth — invariably glamorously dressed, sometimes in an exotic blue jacket that glittered like the night sky, given to her by her adoring husband. One year he gave her a scarlet satin jumpsuit, in which she looked stunning even in old age. While other voices grew quavery over the years, hers was strong to the last. She usually talked with deep affection of the great Wellingtonia tree that stood before the house, that had been grown from a cutting.

I had known Frank Longford first as a fair, curly-haired don at Oxford, taking part in the Labour election campaign on behalf of Dr Lindsay, the Master of Balliol and Popular Front candidate against Quintin Hogg in the Oxford by-election of 1938. I had always admired his work for prisoners, his insistence on loving the sinner, though not the sin. I learned to know him better when he was chairman of Sidgwick & Jackson, the publishers of my first book, *Lady Unknown*. He was always kindly encouraging. When I opened the new branch of Hatchard's bookshop in Eastbourne he invited my editor, Margaret Willes, to their home in East Sussex so that she and her assistant could join us for the ceremony. Coming down to join them for an early-morning swim, he threw off his dressing gown and stood stark naked, surprised by Elizabeth's agonized cry as she ran with his trunks: "Frank, your costume!"

Frank's marriage to Elizabeth was the greatest good fortune of his life. She bore his eccentricities with love, patience and humour. She had loved him ever since the night when, at a Commemoration ball in Oxford, she saw him asleep on a sofa and kissed his cherubic face. He converted her to the Labour Party and she in turn converted him to Catholicism. After their marriage she stood as a Labour candidate for a Birmingham constituency until her growing family (they had eight children) stifled her own political ambition. Instead she became a distinguished authoress with a succession of excellent books to her credit, among them biographies of Queen Victoria and the Duke of Wellington. She always combined profound scholarship with sensitivity and humanity.

Frank died first, with Elizabeth beside him and the family around, Antonia bidding the farewell. When they thought all was over, Frank opened his eyes and said, "Tell the *Catholic Times* where I am." They were waiting for an article. After Frank's death there was one more birthday party for Elizabeth, at which the same old friends, Nico Henderson, Nigel Nicolson and Denis, made the annual speeches. This was the last time we saw her; she was as lovely as ever, but growing deaf and not seeing well. Holding my hand, she asked with genuine interest after my current book, encouraging me as she had always done; her reviews had always been generous. Her advice stays with me: "Always keep the story going, whatever else." Even now, increasingly frail, she still made the best speech in a surprisingly strong voice. But she did not stay long; gently she ebbed, growing more deaf and blind. Her son, Tom, told me that at midnight, as she lay dying, he looked out of her bedroom window and saw the moonlight caught in a halo round the great Wellingtonia. It would have given her the greatest joy. That tree was for her a symbol of everlasting life.

I am proud to have known Frank and Elizabeth, and we sorely miss them both. Though no couple could ever replace them, we should all be grateful for the talented family of writers they have left us.

That last birthday celebration for Elizabeth was also Nigel Nicolson's last appearance at the Longfords' parties. We heard of his death with great sadness. He was an old and close friend; Denis had known him at Oxford and afterwards during the war, and they had entered Parliament at the same time on the same day, albeit on different sides. I watched from the gallery as they bowed at the Speaker's Chair and noticed Nigel's high, stiff, white collar, reminding me of Gladstone. Though a Conservative, Nigel shared Denis's fury at the Suez debacle, and on many political issues they had much in common.

The son of Harold Nicolson and Vita Sackville-West, Nigel inherited Sissinghurst Castle, with its magical garden. When we became neighbours in Sussex, he often entertained us there, inviting us to lunch on private days at times when the gardens were at their best. Once we took Denis's mother there; it was a high point of her life, for she had read Harold Nicolson's work at her WEA lectures in Keighley, and Vita's articles. When we went to pick her up she was so excited that she fell downstairs — but nevertheless, gallant as always, though badly bruised she insisted on making the journey. She listened, enraptured, while Nigel told us how he had helped his father get the long walk straight by standing at the end of the vista; how Vita had sat with him on the garden seat shutting her eyes so that he could test her knowledge of the plants by the scent of their leaves. In later years Nigel would talk to us of his parents' extraordinary relationship, regretting that he had not kept control of the television film of their lives. "They made it all about sex," he complained.

I learned to have a deep affection for Nigel, especially at the end of his life. When he was dying of leukaemia he lay in a dark bedroom in the old house, up an ancient wooden stairway, too weak to move but still lively in mind, and still deeply involved in life. We took our daughter Jenny to see him and he was genuinely interested in her teaching, asking her about education. As always, he encouraged my writing and offered critical advice; and he always had a list of political questions ready to discuss with Denis. I could not bear that he could no longer see the garden he loved, especially the exquisite spring garden that his father had called his "life's work". His son and daughters wanted to carry him down to a wheelchair to see it at its best, but he would not — perhaps it would have been too painful: "We love that most which we must leave ere long."

He told us that a mutual neighbouring friend, Lord Gibson, was dying of the same disease but was holding on to life by frequent transfusions of new blood. "But he has his wife Dione to live for," he said. "I don't want to be a burden to my children — they have their lives to live." On our next visit he told us that Pat Gibson's desperate measures had not held back his death. We miss them both sorely; but I am glad we at least have the books Nigel wrote to remind us of a gentle, sensitive and intelligent friend.

The deaths of Jack and Frankie Donaldson were the greatest blow of all. They were, as I have earlier recorded, our dearest friends. I see them now in their cool, white room with its flowers and lovely music, Frankie with her list of questions eagerly badgering Denis, Jack amused, easy in his chair, encouraging me — as did Frankie — in my work. They leave a gap that no one can fill.

However, many dear friends remain. Ever since our first days in Sussex we have spent many happy days with Frank and Kitty Giles and their family. Frank, a former editor of the *Sunday Times*, is another prolific author, including among his books a life of Napoleon. His wife Kitty is one of our dearest friends. The daughter of the late Lord Buckhurst, whose lands include great swathes of Ashdown Forest, she nevertheless spends much of her time in voluntary work with and for prisoners. It is a vocation to which she is passionately dedicated. Their daughter Belinda was a childhood friend of Cressida's when we lived at Withyham; now married to the distinguished broadcaster David Dimbleby, she has made her own successful career as a television producer and is now another neighbour of ours in Sussex.

We enjoy meeting other country friends like Asa (now Lord) Briggs, the distinguished historian, former Dean of Worcester College, Oxford, and Master of Sussex University, and his clever wife Susan, also a writer. I had first heard of Asa in Keighley, where he was at school, and I had taught his sister Emily, who always complained that everyone expected her to be brilliant like her brother. Since then I had admired his works — particularly on the Victorian period — and made constant use of them in my own writing. He has kindly read all my own books in their messy draft state and has given me much invaluable, though sometimes illegible, advice. We delight in visits to and from them here in Sussex.

In 2005 the great reaper felled two former Prime Ministers, Ted Heath and Jim Callaghan, both of whom had been our friends for decades. I had occasionally met Ted in our student days at Oxford. A year older than me, he had been President of the Oxford Union, where I had often heard him speak in his singularly throttled voice, and we had both campaigned for Sandy Lindsay in the Oxford by-election of 1938 — I hardly knew him in those days; but Denis, who succeeded him as president of the Balliol Junior Common Room, was a friend and they wrote to each other after Oxford at the beginning of the war.

In later years, when Denis was in government and opposition, I frequently met Ted at all-party occasions, often sitting next to him at official meals. Sitting next to Ted presented a challenge: after one such experience Audrey Callaghan swore that she would never go through it again — he had not spoken one word to her. Often he was quite rude to his neighbours, especially towards the end of his life. Indeed, I once saw him across the table fall fast asleep during the soup. However, we always got on famously — I think I must have reminded him of his mother. We met often when the publication of our books coincided, and discussed the pleasure and pains of the book promotion circuit.

In 1979 in Leeds he was asked to present me with the Yorkshire Post Award for my *Lady Unknown*. It was just after the announcement of the general election and, in thanking him, I compared the occasion to Christmas in the First World War trenches, when German and English soldiers had played football together. We were later interviewed by Yorkshire Television when, to my surprise and disbelief, he told them that he had given me good advice about writing. I could not remember it! When we met over the years we always chatted easily; he told me of the pleasure of his visits to China and of his journey to the countryside to select a second panda as companion for the earlier gift, which he had presented to London Zoo. He had developed a surprisingly warm relationship with the Chinese government which was not damaged by the Tiananmen Square incident. I recalled that, during our long session with Chou En-lai in 1972, the Chinese statesman had teased Denis that his government had better relations with the Conservatives than with Labour.

I last met Ted in the year before his death, when he invited us to lunch in Salisbury. I was chilled to see, in the quiet cathedral close, an armed soldier at the closed gate of his elegant house — the lasting legacy of his period in office during the Troubles in Northern Ireland. He was then in a wheelchair and very deaf though, as his secretary assured me, "very much on the ball". He talked of his visits to China, at his Salisbury home and the care he had taken in hanging his Chinese wallpaper there. He loved Chequers and was proud of the improvement he had made in lightening the décor — against the advice of the officials. Unfortunately, I could not ask the personal questions I wished, since he gave us lunch in a crowded neighbouring hotel, and I needed to shout to penetrate his deafness. Afterwards, with great pride, he showed us his immaculate garden with its stunning view of Salisbury Cathedral. Aware that this would be the last goodbye, I gave him a farewell kiss. In July I watched on television his funeral in Salisbury Cathedral, where he is buried, a unique honour for a politician. Ted would have appreciated the distinction. He liked to be different.

April 2005 proved indeed to be "the cruellest month", when in less than two weeks we lost both Jim and Audrey Callaghan. I look more closely here at their lives because I count myself privileged to have been included among the friends of one of the most remarkable couples we have ever met.

I have recalled in earlier chapters Jim's progress from MP for Cardiff in the Attlee government of 1945–51 to Chancellor of the Exchequer, Home Secretary, Foreign Secretary and finally Prime Minister — a unique record for one who, as he often ruefully remarked, never went to university. Audrey was one of a group of dedicated women who helped transform the London County Council, as it was then called, through voluntary work that has often gone unrecognized. I had admired them at a distance, often meeting them at informal lunches given in Highgate by Bess Fletcher, the elegant and hospitable wife of Eric Fletcher MP (later Lord Fletcher). Not a politician herself, Bess had decided to make her contribution to public life in this way, enabling busy councillors to discuss their problems in relaxed and friendly meetings. In later generations, these women would have gone to university and made their own distinguished professional careers. It was partly due to the work of Hugh Dalton's wife, Ruth, that Hampstead Heath was acquired for London. Douglas Jay's first wife, Peggy — a public-spirited, tireless worker on the Inner London Education Authority — could also have made an important contribution in the House of Lords, but was never given the opportunity.

Bea Serota, however, was rewarded. She was made Minister of Health in Wilson's Labour government, a vantage point from which she watched with admiration Audrey's quiet efficiency on the London County Council, where from 1959, as chairman of the South East London Children's Committee, she had been responsible for three thousand children in the council's care. Impressed, Lady Serota appointed Audrey chairman of the Trustees of the Great Ormond Street Hospital for Sick Children, where for many years she served with distinction. Under Audrey's chairmanship, millions were raised for the hospital through the Wishing Well Appeal. Later she became vice-chairman of the National Children's Bureau, though when Jim became a Cabinet minister she resigned from the Bureau and concentrated her efforts on Great Ormond Street. Through her influence and Jim's efforts in the House of Lords, the profits from *Peter Pan*, bequeathed by James Barrie to the hospital, were safeguarded in perpetuity by law.

Audrey gave years of her life to dedicated public work, not for financial reward, nor even for public recognition — she refused Lady Thatcher's offer to make her a Dame; her success, she said, was her reward. As chairman of the hospital's trustees, she was much admired. Sir Anthony Tippet wrote of her "quiet imperturbable gentleness, her absolute sincerity, her uprightness and lack of self regard". Other members of the committee remembered her "lovely sense of humour"; "things very easily made her laugh", and she'd "always be smiling", "she's got the most wonderful smile". Jim told me how a guest at an official dinner had asked who was the lady "with the lovely smile", and how he answered with pride: "That's my wife." It was a smile that, as I always noticed, began with the eyes.

For many years, then, I had watched and admired Jim the politician and Audrey the efficient and tireless administrator. We had been neighbours in London: when Denis was Secretary of State for Defence and we lived at Admiralty House, Jim was along the street at 11 Downing Street as Chancellor of the Exchequer; in opposition from 1970, we lived nearby in West Square near the Elephant and Castle, together with Merlyn and Colleen Rees, the Callaghans' closest friends; and from 1976 to 1979, when Jim was Prime Minister and lived at 10 Downing Street, we were next door at No. 11. But though Denis and Jim met almost every day, Audrey and I were so busy in our own lives that we met less than I would have wished. It was not until we became neighbours in Sussex that they became true friends.

When we moved to Alfriston in 1978 Jim and Audrey were living in a neighbouring village. Jim had longed for many years to take up farming, and Audrey liked the idea of having a rambling old house where her growing family of grandchildren could visit; so when he had resigned as Chancellor of the Exchequer in November 1967 and given up 11 Downing Street, they decided to make their home in the country. Jim bought a rundown Georgian farmhouse and by the time we arrived was farming 130 acres with the help of an old friend, Gordon Denniss. Neither he nor Audrey ever regretted the move. Audrey bred pigs in the old stables, raised bullocks and cultivated a kitchen garden. When in 1979 Jim finally left 10 Downing Street and could read the *Farmers' Weekly* instead of the *Financial Times*, the farm became a haven and an inspiration. As Jim wrote, "to grow and harvest fields of wheat, barley or oats, to rear a good crop of lambs or some sturdy bullocks, satisfies a deep instinct and the occasional successes bring so much pleasure that they offset the winter mud and the inevitable failures". It was a more profoundly rewarding life than politics. At the end of his life, although he was pleased with praise for his political career, he was equally proud that his fellow Sussex agriculturalists praised him as "a good farmer".

So for many years we visited each other, admiring Audrey's flourishing fruit bushes in their cage, marvelling that she could bear to rear pigs — a hobby she shared with Robert Runcie, the Archbishop of Canterbury — and enjoying her superb cooking, which she claimed took no time because she took all the short cuts — she had studied domestic science after leaving school. We followed the fortunes of their growing family with interest. Michael, who made his career in the world of finance, had met at Cardiff University a Welsh girl, Jenny Morris, who had shared a flat with a pretty student from Anglesey: Glenys Parry, who had a "ginger-headed freckled argumentative companion,

Neil Kinnock". All four of them had canvassed for Jim in the 1964 election.

We followed the successful career of their daughter Margaret with particular interest. At Oxford, where she read PPE, she met and in 1961 married Peter Jay, the brilliant son of Peggy and Douglas Jay, by whom she had three children. As Prime Minister, Jim had appointed the young David Owen Foreign Secretary, and after much hesitation selected Peter Jay as ambassador at the British Embassy in Washington, as David had asked. Accused of nepotism, Jim replied that it was the right appointment; if he hesitated only because the candidate was his son-in-law, he had no right to block his career. We once stayed at the British Embassy when, as Chancellor, Denis was in Washington for an IMF conference. I was interested to see in Margaret Audrey's directness and easy grace as a hostess.

Margaret became a life peer in 1992 and in 1998 Tony Blair made her Leader of the House of Lords and Minister for Women. Her difficult task of piloting the reform of the House of Lords through Parliament earned her much praise — though also some opposition, partly because of the quiet strength of her personality. After the dissolution of her marriage to Peter, in 1994 she married Professor Michael Adler, chairman of the National AIDS Trust. The obvious happiness of her second marriage, and her retirement from the stress of her position as Leader of the Lords, made her a great consolation to her father during the sad years of Audrey's illness.

It was in the last years of their lives that I really began to understand and love Audrey and Jim Callaghan. Historians will analyse Jim the politician, will argue about him as Chancellor of the Exchequer. Most will agree that as Home Secretary he combined firmness with tolerance, and that he dealt with Northern Ireland with admirable calm. As Foreign Secretary, his natural cheerful friendliness made allies among leaders in government all over the world — as I often witnessed. I accept Denis's judgement that, as Prime Minister, he handled his Cabinet better than any other since Attlee. Certainly his description in his autobiography of his technique of leading a government should be textbook advice for all prime ministers. But on none of these issues am I competent to judge. What I can record with admiration and affection is his love for Audrey — and her importance in their partnership. Historians may fret over the politics of this period. I would like this "marriage of true minds" which looked "on tempests and was never shaken" to be remembered.

I had noticed that in her later life Audrey was beginning to lose her memory. That she had been mugged in London did not help; and operations had gone wrong. But at no time either then or through the years of affliction that followed did Jim ever show impatience. "You remember, dear," he would encourage her, and pat her hand. We took her to the beach at Seaford where, when their children were young, they had had a beach hut, to remind her of happy times. Gradually, however, she lost her grasp on reality. Jim cared for her himself as long as possible, but the time

421

came when he could no longer manage and he had to place her in the kindly care of nurses at the Catholic St George's Retreat. I shall never forget his stricken face when he next came to lunch with us — nor his broken "I miss her so much". Now, as he often said, he would give up everything to care for her as she had done for him.

Orderly as always, Jim organized his life around daily visits to Audrey; he took her photographs and read to her in the vain attempt to stimulate her failing memory. Sometimes he was rewarded with the old smile; but often she failed to recognize even members of the family. Yet when we visited her I felt so strongly that the old, competent Audrey was still there, though agonizingly dumb and drawn away. Denis even made her smile again. Once Jim came to us from her with a radiant smile because she had spoken a whole loving sentence to him.

For many months he kept the regular routine of visits, until his own health began to fail; even then, except when in hospital, he regularly visited her. Fortunately, ex-prime ministers are permanently given a car and driver, so that right until the end he could make the short journey to see her. The last time he came to us he was very frail and could scarcely walk. At his request, I just gave him sandwiches in his chair. But there were still flashes of the old "Sunny Jim", when he and Denis chanted together poems remembered from childhood.

In 2005 he was determined to keep going until his ninety-third birthday, when he would have lived longer than any other British prime minister. He celebrated the achievement with a small party for close friends and family at the farmhouse. Typically, he reminded Denis: "Look smart; there will be cameras." Jim himself, to his dying day, was always "shipshape and Bristol fashion", shoes polished, trousers pressed. His family were there, along with old friends Merlyn and Colleen Rees, and his biographer Ken Morgan; Margaret did the honours with a quiet grace that once again reminded me of Audrey. Jim was tired, but still his cheerful old self.

We gathered again a few weeks later for Audrey's funeral in the little chapel at St George's Retreat. Jim came to the service from hospital, and this time we were all shocked at the change in him. He had suddenly given up. At least he had been able to read the newspaper tributes to Audrey. Her long support for him, her work for the community, had been recognized. Now he could say goodbye. Once again Margaret presided, and once again his close friends gathered — Merlyn and Colleen Rees; Gordon Denniss, who had jointly owned the farm with him — alongside their beloved children, grandchildren and great-grand-children. The little ones brought posies of spring flowers to lay on the coffin. Jim had chosen the hymns: the movingly simple hymn of praise, "For the beauty of the earth, for the beauty of the skies, for the love which from our birth, over and above us lies," which they had sung so often in their Baptist youth; and "Love divine, all loves excelling", which they had sung at their wedding in Maidstone Baptist Chapel. Although they had long since moved away from their old beliefs, both

423

had always recognized that the values learned in childhood had helped to shape their lives. I sat behind Jim as he followed the words on the hymn sheet with unseeing eyes, knowing that his heart was in the coffin before us. He had seen Audrey safely out. Now he could follow her.

Afterwards at the tea party he sat quietly in his wheelchair, while, one by one, children, family and friends came to say goodbye. It was, as he would have wished, a tidy end. The corn was cut; "all was safely gathered in". Once he had written of the "closing rituals of the farming year . . . to walk to the stubble in empty fields . . . the rhythm of the seasons meets a deep felt need". He would not see the next year's harvest; but with his family around him he knew it was safe. When I kissed him, I said, "Come to us when all this is over," but as he shook his head we both knew it was goodbye.

After the funeral he was taken back to his hospital bed, but he chose then to go back to the home they had loved, where he quietly died eleven days after Audrey. Once again, old friends gathered with the family at the little chapel at St George's for the service he had planned. Some years before his death he was delighted when someone wrote to him praising his "humanity". "I will settle for that as my epitaph," he wrote.

On 28 July 2005 we were all together again: at Westminster Abbey for the thanksgiving service for the lives and work of Lord and Lady Callaghan. The Abbey was filled: Prince Charles represented the Queen and other members of the royal family; politicians, diplomats, many of the "great and good" were present; and hundreds of friends joined the family of a much-loved couple in celebrating their remarkable lives. Margaret Thatcher and John Major represented the Conservative Party; Prime Minister Tony Blair read the lesson. Baroness Williams, Denis and Sir Cyril Chantler, the chairman of the Trustees of Great Ormond Street Hospital, paid their tributes.

Shirley spoke of Jim's "passionate belief in social justice, his belief in democracy with dialogue, in straight and honest responses that made him a hugely popular Prime Minister, and above all in education". She remembered his courage during the Vietnam War when, as Home Secretary, he calmly walked down the Embankment to greet the thousands of demonstrators on their way to the American Embassy, with a cheerful "Nice day, no need to get too rough." He was also, she said, "a canny trades union organizer ... a consummate politician who could be very tough but ... also willing to learn".

As Shirley spoke of Jim's personal popularity in the country, which "outstripped by far that of Margaret Thatcher", I looked across the aisle to the former Conservative Prime Minister sitting — elegant in black, and expressionless — next to Norma and John Major. I remembered how, twenty-six years ago, I had watched from the kitchen window at No. 11 as Jim had left Downing Street and she had made her triumphant entrance. Now she had come to mourn his final exit.

Denis spoke of our close personal friendship with Jim and Audrey through the whole of his political career, and especially during their last years. I was touched that he added: "Their marriage, like ours, was always close and central to their lives." With the present Prime Minister and two former prime ministers in the congregation, he praised Jim as the best prime minister since Clement Attlee. He spoke of Jim's career as Foreign Secretary, Chancellor of the Exchequer and Home Secretary, and of his own gratitude for his support and understanding during Denis's time as Chancellor; of his love of his family and pride in his daughter's career as Leader of the House of Lords; but above all of his love and loyalty to Audrey during their long life together and especially during her last illness. "He was a great man, with a great wife and a great marriage."

Sir Cyril Chantler added his praise for Audrey's years of competent, caring work at Great Ormond Street hospital. The service ended with the "Battle Hymn of the Republic". Jim would have enjoyed the occasion, and especially that it had been a thanksgiving for the lives of both himself and Audrey. Characteristically, he had left a note in his papers: "I would like any Memorial Service for me to be cheerful and joyful. The last hymn could be that splendid American one: 'Mine Eyes Have Seen the Glory of the Coming of the Lord. Hallelujah!' The congregation all singing. The great organ chords crashing out. The Marines on trumpets. That would be a splendid finish!" There were indeed trumpets from the band of the Royal Marines, playing Elgar, and we all sang with great enthusiasm and joy. At the very end, Audrey's niece played Welsh airs on the harp, bringing calm and solace.

At the end of a long life there is inevitably some sadness, but in 2005 I received an email that brought me the greatest joy and hope. I had written to the disabled writer, Christy Nolan, asking permission to quote from his book *Damburst of Dreams*, in which he describes the poetry award given by the Spastic Society, for which I, as one of the judges, recommended him for a special award almost thirty years ago, when he was a little boy.

Since then I have kept in touch and have followed his successful career with delight. Though still severely disabled, he has been able to enjoy some remarkable triumphs. He is now world famous, has won the Whitbread Prize for Literature, has been awarded an honorary doctorate from Lancaster University, has received the Medal of Excellence from the United Nations Society of Writers, and out in China a grove of trees has been planted in his name. He tells me that "just very recently Bono composed a lyric about me and has included it on U2's latest album, 'How to Dismantle an Atomic Bomb'. On 27 June, in Croke Park here in Dublin, he invited me along and there in front of 82,000 fans he introduced me, spoke of my work, recited my poem 'I Learnt to Bow', told his audience that he and the other members of the band went to the same school as me — Mount Temple Comprehensive — and then he sang his tribute song to me, 'The Miracle Drug' . . . but, Edna Healey, don't

427

you ever forget that my literary birth began with your judgement of my very early writings. I am still trying to live up to your expectations and I am busy working on book four."

I did very little, merely shone a small candle on his extraordinary talent. He owes his success to his own indomitable courage and also to teachers and school mates who understood and encouraged him, to medical and technical scientists who have helped him break out of his silent world, and above all to the love and support of his devoted family, father, mother and sister, who love and understand him. When that all works together miracles can happen.

EPILOGUE

The Glories of our blood and state
Are shadows, not substantial things;
There is no armour against Fate;
Death lays his icy hand on kings:
Sceptre and crown
Must tumble down,
And in the dust be equal made
With the poor crooked scythe and spade . . .

The garlands wither on your brow;
Then boast no more your mighty deeds!
Upon Death's purple altar now
See where the victor-victim bleeds.
Your heads must come
To the cold tomb:
Only the actions of the just
Smell sweet and blossom in their dust.

James Shirley

June 2004: Poets' Corner, Westminster Abbey

I sat with my wreath beside Charles Dickens's tomb, waiting as the vergers brought chairs for members of the Dickens Fellowship and the gathering crowd of curious onlookers. As a past president of the Fellowship, I had been invited to lay the wreath at the annual ceremony to commemorate his death in June 1872. Around me in Poets' Corner were memorials to men and women about whom I had written. I knew their faces, recognized their handwriting; but at this moment realized how little I had really known them. So how could I truly tell their lives? At least, I told their marble busts, I had tried.

Beneath my feet lay Charles Dickens. I had read hundreds of his letters to Angela Burdett-Coutts — the inspiration of my first book and, as he called her, his "dearest friend". She lay beneath the stone slab by the great west door, the first woman to be buried in the Abbey in her own right. I had read his letters to her on microfilm in a darkened room and felt I knew them both. Now in death they were united again.

Nearby, under the aisle, a black slab marked the grave of Angela's friend David Livingstone. Researching his wife, Mary, I had followed their trail to the Kalahari Desert and had touched his great bronze statue beside the Victoria Falls. I had found in Scotland the microscope Angela had sent him and recognized it. Angela had sent flowers from my garden at Highgate for the funeral of Charles Darwin, whose grandfather, the great Erasmus Darwin, had been her family's doctor in Derbyshire.

As I waited in the echoing Abbey, I thought of forgotten wives. Catherine Dickens lies in the tangled wilderness of Highgate Cemetery, over the wall from our old home. I had laid a wreath on her grave there on the anniversary of her death. Mary Livingstone was buried, unremembered, on the banks of the Zambezi in Africa. Emma Darwin lies in a simple grave in a quiet Kentish churchyard.

On this June evening I remembered how so many strands of my life had woven together. Here, half a century ago, I had sat with Denis, a new MP, high up in the gallery on blue velvet chairs, and watched a tiny Queen robed with brocade and crowned with a weight of gold, heard the triumphant shout "*Vivat Regina!*" echo around us.

I have watched so many great ceremonies here, witnessed such splendid processions, seen great men I had known borne to the altar and heard their funeral music beautifully played. In recent years I have heard old friends speak in praise of dead friends: when I listened to Shirley Williams and Sir Nicholas Henderson remembering Lord Jenkins, it seemed only yesterday that I saw Nico and Roy — slim young students — walking through Oxford together.

As I walked out of the shadow of the Abbey into the sunlight, I thought, too, of those who have no memorial, yet who, in their day, changed my life; and of all those who, in chapels and churches and schools, opened eyes and minds and hearts and set values that would be remembered lifelong. I have remembered with gratitude some of them: for me they still blossom in the dust.